LONE
RIDER

LONE RIDER

THE FIRST BRITISH WOMAN TO MOTORCYCLE AROUND THE WORLD

ELSPETH BEARD

Michael O'Mara Books Limited

Some names of certain individuals in this book have been changed
to protect their privacy.

This paperback edition first published in 2018

First published in Great Britain in 2017 by
Michael O'Mara Books Limited
9 Lion Yard
Tremadoc Road
London SW4 7NQ

A CIP catalogue record for this book is available from the British Library.

Papers used by Michael O'Mara Books Limited are natural, recyclable
products made from wood grown in sustainable forests.
The manufacturing processes conform to the environmental
regulations of the country of origin.

ISBN: 978-1-78243-962-2 in paperback print format
ISBN: 978-1-78243-805-2 in ebook format

1 2 3 4 5 6 7 8 9 10

www.mombooks.com

Designed and typeset by Ed Pickford

Printed and bound by CPI Group (UK) Ltd, Croydon, CR0 4YY

In memory of

Wijnand Joris Robert Albregts

1955–2009

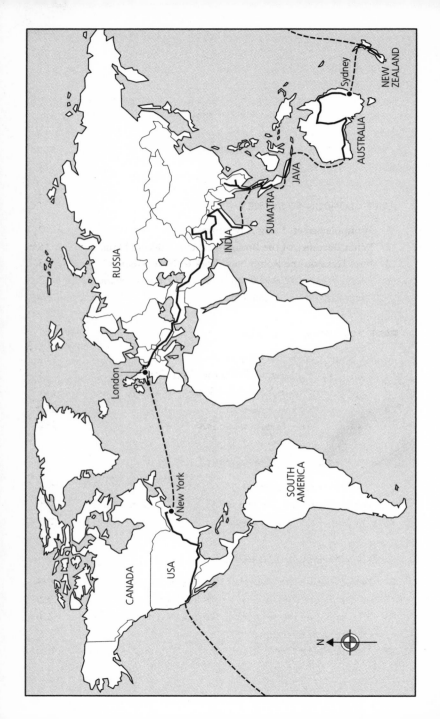

CONTENTS

Prologue   1

PART 1: LONDON TO SYDNEY

1   Wimpole Street: Early Adventures   7
2   What Becomes of the Broken-hearted: Making Plans   18
3   First Days on the Road: New York to New Mexico   35
4   Pretty Boys and Biker Gangs: New Mexico to California   52
5   Part of Me: New Zealand   63

PART 2: SYDNEY TO MADRAS

6   Pit Stop in Sydney: Australia   75
7   Surviving the Outback: Sydney to Alice Springs   91
8   Laying Demons to Rest: Alice Springs to Perth   106
9   All is Lost: Bali to Singapore   119
10 It's a Dog's Life: Singapore to India   130

PART 3: MADRAS TO KATHMANDU

11 Welcome to India!: Madras to Calcutta   155
12 Double Engine, Selfie Start: Calcutta to Kathmandu   170
13 On Top of the World: Nepal   181

PART 4: KATHMANDU TO HOME

14 From Serenity to Chaos: Kathmandu to Varanasi   195
15 No More Lonely Girl: Agra to Rajasthan   205
16 Through the Storm: Delhi to Srinagar   216
17 Falling Again: Kashmir   229
18 No Exit: New Delhi   240

19 Road to Revolution: Pakistan to Iran   249
20 Bell Helmet For a Burka: Iran to Istanbul   261
21 Home Alone: Turkey to London   275

PART 5: THE AFTERMATH

22 All Things Must Pass   287

Appendix: Excerpts from my Journal   305
Acknowledgements   311

PROLOGUE

Southern Thailand, 10 April 1984

For five long, hot, tiring days I'd ridden towards the equator, skimming the Burmese border on the skinny section of the Thai peninsula, somewhere between the lazy beaches of the south and bustling Bangkok and the plains to the north. I had to be in Penang in three days to catch a cargo ship across the Bay of Bengal to Madras.

I had ridden up to the Thai–Burma border in search of a route through to India and onto Nepal. Until now, I'd travelled rich in time, but poor in money. Now, for the first time, I had a deadline and a direct overland route that promised considerable savings of both when they were running out fast. Largely ignorant of what might lie ahead, I'd arrived at the border having heard conflicting reports about a possible route through Burma, as Myanmar was then known. But as I stood gazing at Burma, hazy in the distance on that sweaty, overcast afternoon, I didn't need my makeshift map to tell me that the roadblock in front of me marked more than the end of this particular road. I'd run out of road and options. With nowhere else to go I began the long journey to Penang in Malaysia, more than 1,200 sticky miles ahead.

It was for times like this that I loved riding my bike. Those moments when all thoughts of the past and future slipped away and I existed entirely in the present, the miles rolling past beneath the wheels of my big BMW, the morning light clear and golden, throwing shadow bands across the road as I carved my way around the world.

As I rode and the days and miles ticked past, I spoke to my bike, cajoling her with promises of an oil change and a clean air filter if she got me to Penang in time. It was the kind of bargain I'd struck many times since leaving London nearly eighteen months earlier. With a couple of bags over my shoulder, the takings of a summer's pub work in my pocket and yearnings for my ex-boyfriend in my heart, I'd departed carrying a widely ridiculed dream of riding a motorcycle right around the globe, something which, to my knowledge, no woman and few men had ever done.

I treated my nine-year-old BMW R60/6 well, cared for my darling as I would any old lady with too many miles on the clock. More than 18,000 miles together; another 15,000 to go, just me and my girl. Five nights earlier I'd been in Chiang Rai, as far north as most travellers ventured in Southeast Asia in 1983. There, in the Golden Triangle of Laos, Burma and northern Thailand, the mountain pastures were dominated by opium poppy growing and heroin production, scaring off most outsiders.

But not me.

On that golden southern Thai morning, I was riding on a small dusty country road between fields a few miles from the main highway that carried all the traffic up the peninsula from Malaysia, Singapore and Indonesia to Bangkok. My speed was creeping towards 60 mph; too fast and I knew it. But, as on every previous day, I'd convinced myself that I was safe – so safe I'd capitulated to the heat by removing my gloves. 'We got away with it yesterday,' I said to my girl, even though we'd shared dozens of near misses already.

That's when I hit the dog.

A flash of brown and white fur. Two black eyes filled with terror. A thud. I didn't even brake. It appeared from nowhere and disappeared immediately. All I saw was a blurred collision of metal and hair.

A dark green truck, stacked high with baled goods, had been approaching on the opposite carriageway, blocking my view of the far side of the road. As it passed, the dog shot out from behind it into my path. It never stood a chance, but it was big enough – a standard-issue Thai mongrel the size of a German Shepherd – to knock me clean off my bike.

I smacked onto the tarmac. My breath catapulted out of me and everything slipped into slow motion as I slid on my back across the road, watching my bike trundle, upright and riderless, ahead of me into a ditch, out of sight.

Dazed and breathless, I pushed myself up and stumbled to my feet, my ears ringing as I looked around for some remains of the dog.

Nothing.

My bike, however, was wedged against a tree in the ditch. My chances of reaching that boat in time no longer looked so good. I rushed over to my BMW, wanting to pull her free. I grabbed her front wheel, which was jammed against the tree, clasping the trunk between her front tyre and her exhaust outlets. I tugged as hard as I could. That's when the adrenaline wore off and I suddenly felt the pain.

My hands, red raw, the skin scraped off both palms, were bleeding and screamed sore. I tried to ignore it, tried to tug again at the front wheel, but the pain was too much. I stopped and looked at myself properly for the first time. My trousers were badly torn, my thighs grazed, my right foot smashed up, but my leather jacket had saved my arms and shoulders. Thank god I'd been wearing my helmet. I was cut and bruised and smashed about, with a bike I feared was wrecked, at a time long before the advent of mobile phones, internet and email.

I was twenty-four years old, a young architecture graduate with little experience of the world and hardly any money in my pocket. I was alone, a thousand miles from anyone I knew, in a country whose language I didn't speak and couldn't read, on a road I didn't know.

PART 1

LONDON TO SYDNEY

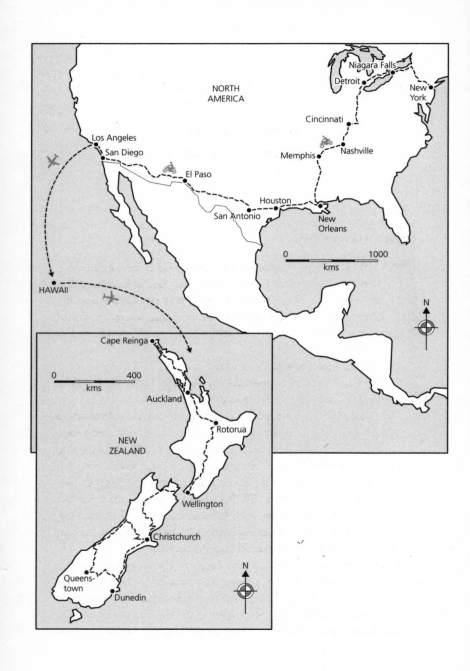

1

WIMPOLE STREET:

EARLY ADVENTURES

London, 3 October 1982

The beginning of my great adventure and I was sitting on a bench in a corner of Heathrow airport, face in hands, crying my eyes out. Three hours of tear tracks streaked across my face. After years of dreaming, months of preparation, weeks of longing to be gone, suddenly I knew what it really meant to feel totally alone.

Turn back, I told myself. *It's not too late.*

Go home, a persistent voice in my head insisted, *back to the family and friends who never wanted you to leave.*

I was tempted. So tempted I was giving serious consideration to reversing the events of a day for which I'd spent so long preparing.

Now, almost three years after I bought my BMW, the morning of my departure had finally arrived and all I could think was that I really wished it hadn't. I'd packed my few items of luggage into my mother's rusted, dented VW Polo before standing in the street outside my childhood home, feeling more awkward than thrilled, my parents either side of me as my brother snapped a last momentous picture of us before we crammed into the tiny car.

By the time we arrived at the airport, I was feeling no less apprehensive, only now my parents and brother looked as if they felt the same way. To one side stood Justin, his eyes flickering from departure board to passing passengers to the floor as my father and I racked our brains for something to say while we waited to hear whether a standby seat was available on the next flight to New York and an uncertain life on the open road.

It's not too late, the voice in my head said again. *You can go back.*

Going back would mean a welcome return into the arms of my mother, who a few minutes earlier had for the last desperate time asked a question that had become a miserable mantra in our house.

'Do you really need to do this?'

I'd said nothing, just nodded as my mother burst into tears, hugged me quickly, then rushed, without a glance back at me, out of the terminal. And out of my life for the next three years, maybe longer.

But going back would also mean capitulating to all the detractors and cynics who had poured scorn on my ambition, including, at their head, Dave Calderwood, the editor of *Bike* magazine. Having sent him a letter and a photograph, I'd hoped for some publicity and advice, but received only mocking male chauvinism in return. Now, as I crouched, crying in the corner of the terminal, reflecting that Calderwood was one of only two correspondents who bothered to answer my many assistance-seeking letters, I wondered if he might have had a point. Maybe, like all the others – the potential sponsors who never replied, the bike manufacturers who shook their heads, the accessory makers who shrugged awkwardly, the shipping companies who patronized me, the officials who rejected my visa applications – he sensed that I was out of my depth.

After all, I was leaving with little more than a vague plan to fly to New York, where I intended to pick up my bike from the docks, ride to my aunt's home in Detroit, then continue west to California, where I hoped to ship my bike to New Zealand or Australia and see where the road took me next.

Apart from buying a standby ticket to New York and packing up my bike for its passage on a cargo ship, I'd done very little preparation, certainly none of the years of research, fund-raising, physical training and logistics planning that I'd noticed other serious travellers had undertaken. I'd spent the previous months working in a pub to amass some savings and when I wasn't working I'd practised repairing my bike using the instructions in a Haynes manual. That was it. No wonder my friends laughed when I first told them I was going to ride my bike around the world.

In fact, I wasn't even sure why I was doing this trip, other than as a distraction from the heartbreak of being dumped by Alex, the guy I thought was going to be the love of my life. That, and a yearning for some adventure and unpredictability in my life after three years spent in stuffy classrooms studying for an architecture degree, had brought me to this place.

So maybe I shouldn't have been surprised that so few people had any faith in me to complete a journey that few men and even fewer women had ever undertaken. Maybe they were right to point out that a relatively privileged young woman from a comfortable home in the heart of the city was unlikely to survive a week in the outback of third-world roads, back in the days before satellite navigation and electronic communication. Back when even maps were sometimes hard to get.

It was a hell of a time to be having doubts.

I really don't know where I got the idea to ride my bike around the world, but it had been in the back of my mind for years. I think it first occurred to me soon after I learnt to ride a motorbike, which might never have happened if I hadn't been thrown out of school midway through my A-levels. By my mid-teens I had become quite disenchanted by my school and was relieved to be going.

I'd arrived at Roedean, a quintessential all-girls boarding school in a foreboding windswept building at the top of the cliffs on the outskirts of Brighton, shortly after my tenth birthday. Leaving home to start there was such a momentous event in my young life that I cannot remember anything before it, other than that I'd grown up in Finchley, north London, with an older sister, Poppy, and a younger brother, Justin.

My mother, who had studied medicine in Edinburgh in the late 1940s, was a bit of a pioneer in her own quiet way. Very few women were accepted into the medical profession back then and she attained the highest grades, qualifying when she was only twenty-four. Now working as a chest specialist at a nearby hospital, she was a selfless quiet achiever who devoted her life to the well-being of her friends and particularly her family, which was a bit of a blessing as my father had very little interest in young children.

The only child of a poor family whose father had worked on the railways in Derby, my dad had dropped out of school with very few qualifications to his name. A year later, finding himself in hospital after a serious car accident, Dad became fascinated by the doctors and nurses scurrying around the wards and realized medicine was what he wanted to do with his life. As soon as he was discharged, he started teaching himself for the O-levels and A-levels he needed to study medicine. He passed his exams with the highest grades, then went on to Oxford to train as a doctor and Cambridge to specialize as a psychiatrist.

At about the time I started at Roedean, Dad published a highly controversial academic paper that made his name. Called the McEvedy & Beard paper and still part of psychiatrists' training, it attributed an outbreak of debilitating illness among nurses at the Royal Free Hospital to mass hysteria. At the time, Dad's paper caused a huge furore, making his reputation and enabling him to branch out into private practice as well as continuing his NHS work, which remained most important to him.

By the time I returned from my first term at Roedean my parents had moved from Finchley to a house in Upper Wimpole Street in the heart of London, a big six-storey Georgian house which had consulting rooms for my dad's private practice. In effect, we lived above the shop, Justin, Poppy and I in the attic rooms on the fourth floor, previously the servants' quarters. The third floor housed our kitchen, the main living room and a dining room. My parents lived on the second floor, which had their bedroom, bathroom, a small TV room and my dad's office. Three consulting rooms on the first floor were rented out to other doctors, while the ground floor had Dad's consulting room, a waiting room and a huge room at the back of the house used by a radiographer. There were two flats in the basement and a mews cottage at the back, which were rented to tenants until my siblings and I were old enough to move into them.

It was a very happy family home, although we all tended to do our own things, bumping into each other occasionally between meals. Family life was very harmonious – although they had lively discussions, usually about medicine, I never heard my parents argue – but Central London was not the easiest place for making friends with other children, so when I wasn't playing in Regent's Park or roaming around the West End, I'd stay in my room, constructing model aeroplanes and ships from kits or matchsticks that I spent months collecting from local pub ashtrays.

From a young age I often worked as a receptionist for my father in the holidays, keeping an eye on his patients in the waiting room. One of them, an extremely rich woman, was a kleptomaniac. Every time she came out of the waiting room, I'd have to open her bag and extract all the ashtrays and vases she'd attempted to steal. Once she went past my desk to the toilet and I heard her rummaging in a cupboard, putting all the bleach and toilet cleaner in her bag, which was bulging when she came out. Another patient was a very wealthy manic-depressive who would walk the streets with great wads of cash, giving it away to passers-by. He credited my father with saving him a fortune.

I greatly admired my father, who didn't care what people thought of him, or what he looked like as long as it was practical and thrifty. Dad would happily walk down Marylebone High Street, pipe in mouth, hair greased back, dressed in ex-army shorts, over which, for reasons only he understood, he wore baggy army underpants. On top, he had a shirt customized using pinking shears to shorten its length and remove the arms. By any standards he cut an eccentric figure, forever in his own world, but we found it very endearing.

Having grown up with very little, reliant entirely on his brilliant brain and a lot of determination, Dad was obsessed with money, putting a lock on the phone and charging us for postage stamps. I think Poppy and Justin felt he was mean, but I thought Dad was simply careful with money, a virtue I shared because I was always short of it. And even though he watched every penny, I always knew he wouldn't hesitate to lend or give us large sums, no questions asked, if we really needed it.

Unable to resist a bargain, Dad somehow accrued seventeen Rolls-Royces, a hearse and an ambulance when we still lived in Finchley. All in terrible condition, parked in the back garden, the drive and the road, they were part of Dad's moneymaking schemes, possibly involving cannibalizing some of them to rebuild others. The ambulance eventually went to a bunch of hippies in the late 1960s, the others sold for no more than £50 each.

Dad's canniness even extended to his private practice. One patient was an antiques dealer, so Dad accepted furniture as payment. Another patient, a shopkeeper in Brighton, gave Dad bent tins of food, thousands of which were stacked in the house – baked beans, fruit cocktail, corned beef, even tinned cheese. Meals would be devised according to the 'eat by' dates on the top of the cans, none of which were labelled, but instead had a reference code stamped on the top of the tins. We were given a list of the codes so we knew what food they related to. Unfortunately we lost the list so we'd pass around the tins, shaking them, trying to determine if a particular tin contained fruit cocktail or spinach, potatoes or cheese. Eventually we gave up and would simply eat whatever was disgorged by each tin. Meals could be very strange.

Some of the tins were stored in Formica-clad kitchen units my father had constructed without realizing he'd put them directly above the boiler. The tins regularly exploded, sugary fruits streaking down our walls. And yet, for some reason they were never moved to a cooler place. The explosions continued regularly until Dad turned to making wine from potatoes, spinach, figs and other canned fruits and vegetables.

Bubbling in huge plastic vats in the kitchen, Dad's strange concoctions tasted like firewater and were drunk by no one but him and some unsuspecting guests.

Even when we went on holiday to France, the tins came with us, packed in a trailer behind the car. Arriving at campsites, we were regarded by the French as very odd when they saw how we brought our own tinned food to the land of haute cuisine and exotic fresh produce.

Holidays were always quite something. Dad invariably bought

second-hand cars from my uncle and put Poppy, Justin and me in the back with a supply of bread, fruit, chocolate and the appropriate Michelin guide for our destination. Every day was spent ticking off sights in the guide. Churches, castles, altarpieces, rare rock formations – if they featured in the Michelin guide we visited them. Normandy, Brittany, various other obscure parts of France and Scandinavia – my siblings and I saw them all, never questioning my father's obsessive need to tick off every entry in the guide.

Every night we'd arrive at a new campsite, erect our tent, usually in the dark, eat from our tins and go to sleep. In the morning, we'd pack away the tent, get back in the car and do it all again, every day for a fortnight, every year without fail, except when my father once got sunstroke and we stayed at one campsite for two nights. It was bliss.

Outside holidays, Dad worked obsessively and had very little to do with us until we were teenagers, when he mellowed slightly and we became more interesting to him. So our upbringing was down to my mother until Poppy and I were sent off to Roedean, where I muddled my way through the junior house, my sister two years ahead of me as a guiding light and protector from bullying because I'd been written off as a 'thicky', a label that stuck until I was sixteen, when it was discovered that I was dyslexic.

I lost count of the number of times I was told I was stupid, and even though I often knew the answers to questions in class before anyone else, I didn't have the confidence to put up my hand. I'd sit there, saying nothing, frustrated because I didn't understand why I couldn't read or write fluently and needed to work twice as long and hard as my classmates to cover it up. At night, after lights out, I'd take whichever book we'd be reading the next day to the toilet, and read the appropriate passage fifteen to twenty times, until I'd almost memorized it, so I'd be able to get through it in class. I'd still stammer and hesitate, but it wasn't as bad as it might have been.

Meanwhile, my sister was considered very bright, the teachers never hesitating in comparing us, tolerating my supposed stupidity only because I was a county lacrosse player and captain of numerous sports teams. However, everything changed when a new housemistress joined the school. From the day she arrived, she had it in for me. She knew I smoked but could never catch me at it, so whenever I walked past her, she'd tell me off. 'Tie your hair up, Elspeth . . . clean your shoes, girl . . . pull your socks up . . . straighten your tie.'

She niggled at me until I decided I'd had enough. Too old to be incessantly told what to do, I rebelled. It was nothing serious, just minor defiance and dissent, but I avoided serious repercussions until one day when I'd bunked off school and was seen in Brighton by one of the staff. Caught sneaking back into the school, I was called down to the headmistress. My parents were waiting in her office and she got straight to the point.

'I think it might be better if Elspeth didn't come back.'

Leaving Roedean transformed my life. If they were disappointed, my parents hid it well. They believed in letting their children make their own mistakes so that we'd learn from them. When I arrived home from Roedean, nothing was said. Instead, I was immediately enrolled at a sixth-form college in South Kensington for the second year of my A-levels.

Mander Portman Woodward was a crammer college, its teaching structured to cater for students who were retaking their A-levels, which made things difficult for someone like me who was starting their second year and hadn't completed the syllabus. I found the lessons boring, but I loved being at home, cycling across Hyde Park and Kensington Gardens to the college, where I met a bunch of students who became the core friends I've kept for life.

Annie, an Australian, was in my Art class, I met Simon in Biology, and Rick and Nick in Geography who introduced me to their younger brother Johnny, who also became a very close friend.

My new friends always seemed to have small amounts of money to buy things, but the concept of pocket money was completely alien to my parents, so I got a job at the Barley Mow, a pub just off Baker Street. Although only sixteen, I looked old enough to work behind the bar, where I gained a crash course in the drinking habits of local workers. Situated opposite a famous advertising agency, the Barley Mow's doors would burst open on the dot of eleven o'clock every morning, when half the agency's staff would storm in, telling us they needed a drink to fire up their creativity. At half past two, they'd still be there and we'd have to interrupt their love affair with the bottle, throwing them out to comply with licensing laws until they were back at 5.30, hammering on the door again to recommence drinking until shortly before midnight, when we physically had to eject them again. Watching the ad men stocking up on inspiration while I gasped for air in the fug of smoke and alcohol fumes put me off serious drinking and heavy smoking for life.

One Saturday, Nick invited me to travel down to Salisbury Plain with him and Rick to try out his Husqvarna. The name was meaningless to me until he turned up with a trailer behind his dad's Volvo and I discovered it was an off-road bike. After a couple of hours watching Nick and Rick riding around, they asked me if I wanted a go. It was my first time on a motorbike and, if I'm honest, I thought it was okay, but nothing more.

A few months later, Simon offered to sell me his first bike. Again, I was fairly uninterested in the bike itself, seeing it simply as a cheap and efficient way of getting around London. Unlike Rick, who spent more time polishing his bike than riding it, Simon had a reputation for trashing and crashing bikes frequently, but the bike he offered me was an exception, a mint-condition Yamaha YB100 that he'd barely ridden. Having saved some money from the pub, I drove a hard bargain. Simon still says I got it for a song only because we were approaching the end of our year together and selling it to me would ensure we stayed in touch because I'd need his advice on repairs and maintenance.

The next weekend, I stuck an L-plate on the YB100 and Rick and Nick showed me the clutch, brake and throttle, explained what the gears did, then left me to spend Saturday wobbling up and down the mews behind my parents' house. On Sunday I rode it out into Marylebone and Regent's Park (in the late 1970s, central London was empty on Sunday mornings), then ventured into proper traffic for the first time on Monday, riding it to college. It felt like a foreign thing with a mind of its own, but when I learnt how every part of it worked, I shook off my fear and became one with it, confident that I knew it like a reliable friend.

My father, impressed by my bike's money-saving qualities, welcomed it, but Mum, who had treated dozens of unconscious motorcyclists in A&E, was less impressed. To her annoyance, I soon taught Poppy to ride, selling her my Yamaha in order to buy a Honda 250. For a while I rode it on L-plates, then I took my test in Golders Green, an event that involved little more than circling the test centre in both directions until the examiner leapt out in front of me. My emergency stop having spared him from being run over, the examiner passed me with flying colours.

I celebrated by riding down to Brighton to see my grandmother. A few weeks later I visited a friend eighty miles out of London. Suddenly aware of the travelling potential of a bike, I started to think about riding around Europe, then the world. Not knowing if a circumnavigation was even possible, I mentioned my embryonic plan to Nick, Rick, Johnny and Simon when we were sitting outside the Devonshire, a pub at the end of our street. Their response was a surprise.

Mouths dropped. Glasses froze in mid-air. Everyone, including me, burst into laughter.

Of course we were all vaguely aware of Ted Simon, a journalist who'd recently returned from a four-year ride around the world on a Triumph Tiger, but since then an Islamic Revolution had toppled the Shah in Iran and things were looking dodgy in Afghanistan. So the thought of me, a seventeen-year-old girl who'd ventured only as far as the south coast, now riding around the world on her own?

Ridiculous.

I wondered if it was the fact that I was female. My friends weren't chauvinists, but 1970s biker culture was quite primitive. Other than Poppy, I knew no other female riders. I'd never seen another woman on a bike around town, and bike shops were a daunting and entirely male domain. Sometimes, turning up to buy a replacement part, I'd have to battle the staff to convince them that I knew which part I needed for my bike.

Biking was a male-only club and I was definitely not a member. But I was happy to be on the outside, nose pressed up against the window, not caring if I was let through the door, because I'd always ridden my own path. I knew that in spite of the rigours of my father's holiday regimes, I really enjoyed travelling. Poppy and I had been to Egypt together, a tough destination for two young female travellers in the late 1970s, and the following year I'd dragged a boyfriend, Andrew, around Europe for a month on an Interrail train pass. If I could survive those excursions, surely I had a chance of a ride around the world.

But first I had to finish my education.

2

WHAT BECOMES OF THE BROKEN-HEARTED:
MAKING PLANS

London, September 1978

Having struggled through A-levels and enjoyed only Art, I decided to enrol in a foundation course at Chelsea Art College, a decision greeted by my father in typical fashion. 'The only time an artist ever makes any money is when they're dead,' he harrumphed. 'What's the point of that?'

While at Chelsea, I met Mike, who became my boyfriend for more than a year. Not a biker, Mike would ride around town behind me on my pillion and again I'd suffer the disbelief of onlookers that a woman was riding the bike instead of a man. On one occasion we were knocked off the bike by a big black diplomatic car. At first the driver refused to pay for the damage as he was convinced that I could not possibly be the owner of such a big bike. Meanwhile, Dad's mantra that I needed to acquire some kind of skill for which people would one day want to pay me played on my mind. As the end of my foundation year approached, I started to think about my next step. Having discovered at Chelsea that I was good at making things, I thought about sculpture, then decided on a whim to study architecture. Beyond knowing that it had something to do with buildings, I understood very little about the subject, but I thought it might possibly satisfy my father, who thought medicine, law or dentistry were the only three professions worth pursuing.

That autumn, I started at Central London Polytechnic, a college with a well-regarded architecture department conveniently close to home. Joining a queue to enrol during Freshers' Week, I found myself standing behind a tall fair-haired boy who, like me, had a bike helmet hooked over one arm. We got talking. He had a big blue Suzuki two-stroke that I suspected (correctly) would be noisy and smelly, but probably very fast. His name was Alex.

Over the next few weeks, Alex and I got to know each other better. By now I was living in the small single-room flat in the basement of Wimpole Street, my parents as usual leaving me to my own devices, happy to provide a roof over my head and pay the utility bills. I received the minimum student grant of £410 a year, but everything else was my responsibility. Knowing I'd need money for food, clothes, books and petrol for my bike, I'd taken a job working three or four nights a week at the Devonshire Arms.

Although I liked PCL, I was never the type of sociable student who would spend hours hanging around the bar or halls of residence. I had enough friends in London and I lived only a few minutes' walk away, so I would go home at lunch to eat plain spaghetti, not least because it was much cheaper than the student canteen. And as the term progressed, Alex would come back with me more often than not for something to eat, a chat, a roll-up and endless cups of tea in my little kitchen, which he christened El's Café.

Alex was different from any other boy I'd met previously and I started to realize that I liked him a lot. We got on really well, laughing about so much. He had an ear for picking up on the absurdities of things I said that I thought sounded really normal, which he parodied in sketches of me. In one of them, he drew me sitting in my kilt and clogs, sipping tea, smoking a roll-up, a speech bubble coming out of my mouth: 'Piss probably wouldn't taste too bad . . . chilled.'

He also laughed at my way of never spending any money on anything I thought was unnecessary. All my clothes came from the Oxfam second-hand shop and my meals were very simple. If they fuelled me cheaply and efficiently, I was happy and could still afford petrol and oil for my bike.

Like me, Alex came from a slightly unconventional family. His father was a tall, shouty Dutchman whose eccentricity rivalled even my own father's habits. When I phoned Alex at home his father would pick up the phone and, without any preamble, yell: 'Speak to me!'

Some time in our first term, Alex mentioned he'd heard of an old BMW for sale near his home in Plymouth. Bored with my Honda 250, I fancied something bigger. I knew little about BMW bikes, except that they had two big lumps for cylinders, one sticking out on each　side, but I'd always wanted one. There was something about their reputation for well-built solid engineering and reliability that appealed to my practical nature.

Alex suggested that we went down to see the bike, and although I wasn't sure that I was quite ready yet for a bigger bike, I found myself immediately agreeing just to impress and be with him – a sign, I realized, that I was falling in love with him, hoping that someday something more would come of our friendship.

The timing was right. I'd taught my brother to ride and had sold him my Honda, so a few days later I found myself in a van with Alex, travelling down to Plymouth to have a look at the BMW.

The sellers, two middle-aged men with sensible clothes and neat haircuts, lived in a sparsely populated street on the edge of Saltash in Cornwall, across the Tamar from Plymouth. Standing outside their house, looking at the bike, I wondered if I'd ever be able to ride it.

Then I noticed them exchanging glances. They didn't need to say anything; I could guess what they were thinking: 'Who does she think she is, buying a proper bike?'

'I'll have it,' I said.

'You sure?' said one of the men, a smirk curling the corner of his mouth. 'Don't you want a test ride?'

I looked at the BMW. It seemed huge to me, but I didn't want to give them the satisfaction of seeing me struggle.

'No. It's okay.'

And I knew it would be okay. I trusted Alex's judgement and it was a BMW after all, a beautiful 1974 R60/6 with 35,000 miles on the clock.

Alex rode it for me to Dartmoor, where I then practised riding it on the empty roads over the moors. The winter sun was casting long shadows as I slowly, gingerly moved off, surprised at how it didn't feel that heavy because the engine had a much lower centre of gravity than my Honda. I knew I would be fine with it. Alex agreed to ride the bike back to London, and, as I got onto the pillion and pulled myself close to him, I tried to suppress a huge smile.

Shortly before Christmas, Alex and I turned a corner, easing from friendship into something more intimate. I couldn't have been happier.

As soon as I could, I took the BMW for a long trip, riding up to Scotland over the Easter holiday, staying in youth hostels. As a young woman on a big motorbike I encountered even more strange looks and double takes than I had done before.

Riding several hundred miles every day, I learnt a lot, like how much oil the BMW needed and that I was comfortable in my own company. Travelling on my own, I felt a great sense of freedom. I could go where I wanted, when I wanted, stop when it suited me. And although the journey was primarily about riding the bike, I stopped off to see many castles, abbeys and churches. Clearly my dad's obsessions had rubbed off on me.

A few months later, I took off on a tour of Europe with Rick on his Norton Commando, which looked great and sounded wonderful but convinced me never to ride a British bike. It vibrated so much, bits regularly falling off it, that I had to ride behind Rick, picking up the parts that his bike shed in its wake. The indicator, the backlight and the number plate all shook themselves free, some of them more than once. I would have found it funny had it not been such a sad lesson in why British bikes no longer led the world.

We rode down through France, crossed the Mediterranean on a ferry from Marseille to Corsica. After spending several weeks riding around the island we took another ferry to Pisa, then rode down to the heel of Italy, before turning back for home via Austria and Germany, by which time I was fully convinced I'd made the right choice of bike. Whereas Rick could hardly walk at the end of each day, I arrived back in London feeling like I'd barely left home. It was a powerful testament to the qualities of impeccable German engineering.

Riding around Europe with Rick, I contemplated the logistics of a round-the-world trip. Having survived on very little money, I was reassured I could get by on a longer trip on the meagre funds I might be able to raise from my pub work, although the dangers of a frugal lifestyle were made clear when I went to see my dentist for a routine check-up.

'If you continue like this, your teeth will fall out.'

He explained that I was deficient in vitamin C and asked again what I was eating.

'Banana custard . . . mashed potato . . . spaghetti . . .'

'What do you have with the spaghetti? Vegetables?'

'Margarine and black pepper.'

'Long term, you need a balanced diet. Right now, you need more vitamin C.' Rather than change my pauper diet, I bought some vitamin tablets, which seemed to solve the problem.

The following Easter I took off on the BMW to Ireland with Mike (who I'd also met at Chelsea) – or as I called him, Mike the Bike, to distinguish him from Mike the Artist, my former boyfriend at Chelsea Art College. Compared to my other motorbiking friends, Mike the Bike was more of a proper biker. He lived in Wandsworth and had a Triumph and a Guzzi Le Mans, of which he was very proud, even if it rarely actually went anywhere.

Mike rode his Triumph to Ireland and seemed to spend most of his time fettling with it, trying to keep the oil in the engine. Wherever we stopped, his Triumph would always leave its mark. In contrast, I barely had to touch my BMW apart from putting petrol in it, and checking the tyre pressures and oil, which was always dead on the mark.

Halfway through our trip, Mike left to return home for work, so I continued on my own until I met John, an Australian on a Velocette. He was great company and had a beautiful bike.

After Ireland I returned to my degree at PCL. Then, in the summer holidays, I flew out to Los Angeles to meet up with my brother Justin, who had taken a year off after school and was returning from picking apples in New Zealand. With plans to ride east across the States to New York, we trudged around LA trying to find a bike, growing more despondent as our search dragged on.

Friends had suggested I took the easy option by riding an American bike, but I wasn't so sure. I wanted a BMW. I trusted them more and I knew how to repair them, but Americans didn't seem to appreciate BMWs, thinking they were quiet and bereft of the chrome they liked on Harleys. After a couple of days searching I was starting to resign myself to riding some big American hog. Then, poking around in a garage next to a large bike shop, I spotted the back of a familiar-looking seat half-hidden in a dark corner.

'What's that?' I asked a garage hand.

'You don't want that, miss.' The garage hand shook his head. 'We took it part exchange, but it's not . . .'

I didn't let him finish his sentence. 'Can I just have a look at it?'

As I pulled the junk and boxes off the bike, I felt my pulse start to race. It was an old BMW R75/5.

'I'll have this.' I could feel a smile widening on my face. 'How much do you want for it?'

Justin and I eventually paid $1,500, the limit of our budget. Their loss was our gain, we soon realized. The bike was an absolute bargain. We loaded it with our twenty-year-old thick canvas tent with heavy wooden poles and took turns to ride pillion as we headed from California through Arizona to New Mexico, where we turned back on ourselves, north-west to Utah, Nevada and Oregon. When we reached Washington State, we turned east to ride across the northern states to Detroit, where we stopped with Renee, Mum's sister, before flying home. We left the bike with her and she eventually sold it for us the following year.

For very little money, we managed to cover a vast mileage, an achievement that appealed more to me than to Justy, who frequently thought my fiscal caution was unnecessary. Stopping at a petrol station in Arizona on a midsummer day when thermometers had passed the 40-degree mark, he asked if we might dip into the kitty we kept to pay bills.

'I want a Coke,' said Justy, the sweat running down his face like he was standing under a shower.

'No.'

'Just one ice-cold Coke.'

I shook my head. I had control of the kitty and I wasn't going to allow a temporary desire for a cold drink push us over our daily budget.

'Bugger it,' said Justy. 'I'm having one.'

He got out his own money, bought a Coke, sat in front of me relishing every cold, refreshing sip. I was desperate for one too, but I wouldn't allow myself the luxury. However wonderful the immediate satisfaction of a cold drink, it didn't appeal as much to me as the satisfaction of staying within my means.

There was, however, a serious edge to my parsimony. If I was going to succeed in my dream of riding around the world, I'd have very limited funds for a journey that would last an indeterminate time and inevitably involve numerous unforeseen events. I had to learn to exist on the bare minimum.

After America, I returned to PCL for my final year, knowing it would be a year of big decisions about my future. I needed to secure a good degree and find somewhere to undertake a year of work experience so that I could progress to my Part II, the second degree that all architects need to qualify. Although the thought of working in an office followed by two further years in classrooms didn't appeal, I accepted it as a necessary part of joining the kind of profession that my father might respect.

Returning to London also meant a return to Alex, who I now loved so deeply I was seriously considering postponing, even abandoning, my dream of riding around the world in order to build a life after college with him.

In many ways, Alex was the ideal boyfriend, very happy to spend days on end together doing little more than hanging out in my kitchen, chatting and laughing, but equally happy for me to go off with my biker friends for weeks at a time, never becoming jealous or demanding if my attention was elsewhere.

However, Alex's easy-going nature also left me feeling slightly on edge, wondering if he wasn't fully committed to our relationship. And as the stress of our approaching finals increased, our commitment to one another faltered. For no particular reason, we split up a couple of times, our on–off relationship leaving me wondering what was happening, where we were headed and in which direction I should look to the future.

My trip across America with Justin had convinced me that I could now ride across the continent on my own. And if I could get from New York to Los Angeles, then I could ship the bike to Sydney, where I might be able to earn some money to fund the next leg of my trip. Breaking down the trip into sections made it more manageable, more easily envisaged, and by early autumn I'd started preparing seriously, writing to shipping companies.

A few months after my and Alex's second anniversary, and a week before Valentine's Day (not that we were in the habit of celebrating such conventions), I found a letter on my kitchen table.

'Dear Elspeth,' it began. 'Here I am upstairs writing to you downstairs, because when I see you now my heart is so confused my head can't think of anything to say.'

I read these opening words, written by Alex in red ink on a page torn from a spiral-bound notebook, and although they confused me, I instantly knew what was coming next.

'You cannot tell how much pleasure you have given me just being with you. You are beautiful, but beyond that you have a beauty which comes from within, very strong, which can only be described as good. You are a very special person. Thank you.'

Insisting his intentions were good, Alex told me the relationship was over without ever saying it in so many words. Instead he left me confused, struggling to understand what he meant when he wrote: 'We have so much in common in the way we see and feel things sometimes it shocks me, but in other ways we are so different it hurts.'

Bewildered, I read on. Alex gave no reason for wanting us to split. He offered no explanation, no request for forgiveness. Instead he wrote about the awkwardness he felt about writing the letter, then ended his note in the same simple-worded ambiguous tone as he'd started it.

'I know it will take time. It's always worth looking forward to better times, surely? Love from A.'

Confused and devastated, I went upstairs to where I guessed Alex had written the letter, thinking, hoping, wishing he might still be there.

Instead of Alex, I found another copy of the letter screwed up in a bin in the corner of a room. It was identical in every respect to the letter he'd left for me, except for the last sentence, which he'd omitted from the letter he left on my kitchen table: 'I love you Elspeth, I always will. Sadly, A.'

I couldn't understand why Alex had initially written he loved me, then decided it was better not to say so, but I decided then and there I would never tackle him on it. It was his decision and it wasn't my business to ask him, or to tell him I'd found both letters. Instead I folded the letters together, tucked them in a pocket.

The split hit me hard. It was the first time I'd been dumped and I was really in love with Alex. I'd always remained friends with ex-boyfriends, but this time I knew it was going to be different. Alex wasn't going to figure in my future life and the thought of that tore me apart. Desperately unhappy and lonely, I looked for distractions.

To get away from Alex, maybe to prove something to him, I decided I'd definitely now go away. I had just over three months until I finished my degree in June and I'd already managed to save £2,000 during three years at college. If I started working straight away, I might be able to double that by the end of the summer.

Riding a bike around the world was probably an extreme reaction to heartbreak. Other people might have considered going somewhere hot for a fortnight, got drunk, let their hair down in a new environment. But I knew that wasn't for me because when it was over I'd have to return home, where I'd still be confronted by my feelings for Alex.

A short break wouldn't be enough, I decided. I needed a proper distraction.

*

Within days of being dumped by Alex, I started a letter-writing campaign to seek sponsorship and advice for my trip. I wrote to anyone – accessory manufacturers, bike magazines, BMW in Germany – who I thought might be vaguely interested in helping a young, inexperienced female biker to do something that few people had achieved. To all the letters written, I received only two replies.

One of the letters, a very polite rejection, came from BMW Germany. The other was sent by the editor of *Bike* magazine, who made it very obvious that he and the rest of his chauvinist colleagues found the whole idea extremely amusing.

'Dear Elspeth,' the editor replied on a typewriter with wonky letters and uneven spacing.

Brecon said he'd write this letter but he can't 'cos his tongues [sic] jammed his typewriter.

Julian asks if you've got a eight feet tall husband who's also a karate expert?

Mike Clements has already formed the Elspeth Beard Appreciation Society and wants to know where in the world you're going to be so he can get there first.

Me? I'd like to offer you sponsorship 'around the world' but I think that'd be a waste and a shame for London.

Best wishes,
Dave Calderwood

Reading the letter, I could imagine the jeering laughs *Bike*'s editorial team had at my expense. I imagined them returning from lunch at a pub near their office and sitting down to compose their letter, each of them trying to contribute a more mocking response than their predecessor.

The thought of the banter going round the office at my expense made me seethe. At that moment I became more determined than ever to show them and other doubters that I could do it without their help.

But before I could do that, I composed a reply. 'Dear Boys . . .' I started. I thanked them for interrupting their busy days stuck behind their desks to reply to a reader who was going to do something of which they only dreamt. Then I picked off each of my detractors in turn.

'Brecon,' I wrote. 'Don't bother getting your tongue out of your typewriter as I'm sure you wouldn't know what to do with it.'

I continued in the same sarcastic fashion, the letter firing up a fury that they could dismiss me so casually. But it also made me feel quite alone. Rick, Nick, Johnny, Simon, Mike and Annie had dispersed from London to study or work. And whenever I mentioned my trip plans to any of them, I got the feeling it distanced me from them. After all, few people went round the world in those days, let alone by motorbike. Even my parents were turning against the idea.

I tried not to let the detractors bother me too much and concentrated on getting my bike prepared for the trip. Following the instructions in my Haynes manual, I stripped down the cylinder heads, replaced all the seals and gaskets, installed an extra base gasket to lower the compression. Replacing the three-gallon tank with a £20 second-hand five-gallon tank increased my range from 180 miles to 300 miles. I changed the handlebars from Laverda Jota drops to the standard BMW bars, which would be a lot more comfortable for the long distances. I put on new tyres, fitted a new battery, replaced all the cables and generally gave the bike a thorough service. I also removed anything that wasn't absolutely essential, such as the clock, hazard warning lights, spotlights and the side covers.

As I worked in the garage below my parents' mews cottage, my mind ran through which route to take. In 1982 there were very few guidebooks. With a school atlas open on the garage floor, I could see that the logical direction was east through Turkey, Iran, India and Southeast Asia to Australia. Riding towards the morning sun, it would take me maybe a year to reach Oz, which was a problem. Although I could afford the time, I didn't have enough money to last that long. And riding through countries where I didn't speak the language, where the culture often discriminated against women, would be a challenge that might prompt me to turn home.

By contrast, starting my ride in America and riding west was more manageable. I knew how to minimize expenditure in the States and I knew the language. If I worked seven days a week from the end of my finals in June until I departed in October, I reckoned I could save another £600, which would take my budget up to £2,600 (approximately £6,500 in 2017). If I was careful, it ought to get me across America, then I'd fly and my bike would sail to Australia, where I could work for six months to raise funds for the next leg of my journey.

I phoned around some shipping companies, nervous and apprehensive because it was the first real commitment to doing the trip. I also got myself a temporary New York State Insurance ID card. In the midst of all this, I completed my Architecture degree, a struggle because it involved bumping into Alex, whom I wanted to avoid at all costs.

By mid-June I'd finished my exams and was working at the Devonshire Arms seven days a week. Starting at 8.30 a.m., I made sandwiches and salads until 11.30 a.m., when I would go behind the bar to serve the lunchtime rush of office workers, doctors, radiographers, shopkeepers and journalists from the local BBC radio station. At 3.30 p.m. I had two hours' rest before returning to the pub to work until midnight.

The pay was pitiful, the hours nearly killed me and I hated having to be polite to drunken idiots who would either shower me with abuse or try to chat me up when I was still pining for Alex.

The alternative, of getting a proper job and settling down, offered very little to get excited about. By August, I had the results of my Architecture finals, a disappointing third-class honours degree. Dejected, questioning whether I should continue with architecture at all, I felt an even stronger need to get away and leave everything behind me. Margaret Thatcher's first term as prime minister was approaching its end. It was a time of stark recession, 12 per cent unemployment and bleak prospects for graduates. My friends were scrabbling around for jobs, but I couldn't see myself sitting in a city architect's office, toeing the nine to five line. Hoping Australia might offer better prospects for a young woman, I wrote to a Sydney architect called Harry Seidler to ask for work experience. He agreed, so I applied for an Australian working holiday visa.

Big mistake.

Working holiday visas were intended for travellers picking up short-term jobs here and there before moving on. They weren't intended for people like me who wanted to work in one place for six months before continuing their trip. If I'd lied and said I was going to be an itinerant worker, I would have got the visa I needed, but my honesty got my application rejected. Now I was stuck with nowhere to earn the funds to finish my trip. I wrote to several shipping companies providing them with details of my bike, my intended route and my first port of call. A few weeks later, the shipping company sent me a quote with a terse warning: *The prices are estimated on today's tariffs and rates of exchange and exclude insurance, packing, customs documentation, clearance, quay rent, demurrage, duty, local taxes and dues, chamber fees, import licences, export licences, surveys, penalties and fines.*

Wondering what exactly I was paying for, I booked a passage for my bike to New York in early September.

With less than a month to go to my planned departure at the end of September, all my attention focused on preparing for my trip while sidestepping the parade of drunken passes I received behind the bar at the Devonshire Arms. Evenings, when regulars and locals filled the pub, were generally less hassle than daytime, when office staff formed most of the clientele, like the three engineers who turned up one manic lunchtime. Two of them immediately tried to chat me up even though it was obvious I was really busy.

Smiling, I stood there patiently as the pair took ages to find their money in their pockets while, behind them, a queue of customers waited to be served. But my patience ran out when they decided that it would be funny and flirtatious to throw their money at me.

Turning away from them, I mouthed a single word at one of the other bar staff.

'Arseholes.'

When I turned back to the group, its third member, who hadn't thrown money, was looking very embarrassed.

'I'm sorry,' he said.

I smiled weakly.

'Do you work in the evenings?'

'Usually.' I smiled again. 'I'm trying to save money to go away travelling.'

The young engineer turned away and joined his colleagues for a drink and some food, but as he was leaving, he leant over the bar.

'I'll see you again.'

I nodded, thought nothing more of it until the pub phone rang three days later.

'It's Mark here,' said a voice. 'I came in the other day with those two idiots. I wondered if you'd like to go for a drink.'

A date was the last thing I needed, but I had nothing to lose and nothing happening outside work that week. 'Why not?'

We met the following weekend. Focused entirely on my trip and still getting over Alex, the thought of romance was very far from my mind, but Mark was extremely persistent, phoning regularly after our first date, asking to see me.

'I'm going off in a month's time,' I told him repeatedly.

'That's okay . . . I don't mind,' he said.

I liked Mark, but I was still reeling from Alex. So, not wanting to hurt his feelings, I decided to be straight with Mark. 'I can't get involved,' I said. 'This is the wrong time and wrong place for me.'

But Mark didn't seem to care. When I wasn't working, he would come over to my flat, watch while I serviced the bike, wrote letters, made arrangements for my trip. So I let him. It was hardly a heady whirlwind romance.

On 10 September 1982, I rode my bike out to a warehouse near the Thames docks at Dartford in Kent. Standing in the warehouse, I wrapped up my bike, then watched as two dockhands pushed her into a wooden crate. I placed some spare parts and tools beside her, gave her a fond pat, then stood back as the dockhands nailed on the crate's cover.

Suddenly there was no turning back. I was actually going.

I left the warehouse in a daze, a mix of nerves and excitement made worse by the exhaustion of working more than a hundred hours a week while memories of Alex still haunted me.

When I got home, I told my parents and friends about my bike's departure. Most of them looked at me wide-eyed. All of them responded similarly. 'So . . . does that mean you're really going then?' Even now they were expecting me to chicken out, but as I explained to them, it was far too late for that. My bike was on its way and so was I.

To Mark's great credit, he didn't try to dissuade me. He didn't understand what I was doing or why, but he accepted it. He even seemed slightly bemused by it all. Dad said nothing, but that was normal for him. He left it all to Mum, who stepped up her campaign to discourage me. For months it had been 'Do you *really* need to do this, Elspeth?' Now, as the day of departure approached, she became more desperate to stop me. 'If you leave, don't think of darkening our doorstep again' turned a few days before my departure date into a not entirely serious threat to disinherit me if I left.

'Why, when you have a choice, do you have to choose the difficult path over the easy one?' she said. Not having an easy answer, I shrugged. 'Elspeth, dear . . . your wandering spirit . . .' Mum sighed. 'I just worry where it might lead you in life.' I knew Mum's kind, caring wisdom lay behind her questioning of my character. If she sounded harsh or judgemental, she certainly didn't mean it. It was simply a sign of her wanting me to be what she considered normal. Like any mother, she worried that something might go wrong when I was a long way from home and from her.

On 2 October I awoke with butterflies in my stomach. I'd spent the previous days packing and repacking my belongings repeatedly, trying to decide what to take, not just for myself, but for my bike. By late afternoon, a small collection of bags was piled by the door to my flat. A red sausage-shaped nylon holdall contained my clothes and camping gear, which amounted to very little: a pair of soft shoes; a pair of waxed Belstaff waterproof trousers and a pair of shorts; a couple of T-shirts; a jumper; some socks and underwear. I'd wear my leather jacket, jeans and bike boots on the plane and carry a small tank bag in which I kept my valuables – maps, camera, passport and money, basic tools. In two fold-over plastic panniers I put the larger tools and spares for my bike that I'd not packed in the crate with my bike.

That evening I had a few friends round to the flat. Mark, Mike the Artist, Aussie John, Nick and Rick's younger brother Johnny, Justin and my parents. We were meant to be celebrating my departure, but it was a strangely subdued affair. Even now, my friends and parents were still not entirely resigned to the fact I was leaving, and I was in such a daze I found it difficult to relax or enjoy my last evening at home. The following morning Mark and I said our awkward goodbyes, not knowing when we would see each other again. I felt a sense of relief at leaving and I hoped he'd forget me and get on with his life in London. All my thoughts were of what now lay ahead.

Twelve hours later I was at Heathrow. From my seat in the corner of the terminal, I peered at the departures board. Only one more PanAm flight to New York was showing and I was on standby. I didn't fancy my chances of getting a seat. Actually, I was betting against it, more out of hope than conviction.

A deep breath. I wiped tears from my face, rubbed wet palms against my jeans as I stood up, pulled on my biker jacket. The PanAm desk was just in sight, a blue-suited member of the ground staff sitting sharp behind it.

I slung my bags over my shoulder – the tank bag, the fold-over panniers, the red holdall – and felt my knees begin to crumple. The weight of the bags wasn't too bad, but their awkward bulkiness was manageable only in short stints. Suddenly the desk felt a lot further away, but I made it, my T-shirt damp beneath my blue leather jacket.

'Any chance of getting on the next flight to JFK?'

Trying not to look too hopeful, I watched the PanAm ground staff look at his clipboard, then flick left to a large, grey plastic box, a computer screen. Leaning over the desk as the employee consulted PanAm's computer, I prayed silently.

Don't let there be a spare seat, I said to myself. *Don't tell me I'm going.*

The PanAm man looked at me. 'Yup, we got a space.'

My heart sank.

'You sure?'

A smile and a nod. 'Definite.'

I tried to sound pleased. 'Oh . . . excellent.'

But it didn't feel excellent.

I really couldn't turn back now. Not after everything I'd said. *No choice but to carry on*, I told myself. *Better that than going back and losing face.*

But in truth, I was kidding myself. My destiny had been decided days earlier. I went wherever my bike led me. And my big Beemer was already in the Big Apple.

3

FIRST DAYS ON THE ROAD:
NEW YORK TO NEW MEXICO

New York, 3 October 1982

Strapped into my seat on the last flight to New York, some of the doubts I'd had earlier began to fade away. It was a relief not to have to do much for the next seven hours, except think about what lay ahead. Almost immediately my thoughts turned to Mark and I wished I hadn't been quite so distant towards him. He'd been so generous and sweet to me, while I'd been selfish and single-minded. I worried sometimes that I'd made him feel as if he was more of an irritation than a boyfriend. I decided to write to him when I got to New York, just to apologize for not treating him very well. I'd tell him I wasn't worth waiting for.

Arriving in New York at 10 p.m., I got myself to a cheap hotel in midtown Manhattan, then crawled into bed for a longer sleep than I'd had in the past week. Weeks of working solidly at the pub, preparing and packing for the trip, clearing out my flat and saying goodbye to everyone had finally caught up with me. The next morning, after waking feeling refreshed for the first time in ages, I decided to waste no time in finding my bike at the docks.

Several subway train journeys later, I was in the shipping agent's office in Brooklyn, shocked to discover that my insurance for New York State alone would cost me $195 and questioning why it would take three days to process my bike through customs. I'd intended to leave New York that afternoon for somewhere that was cheaper than a Manhattan hotel. Worried that I'd run out of money sooner than anticipated, I decided to walk back to the hotel, a journey that took more than two hours, but saved me seventy-five cents. If I saved that much three times a day I'd have enough to pay for a meal. It all added up.

Having done the sights in New York on a previous visit with Justin and knowing I'd be spending money as soon as I walked out the door, I spent a lot of time in my dark little hotel room, curled up, watching television or hibernating to store up sleep and energy for the journey ahead.

On my second evening in New York, I wrote to Mark, relieved that there were now 4,000 miles between us and I no longer had to go through the motions of a relationship. But I also felt bad that my feelings for Mark did not match his for me and hoped the separation would cause our vague relationship to fizzle out. I had other things on my mind.

By my fourth day in New York, I was losing patience with the customs people. Bored with sitting in my hotel room, staring at the ceiling hour after hour, I decided to hassle the customs officials until they processed my bike simply to get rid of me. I was just about to head down to the customs office to thump on a few desks when the hotel reception called up to my room to say they'd had a call. My shipment was ready for collection at nine o'clock the next morning.

Five days after arriving in New York, I rolled my bike out of the customs warehouse, amazed that it was still in one piece and even had my little green rubber frog, which I'd mounted spread-eagled behind my fairing as a mascot. Wasting no time, I pulled on my helmet and rode back to the hotel, where I made a note of the odometer (45,477 miles), strapped my bags to the bike, then battled my way out of New York City with no more than a rough idea of which way to go. I found my way to the Lincoln Tunnel, then paid a toll to pass under the Hudson River to emerge in New Jersey, where I looked at the sun and headed north. I'd worry about where exactly I was when I ran out of road.

A few hours later, I was on Route 17, heading north through beautiful farming land, past small towns, the road lined with trees in full autumn colours, my bike purring beneath me as if she was delighted to be released onto the open road after captivity in a ship and warehouse.

I pulled into a petrol station on the highway for my first tank of American 'gas', served by an attendant. Having loosened the lid, I waited by my bike, but every attendant pointedly looked the other way, walking stiffly past me to serve customers who'd arrived after me. I raised my hand, tried to get the attention of one of the attendants. I was sure he'd seen me, but he turned away.

Ten minutes passed. Still no service. I was getting hot in my helmet, so I removed it, shook my hair loose and looked around. Was I ever going to get served here? I caught the eye of one of the attendants; could have sworn he did a double take. He nodded at me, smiled. Now I was getting a response. Is that all it took, removing my helmet so they could see I was a girl, that I wasn't a threat and wasn't going to cause problems?

Two of the attendants came over, their body language now relaxed and welcoming.

'Ma'am?'

'Can I get some petrol?' I said.

Their eyes widened. 'You from England?'

I nodded.

'Wow.'

The questions now coming thick and fast, they couldn't serve me fast enough. Nothing was too much trouble. I went to pay inside the petrol station and as soon as I opened my mouth, there were more questions.

'How ya findin' it here?' said the woman behind the cash register.

'I'm not finding the people very friendly.'

I walked out. With my helmet off, I was a source of fascination, but with it over my head, they didn't want to know me. I wondered if it was because bikers didn't have a good image in American culture. Marlon Brando in *The Wild One*, Peter Fonda and Dennis Hopper in *Easy Rider*. Maybe it was no surprise many Americans thought anyone on a bike was definitely male and definitely trouble. I hoped it wouldn't continue like this right across America.

By six o'clock I was in Binghamton, a pleasant college town about 200 miles north-west of New York City. I checked the bike over and, reassured that everything was okay, rode from one motel to another, looking for a bed.

Without a guidebook to hand, I had little idea of what price to expect, but plucking a figure out of the air, I'd budgeted on spending five to ten dollars a night. I was very wide of the mark. If the motel rooms were this expensive I'd run out of money before I got to Australia.

I contemplated finding somewhere to pitch my tiny two-man tent, but it was cold and miserable. After riding 200 miles, I really didn't fancy it.

Tired and needing a bed, I pulled into the forecourt of yet another motel and walked into the reception, where a woman was standing behind a counter.

'Get out!'

I stopped dead, held up both hands in surrender, then loosened the strap under my helmet and removed it.

'Oh!'

I smiled. 'Do you have a room?'

The woman looked flustered. 'I . . .'

'The sign outside says you have vacancies.'

Although reluctant to let me stay, she had a room for $27, a lot of money but cheaper than anywhere else I'd found and it did have a colour television. I took it.

Fifteen minutes later, lying on my bed after a shower, I wondered if I was going to be made to feel unwelcome wherever I went. Justin and I had experienced no problems when we'd ridden from Los Angeles to Detroit, but I had an overwhelming feeling they didn't like bikers much in this part of the States. It seemed they thought anyone on a motorcycle was a dirty, dangerous Hell's Angel.

Interested in very little other than my bed and getting my money's worth from the television, I spent the evening in my room, eventually drifting off to sleep. It felt good to have the first day behind me.

*

Keen to reach Auntie Renee's home in Detroit before dark, I left the motel shortly after 6 a.m. The thought of forking out another $27 for a night's sleep when I could stay with family had me speeding through a flat, featureless landscape. By midday, I was standing beside Niagara Falls, having crossed the border into Canada. The falls were spectacular, but after a quick lunch and the mandatory photo opportunities, I was back on my bike, mindful that I'd completed less than 250 of nearly 500 miles I had to ride that day.

Two hundred miles into Canada, I started to feel extremely tired, my shoulders really aching. Riding long distances after months of bumbling around London, covering only a few miles at a time, was a shock to my system. With every mile, the attraction of pulling over to find a hotel for the night became stronger, but with only another fifty miles of agony to go, I persuaded myself to continue.

Shortly after 8 p.m., I arrived at the border, every part of my body aching with tiredness, desperate to end the day's journey. Pulling up at the US Border Control, I turned off my headlight to avoid blinding the border guard in the darkness, but my gesture was met with frosty suspicion. There was nothing for it. Yet again, I pulled off my helmet to show I was female. Then, when I opened my mouth and he heard my English accent, everything changed. 'Sorry, ma'am. We'll soon have you on your way.'

Finding Renee's house in Detroit was easier than I expected and an hour later I was in the bosom of my extended family, surrounded by her four young children in a wonderfully chaotic household.

Staying with Renee, I did very little except eat, sleep, take stock of my journey and plan my route ahead. My choice influenced by the weather, I decided to avoid the northern states, which were cold and wet in October. Instead, I'd travel through the Deep South. I'd always wanted to see New Orleans.

On the morning of the third day with Renee, I looked up the Australian High Commission in the Detroit phone book, rode into town to ask for a visa, but was turned down again. The next morning I decided to leave and packed up my bike, strapped all my gear on, took a look at my watch and changed my mind. On the fifth day, I did the same. I wasn't spending any money and I really didn't want to leave. On day six, self-motivation kicked in and I finally departed the comforts of my aunt's home, bound for Cincinnati.

Two hundred and seventy miles of desperately dull highways gave me plenty of time to think things over. Inevitably, my thoughts turned to Alex. I was still feeling confused about what had happened between us and wondered if I would even be here if he hadn't dumped me. Riding across the Midwest prairie, surrounded by mile after mile of Ohio maize fields, it was strange to think that if Alex hadn't written me the two notes that were now folded in the breast pocket of my leather jacket, I might now be moving furniture into a one-bedroomed flat, somewhere on the District Line, hoping for a job in an architect's practice in London. Already, London and everyone I'd left behind were starting to feel very far away.

Before leaving Renee's home, I'd located a youth hostel in Cincinnati, but the address I'd noted down proved to be a detached Victorian house in a nondescript street. No youth hostel sign. Nothing to suggest it was anything but a suburban home.

I knocked at the door. A man in his late twenties answered, tall, fair-haired, in jeans and a casual shirt. I asked for directions to the youth hostel.

'Right here.'

I glanced around. Not even a YHA sign on the door.

'I just bought it,' said the man.

'And it's a youth hostel?'

The man nodded. He seemed a nice guy, but something in his manner made me suspicious. He was a bit nervous and his hostel was unlike any other I'd stayed in.

'I'm Philip.' He held out his hand.

'Is anyone else staying here?'

'No.'

I felt uncertain. Surely anyone could say their home was a youth hostel, get young people in, drug them and harvest their organs? I envisaged bodies being shipped out under the cover of darkness.

'Why don't you come in, have a look around, see if you like it?'

Philip showed me the register. It had the proper YHA logo at the top of each page, which reassured me, but there were no names on any of the pages.

I decided to take a chance. Beneath his nervous manner, Philip seemed trustworthy. And his hostel was cheap. It looked comfortable and there was little chance of being disturbed by other rowdy guests.

Philip turned out to be very friendly and welcoming. That afternoon, he showed me around Cincinnati, riding behind on my pillion. We went up a tower and gazed out at the view. Parts of Cincinnati were very beautiful. Later, after returning to the hostel, we went out for several beers, which he bought. We had a few good laughs, talked about many things, and although I sensed he was quite attracted, he didn't try it on. Instead, he persuaded me to stay a second night. He was nice and seemed very pleased to have a guest, so I said yes. At last, someone who wasn't suspicious of bikers.

I left early on the morning of 17 October, the start of my third week on the road. Three hundred miles to Gatlinburg on the edge of the Great Smoky Mountains National Park, where I hoped to save some money by camping that night.

As ever, financial concerns filled my thoughts. As I rode I pondered the old girl's consumption. It was a big country, which meant big distances every day and hefty fuel bills. The BMW was most economical when cruising at about 60 mph, but I got bored, wanted to ride faster, so I tried to calculate the pay-off between slow riding, which incurred greater expenditure on accommodation and food, versus fast riding, which cost more in petrol. There was no easy answer.

After a long hard ride through Kentucky into Tennessee, I arrived at Gatlinburg only to discover that all the campsites and motels were full. Asking around, I discovered I'd chosen the busiest weekend of the entire year, when almost everyone within driving distance came to the park to see the autumn tree colours. Disbelieving my bad luck, I sat down on the side of the road, too tired to ride on any further. I always found that this was the best way to make decisions.

While I was sitting contemplating the situation, an elderly couple stopped beside me. I explained my predicament, hoping that they might have some idea of where I could stay, but they wouldn't hear any of it and offered me a bed in their huge motorhome. Under the circumstances I had little choice, although I felt slightly embarrassed sitting in their pristine motorhome in filthy leathers and duck-oiled cotton trousers. It didn't seem to bother them and I had a very pleasant evening with them.

They asked me where I was headed. When I said Sydney, then London via the Far East, India and Iran, Jack told me he had spent many years travelling. 'When I was young and travelled I think I was just trying to get away from myself,' he said. 'But everywhere I pulled up at night I was always there.' I knew exactly what he meant. Here I was in the middle of Tennessee, on my own, far from home, running away from my problems and trying to get away from my feelings for Alex, which I still carried with me everywhere I went.

Although Alex and Mark were frequently in my thoughts, I felt that the trip was already doing me good. With every passing day and mile, I thought about them slightly less. The simple requirements of my life on the road – calculations of mileage and consumption, considerations of the journey ahead and what I needed to do at my next stop – were pushing thoughts of home out of my head. Before it got too late and the conversation turned to even more weighty matters, I made my excuses and turned in for the night.

'Remember, Elspeth,' said Jack as I was about to leave the room. 'Young people with no friends are nobody.'

The next day, Jack and his wife insisted they chauffeur me around the park, but by midday, realizing one view across the Smoky Mountains was very much like every other, I was on the road again, heading west towards Nashville and Memphis for no particular reason other than I had heard of them.

I didn't know what to expect of Nashville, but as it was the epicentre of Country and Western music, I imagined the locals would all be dressed in huge cowboy hats, fancy boots, shirts with tassels and collar brooches, and jeans with huge belt buckles. Needless to say,

I didn't see a single person dressed like that, not even a hint of the Country and Western music scene at all. Disappointed, I decided to keep moving and stopped that night at a small hotel off the freeway between Nashville and Memphis.

The next day I arrived in Memphis by mid-morning and searched out Elvis Presley's house, Graceland, only to find it was closed to visitors. All I could do was stand outside the iconic wrought-iron gates shaped like a book of sheet music, with green-coloured musical notes and two silhouettes of Elvis. They weren't something I would normally ride out of my way to see, but as I was there I decided to make the most of it, so I bought a sandwich, sat outside the gates, eating it and watching all the other tourists, many of whom were carving or writing their names on the wall.

With nothing else to interest me in Memphis, I turned my bike south and headed towards New Orleans, a place I'd always wanted to visit. As I rode along smaller routes parallel to the Interstate highway, the air felt warmer, the accents sounded broader and the speech became slower the further south I went. Passing through cotton fields, it felt like life was slowing almost to a halt. I stopped to take a photograph and there was total silence, absolute peace, one of those perfect moments, just me on my own in a motionless environment. No cars, no voices. Nobody there. No one wanting anything from me. I loved it. It was exactly what I'd been seeking for the last few months.

By six o'clock darkness was approaching, so I pulled over at Vicksburg, an old pioneering town and the scene of a decisive siege in the American Civil War. Two hundred miles from New Orleans, it left an easy day's ride for the following day, so I drove around the main streets looking for a cheap motel. Hot, sticky and tired, I'd stopped to look at a map of the town when a red Corvette Stingray with white leather seats cruised up.

'Can I help you, honey?'

The voice came from a man dressed entirely in white leaning out of the window of the Stingray, his eyebrows raised suggestively. With a huge gold medallion buried in his hairy chest and eyes like a shark, he immediately reminded me of Burt Reynolds.

'I'm okay, thanks,' I said, feeling like I was a bit-part player in some trashy 1970s Hollywood movie.

'You look more than okay,' said Stingray Man, 'but you don't seem okay.'

I explained I was looking for a cheap motel.

'Follow me, sweetie pie.'

He spoke in a slow southern drawl that in any other circumstances I would have found attractive. I weighed it up: surely there was no harm in taking up his offer? After all, I was on my bike so I could go anywhere I pleased. I agreed.

Five minutes later we were outside a motel with a large neon sign: *Rooms $10 per Nite*. It certainly looked like the kind of place I was after. As I walked towards a hut labelled reception, an obese man in a food-stained nylon shirt over skin slick with sweat pushed open a fly screen on the door.

'Yeah?'

'Are you the owner?' I said.

He nodded slowly. I noticed he had a shotgun hanging casually from his right hand, as if it were an everyday thing. Perhaps it was, here in Vicksburg.

'I'm looking for a room.'

'We got three types – ten dollar, fifteen dollar, twenty dollar.'

'I'll try the ten dollar.'

Without even nodding, the owner lolloped away from me, his feet slapping along the walkway as he led me from the reception hut to the rooms, his gun still in his right hand. The motel seemed empty, no guests loitering around. He stopped at a door, leant his shotgun against its frame, opened the door and flicked a switch inside the room.

'This one's ten dollars.'

I looked inside. It was basic and a bit grubby, but good enough for me, especially at that price.

Behind me, Stingray Man lurked, heavy-lidded, smoking a cigarette. I left him outside the room, followed the obese motel owner back to the reception hut, where I filled out some forms, paid my deposit and got a key. When I returned to my room, Stingray

Man was gone. Relieved that I'd shaken him off, I opened the door, carried my bags into the room. Suddenly Stingray Man was behind me, appearing from heavens know where. He followed me into the room, sitting down in its only chair.

'Well . . .' I said, 'thanks very much for your help.'

I smiled to soften the implication that it was now time for him to leave, but he failed to take the hint. I turned my back.

'You feel like company?'

A hand slid over my bum, round my hips, towards my front.

'No.'

I said it as firmly as I could, but he refused to go. I didn't listen to what he said next. The tone was obvious: lascivious, suggestive, predatory.

'You having any trouble, miss?'

It was Obese Owner. He was in the doorway. I never thought I'd be pleased to see him, but he'd turned up just in time.

'I was just asking this gentleman to leave,' I said.

'You know this *gentleman*?'

I explained that Stingray Man had led me to the motel, but that was all.

'So I guess it's time for you to go,' said Obese Owner, stepping into the room, his shotgun still held in his right hand, hanging loose beside his hip. Stingray Man paused for a moment; then, without saying a word, he left. I expected Obese Owner to follow him out, but he only went as far as the door, from where he watched Stingray Man get into his Corvette, drive out of the motel, out of sight on the highway.

'You need anything from the grocery store?' said Obese Owner.

I told him I was fine, wondered how long I'd have to wait before he left.

'Just say if you need anything.'

'Thanks.' I pulled a polite smile, not too curt, I hoped.

'You mind if I come in and talk?'

I wanted privacy, but Obese Owner had just saved my skin. Thinking it might seem churlish if I was too unfriendly, I shook my head.

'Be my guest.'

He was pleasant enough. We discussed Stingray Man and his wandering hand trouble.

'If that jerk comes back,' said Obese Owner, 'I've got my 12-bore in my office. I'll blow his ass off.'

I didn't know what to say. It seemed wrong to say thanks to an offer of murder, but I appreciated the sentiment.

'That's good to know,' I said.

'Well, what about me then?' said Obese Owner. 'I've never slept with an English girl.'

I looked at him and realized he wasn't joking. A tiny part of me admired the chutzpah of his simple matter-of-fact approach, but I shook my head.

'Thanks, but no thanks,' I said, then reminded myself to smile. He had a gun and I was maybe the only guest in the motel. 'It's been a long day on the road. I need some rest.'

Obese Owner shrugged and left the room. My heart pounding, I bolted the door behind him. I tried to settle down for the night, exhausted after the day's ride. Lying on the bed, studying the map, deciding on the following day's route, I let my eyes wander and noticed the brown pattern on the carpet. It appeared to be moving. For a moment, I thought my eyes were going. Was tiredness playing tricks with my vision? Then I looked at the walls . . . the ceiling . . . the bedspread. They all appeared to be moving.

Cockroaches. Hundreds of them. I leapt off the bed, grabbed my shoes, pulled one on, stopped suddenly when I felt something move beneath my foot. It was a roach, inside my shoe.

Suppressing the urge to scream, I tipped out the cockroach, grabbed as much of my stuff as I could, felt relieved that I'd been too tired to unpack most of it, ran out of the door.

'I can cope with just about anything,' I told Obese Man in the reception hut. 'Spiders, snakes, almost any insect or creepy-crawly. But roaches I hate.'

Obese Owner gave me a new room, a better one for the same $10 price, so I felt I'd scored at least a minor victory, even if I was still finding squashed cockroaches inside my clothes and bags weeks later.

*

I spent a pleasant morning in warm sunshine, wandering around Vicksburg's huge park full of war memorials. Keen to get to New Orleans, I set off before midday, unsure of exactly which route to take, but knowing that New Orleans lay to the south. An hour later I found myself riding through the swamps of the Mississippi delta, the road signs telling me I was about 150 miles from the Big Easy.

The swamps kept my mind busy for fifteen or twenty minutes, but soon grew dull when they continued for hour after hour. With little in the monotonous landscape to occupy me, my mind wandered. And inevitably, it wandered to thoughts of Mark. Approaching a month on the road on my own and I still hadn't managed to work out my feelings about him. He was such a nice person, but somehow his niceness conspired to turn me off. Maybe if Mark hadn't made his love for me so obvious, I'd have found him more attractive. That niceness was a problem. He had no edge, no danger and none of the exciting uncertainty I'd felt with Alex. Whereas Alex always left me guessing, Mark presented his love to me on a plate. Knowing exactly what I was getting made Mark a bit boring to me. Maybe I needed danger more than I needed security.

By late afternoon I was in a New Orleans youth hostel, enjoying the company of other travellers for the first time since I had left home. The city was a great place, compact and manageable on foot, and the hostel, a lovely old French Creole building with wrought-iron balconies, was busy with the usual hostelling people, comparing all their travelling adventures.

Having rolled up on my bike, I felt slightly apart from the other travellers, excluded from their experiences and their need to hook up with other young people on the backpacker trail. They looked at me as if I were slightly strange. A couple of them made it clear they were suspicious of a young woman on a big bike, especially when I told them I was on my way to Sydney, but it was pleasant to be around fellow travellers again.

On the second day, I met a girl from Montreal at breakfast and we went around New Orleans together. Unused to the company of other people, I found myself struggling to talk to her. Still unsure of exactly why I was doing the trip, I found myself clamming up in the company of others, paranoid that everyone thought I was dull and uninteresting.

Fortunately New Orleans was full of life, the streets bustling with music, buskers, jazz halls and bars. Although not somewhere I'd stay for long, it made a pleasant break for a few days. I realized I'd been riding my bike every day since I left Detroit, the thoughts in my head keeping me moving forwards, putting miles under my BMW's wheels as a distraction. Maybe if my head and heart weren't such a swirling mass of thoughts and emotions, I would have ridden slower, stopped more, taken in the sights instead of racing across the continent to Los Angeles.

After three days in New Orleans, I was tiring of a big city and longed to be on my own again. Sometimes solitude was my best companion. I left early the next morning, heading west for Houston, which I hoped to make that night as there was another youth hostel there, across the state line in Texas, a state I'd heard so much about but never experienced. Remembering the boast of a Texan I'd met with Justy in one of the Dakotas the previous summer, I rolled into Texas expecting something special in the land of oil, 100,000-acre ranches and ten-gallon hats.

'You haven't seen America until you've seen the Lone Star State,' that Texan had exclaimed.

After such a build-up it was perhaps inevitable that my first experience of the state, a two-hour ride around Houston in search of a youth hostel after 400 hot and dusty miles from New Orleans, was an anti-climax. As far as I could make out, there was little special about Houston, a vast sprawling city of skyscrapers that seemed to be one huge roadwork surrounded by oil derricks. When I found it, the youth hostel was good. Run by a newly wed English couple who seemed genuinely glad to have someone staying with them, it was a pleasant place to stay the night.

From Houston, I rode to San Antonio to see the lump of rock that I'd seen John Wayne fight for in the *Alamo* movie before continuing to El Paso across 500 miles of flat, empty rocky desert, interspersed with occasional bits of scrub.

Riding through endless nothingness for mile after mile, I wondered how Texas had managed to get its reputation. Sure, it was big. And yes, there was something impressive about an extraordinarily empty, endless landscape split only by the road running ahead to the horizon. But I struggled to see what was great about it. Hot and dust-covered, I decided the sooner I got out of the state the better. With very little traffic in sight, I let rip, speeding through Texas faster than anywhere else so far, stopping only when I spotted a chain motel just outside El Paso. I pulled into the forecourt, took a room, parked my bike outside it and looked around. A gas station, a diner and some tumbleweed. That was it. There was a stark beauty to the vast emptiness, the kind of beauty that looks atmospheric in photographs, but seeing it made me realize it was perhaps not that surprising that El Paso's biggest claim to fame seemed to be the number of illegal immigrants that poured in across the border from Mexico.

After a good night's sleep, I ate breakfast in the diner, then decided to give my bike a quick check over before leaving for Las Cruces in New Mexico. My speedo cable was rubbing on the steering yoke, so I re-routed it, then checked all the other cables as well as the fluids and oils.

Satisfied that everything was in order, I pressed the ignition. For the first time since arriving in America, the old girl didn't want to start. Her engine turned over, but that was all.

I unloaded the BMW and investigated. In rerouting my cable, I had pulled a wire off the ignition coil. I reconnected the wire and prepared to leave again. Just as I was reassembling the final parts of the bike, a guy pulled up on a Honda Gold Wing.

Like my friends, I wasn't a bike snob, but there was something about Gold Wings that irritated me and many other bikers. It wasn't so much the bikes as their riders. Compared to BMWs, Gold Wings looked like motorized easy chairs, often attracting riders who were as brash and flash as their transport.

In his early thirties, reasonably good-looking and far too smooth, the Gold Wing rider who'd pulled up beside me was a perfect case in point. Dressed in a leather flying jacket with a sheepskin collar, he walked with a swagger that said he thought he was something rather special.

He made a few remarks as I reattached my tank to my BMW, offering tips that were of little help to someone who knew their bike considerably better than him, but other than that, he said very little until I'd finished.

'Buy you a coffee?'

It seemed churlish to refuse, so I walked with him to the diner.

'Buddy's the name,' he said. 'Bud for short.'

I nodded and listened as Bud told me at length about himself and asked me nothing about how an Englishwoman on a BMW came to be riding through the Texas desert.

'What do you do?' I asked.

'I cruise,' he said. 'It's cool.'

I could sense the conversation wasn't going to go far unless I kept the questions coming about his favourite subject: Bud.

'And when you're not cruising?'

'I've been cruising for two years now. California, mainly.'

I nodded. 'And what brings you to Texas?'

'The law.'

Bud didn't look the fugitive type. 'The law?'

'You can cruise without a helmet here. It's cool.'

There was something quite comforting about Buddy's simple approach to life, even if it was a bit mindless, so I accepted his offer to ride together for the day. Ground down by the drudgery of hundreds of miles a day, alone on long hot freeways, I would have found anybody good company.

We managed only about seventy miles, stopping at Las Cruces, a pleasant New Mexico city dominated by a spectacular vista of the Organ Mountains. Although Bud's conversation wasn't exactly scintillating I enjoyed having some company; the 1,200-mile ride from New Orleans through Texas into New Mexico had been long and lonely. We checked into a chain motel, where I found myself in a room with Bud, wondering how and why I'd ended up alone with him.

Somewhat reluctantly, I slipped into the embrace of Bud's blond-haired arms. He'd said all the right things, charmed me to where he wanted me, but it wasn't my finest hour. I'd never slept around and yet here I was with a complete stranger, going through the motions in a bland, nondescript motel room on the edge of the New Mexico desert.

Even in the midst of it, I felt really cheap, not like myself at all. Maybe I'd spent too much time on my own, confused thoughts of Alex and Mark whirling round my head. Maybe I just needed human contact, but I didn't even particularly like Buddy, who deep down I knew was a complete jerk. A smooth-talking smarmy Californian pretty boy? On a Gold Wing? What was I thinking?

4

PRETTY BOYS AND BIKER GANGS:
NEW MEXICO TO CALIFORNIA

Las Cruces, 26 October 1982

Buddy and I didn't speak much the following morning. There was nothing that unpleasant about him, but the night spent together had not been particularly pleasurable as Bud was a selfish soul. The previous evening I'd told myself that it would be worth it because the sex would be great, but that was merely a way of pre-empting the guilty feelings I knew I'd have in the morning. And now I felt awkward and regretful. Somehow I'd ended up with the worst of everything: rubbish sex and feeling crap about myself. I wanted to get out of the room and onto the open road as fast as I could just to put the event, rather than Buddy himself, behind me.

Before we parted, Buddy asked if I could lend him some money. His bank was in California, he said, and he wasn't able to withdraw any money in New Mexico.

I watched and listened for several hours as Buddy made phone calls to different banks, trying to find a way to access his bank account in Las Cruces. By the end of it, I felt really sorry for him, so I lent him $40, more than a day's budget for me.

We parted outside the motel and I rode up to White Sands National Monument, an extraordinary 275-square-mile expanse of white gypsum and calcium sulphate dunes in the middle of the New Mexico desert.

I walked for miles across white dunes, stared around, marvelling at their stark whiteness against the dirty scrub of the New

Mexico desert. The sky reflecting in the sand, it looked serene, unworldly.

Taking off my boots, I walked on across the gypsum, felt the fine powder slide between my toes. Because it reflected light instead of absorbing it, the sand felt cool underfoot, quite unlike normal desert sand. It was a very special place.

After a while, I sat down, watched a tarantula spider crawl across the surface and thought through the previous twenty-four hours. Why had I slept with Buddy? What was all that about? And how would it be when I saw Buddy again to collect my $40?

Doubting I'd find the answers in the middle of the world's largest gypsum dune field, I walked back to my bike to continue the long journey west towards Tucson, where I relished a night alone in a bed before climbing back onto my bike for the long haul through Arizona into California, towards San Diego.

I was in the Arizona desert, on the move, when I first saw them. Five dark shadows behind me, approaching fast, the only other living things I could see on a long, flat road, running from horizon to horizon across an empty landscape.

With their long front forks, leather jackets, bandanas in place of helmets, I immediately knew what they were.

A biker gang.

They came up alongside me, one on either side. A third rider positioned himself behind me, his front wheel almost touching the rear of my bike, the other two riders on his flanks. I was trapped on three sides.

I looked across, saw the studs, skulls and swastikas on their jackets, the crucifixes and biker club emblems painted on their petrol tanks.

One of them met my eye, swerved his bike towards me, smiled ominously. Was it my long plait, hanging down my back, beneath my helmet, that was making them do this?

Maybe I should have been scared, but something about them didn't faze me. As long as I kept moving and didn't let them pull ahead of me, I'd be fine.

But the riders on either side edged ahead, the two flank riders to my rear moving forwards to take their spaces. They'd done this before, I realized. And I wondered what usually came next. I had to get out of there before they boxed me in.

I accelerated up to 70 mph. They matched my speed. I twisted the throttle some more, glimpsed at my speedometer, saw the needle push past 80 mph . . . 85 mph . . . 90 mph. Still they stuck to me. But I could sense they were struggling to keep up. I twisted the old girl's throttle further, spied an escape in the distance.

A corner.

If I could make it to the bend before they pushed me off the road, I'd be safe. Their big ugly choppers and Harley-Davidson hogs could match my BMW for speed in a straight line, but cornering was another matter.

I twisted the throttle further, edged slightly ahead, then watched three of the bikes – two on either side; one behind me – match me for speed. But now, only a few hundred yards from the bend, they could see what was coming. They started to slow and I moved ahead of them, taking the corner as fast as I could, glorying in the superior handling of my BMW over their dumb meathead hogs. Another two bends followed in quick succession and I watched them in my mirror, dropping back fast, knowing the game was over and I'd won.

With a further twist of the throttle, I left them far behind me, turned them into dots. The race for the corner had shown them up for what they were – five idiots who wanted to frighten a lone woman rider. Maybe they were just playing with me, but it was all a bit unnecessary. Bullies always travel in packs and pick on easy targets. I felt sure they wouldn't have dared give the same treatment to a man. When I stopped for some petrol a couple of hours later, I made sure to tuck my plait inside my leather jacket. Maybe it was best not to advertise the fact that I was a woman.

And maybe I'd just been shown why many Americans distrusted all bikers.

*

Three weeks after turning my back on the Atlantic Ocean, I crested a hill and there she was in front of me: the blue-green expanse of the Pacific. By six o'clock that evening I was pulling up outside the home of Walter, son of Heddy, a very old friend of my mother. San Diego lay around me. Having reached the coast, North America was done. Three continents to go.

Walter was very kind, squeezing me into his home, but because of the tiny size of his apartment rather than anything to do with him, I felt I was permanently getting in the way there. He gave me a beer and listened as I told him my stories, nodding sympathetically when I came to my encounter with Buddy. I told him about the $40 loan.

'He gave you a number?'

I nodded.

'Want to give him a ring?'

'Yeah.'

I tapped the digits into Walter's phone, waited a few seconds while exchanges clicked and whirled.

A long tone. I sighed.

Walter raised his eyebrows and I shrugged. 'Nothing,' I said. 'It's disconnected.' I felt stupid. It hurt more than the $40 he'd ripped off me.

The next day I decided to give my BMW a mini-service. While adjusting the timing, I ripped the throttle cable by turning over the engine while the Allen key was still in the alternator. I could have kicked myself for being so stupid.

I patched up the cable and rode to a bike shop in San Diego. Standing in line for service, I heard a familiar roar outside the shop and turned around. It was an R90S, just like Alex's bike. I suddenly realized how much less I'd been thinking of him.

'I passed you in Tennessee,' said the rider when he came into the shop and I realized where I'd seen his bike before. He held out his hand. 'Frank.'

We got chatting, exchanged tales from the road. I told him I'd ridden from New York and was on my way to Sydney. He was at the end of a long tour, a rare BMW rider in America.

'There's not many of us on the West Coast,' he said. 'It's all big bikes here. They like to cruise.'

Smiling, I told Frank about Buddy's love of cruising. And the $40 I'd loaned him.

'That's bad. You got an address for Buddy?'

'Yes,' I said.

'Let's go round there.'

We rode around to the address I had noted in my diary. Buddy's home was a genuine address, a small house on a shabby street. I knocked on the door while Frank waited nearby. I didn't need to explain the outcome to him when I returned from the house. He'd seen it all: a woman answering the door, shaking her head when I asked if she knew someone called Buddy, closing the door in my face with an awkward, apologetic smile.

He'd given me a false address. What a surprise.

Frank and I spent the day walking around together. I wasn't cross at Buddy because he'd stolen from me. I just felt sad. My trust in men, fellow travellers and human beings had just taken three steps back. If Buddy had simply asked for the money, I might have given it to him. At least he'd have saved me a wasted journey.

Frank restored a bit of my faith in fellow travelling bikers. We spent a few days on the beach together. He was good company, strictly platonic after my experience with Buddy. At the end of it, he arranged for me to move out of Walter's place to a flat belonging to his friend, Binny, for one night, then we spent a hectic day together, snorkelling in the morning, Sea World in the afternoon. In the evening, a dinner party at Binny's flat, then a film about the Himalayas. After weeks of watching every penny, it was nice to spend a bit of money, feel extravagant. Having made the West Coast with funds to spare, I felt secure paying for a few small luxuries at last.

From San Diego it was a short ride up to Los Angeles, where I stayed with Ford, a former patient and friend of my father, and Twyla, his wife. They were very kind to me, offering me a free bed while I was in Los Angeles, but I had the impression Twyla thought I was a bit odd and quiet. It was a very strange set-up that left me unsure what to do or where to go around the house. Ford and Twyla left me alone for most of the time, but I didn't know if that was because they thought I wanted it or they didn't like me.

Maybe they had good reason to think I was withdrawn. The physical and mental demands of four weeks on the road, most of it entirely on my own, had taken their toll. When I wasn't catching up on sleep, I worked on my bike or watched hour after hour of rubbish television, the most relaxing way I knew to pass time painlessly.

In between, I worked through the thick package of correspondence from home that had been sent to Ford and Twyla's address. There were two tapes from my parents, letters from Justin, Rick and various other friends, but most prominent of all was a stack of letters and postcards from Mark.

I looked at the pile, decided that I needed some light relief first, then family news from home, before confronting the emotional maelstrom I expected in Mark's letters. First I opened Mike the Bike's letter, which I knew would be entertaining. I wasn't disappointed.

Hi there!
Fallen off yet? No? Jolly good.
     Oh dear, having started this, I can't think of anything else to say.
     Yesterday, while travelling through exotic Brighton, I almost ran your dear brother over. However, I missed him and he made me a cup of coffee, so I discovered you'd got the bike and were on your way.
     Friday I was incredibly brave. I went to work by Norton. Amazing – not one breakdown in the whole eight miles!

And so it went on until it ended, 'Right, that's your lot. I've sent Aunt out for stamps, so all I've got to do now is post it. Love n kisses, Mike.'

I sat on my bed, feeling quite emotional as I thought over Mike's news and his accounts of what was going on at home, including his assessment of which pub in London now served the best bacon and eggs.

Next I read Rick's letter, then Justin's before borrowing a tape player from Twyla to listen to my parents' tapes. Having not spoken to them since phoning them from Renee's house in Detroit, it was lovely to hear their voices and I vowed to get a tape recorder of my own in Sydney. Then I turned to the small pile of neatly addressed envelopes from Mark.

After weeks spent riding across the States with conflicting thoughts of Alex and Mark swirling around my head, it felt strange to be confronted by half a dozen letters written in Mark's neat regular hand, the first of them composed at roughly the same time as I was sitting at Heathrow, tears rolling down my face as I agonized over whether I really wanted to do the trip after all. Although they also carried news of things happening at home – Justin's birthday party; Channel 4's launch – when it came to the emotional stuff, Mark's letters pulled no punches.

'You left a big hole in my baggy life, you know, but for some reason I'm really glad you didn't turn back at the airport,' he wrote at the start of his next letter, written a couple of days after we last saw each other at the leaving party in my flat. 'I feel such a part of it that it's really weird not to be over there too.' And then he dropped the bombshell: 'I've now got three out of the seven directors working to get me to their Sydney office and it seems to be pretty certain that I can go.'

Reading Mark's plans to follow me out to Sydney, I didn't know what to think. Although the promise of a familiar face in Sydney was welcome, I had qualms about the intrusion. I'd chosen Sydney as my first pit stop for a very good reason: it was a long way from anywhere and anyone I knew. I'd hoped its physical distance from home would help me gain some mental and emotional separation from the thoughts and feelings that had been bothering me. But that was unlikely if Mark followed me to Sydney, harbouring hopes of romance.

Opening Mark's next letter, written the following day, I found he had continued his theme. 'You know how it is at night when your thoughts are really clear? Well mine are now and I still think you are effing amazing.'

I couldn't help being touched by Mark's sentiment, but as I read on through his letters in the order he'd sent them, they got heavier and I became increasingly concerned that he was carrying hopes that I couldn't possibly fulfil.

I felt guilty. Our separation was having the opposite effect on Mark that I'd hoped for. The distance I'd been seeking had made Mark miss me all the more. It played on my mind. Mark was a lovely man and I didn't want to hurt him.

Deciding I needed to get away from Ford, Twyla and my stack of emotion-laden letters, I travelled by bus down the coast to Mexico, where I spent a few days doing the tourist thing in Baja California. When I got back to LA, I turned my attention to organizing the next leg of my journey.

Shipping my bike to Sydney, I discovered, would cost me $703, cheaper than I'd expected for what was a very long journey and considerably less complicated than getting myself into Australia. I'd visited Australian consulates in New York, Detroit and Houston and been refused a working visa every time. I decided that maybe a tourist visa was a better idea and turned up at the consulate in Los Angeles expecting to be welcomed with open arms into Australia.

'We've got it on record that you've applied for a working visa . . .' – the official looked down at his notes – '. . . four times.'

'Yes.'

'And you said in your previous applications that you needed a working visa because you have insufficient funds to support yourself in Australia on a tourist visa.'

'Yes.' I smiled as sweetly as I could.

'So we can't give you a tourist visa.'

I couldn't believe it. I put all my documents on the official's desk – the letter from Harry Seidler in Sydney offering me work in his architecture practice; a letter from my mother's friend stating I would be able to stay with her in Sydney; my documentation showing my plan to ride across Australia to catch a ship to Indonesia. Surely they proved I wouldn't be a burden on Australia, that I'd actually contribute to the economy and that I wouldn't outstay my welcome.

The official shook his head. 'Can't do it. My hands are tied.'

'But my bike is already on a ship to Sydney.'

'I'm sorry.'

I returned to Ford and Twyla's house despondent, wondering if I'd ever find a way through the strictures of Australian bureaucracy. By the next day I'd hatched a plan. There was one last Australian consulate on US soil I could try before abandoning any hope of working in Sydney. It was in Hawaii, a place I'd always wanted to visit. A final roll of the dice, maybe, but one accompanied by the tempting prospect of a week slobbing on a beach, eating pineapples and tropical fruit, maybe even learning to surf.

With nothing planned in advance, I booked a flight to Hawaii. I had started to feel nauseous but hoped these feelings would dissipate as soon as I'd solved my visa conundrum. My tiredness and general queasiness bothered me though. If it didn't improve in the next few days, I'd seek out a doctor, get something for it before I boarded the flight.

Arriving in Honolulu I checked into a youth hostel near Waikiki beach, a place I'd heard a lot about and assumed would look like the tropical paradise images I'd seen of Hawaii: a horseshoe-shaped palm-tree-fringed crescent of sand beneath blue skies that would fade into a magnificent multicoloured sunset. The reality was quite different. Waikiki beach was a concrete jungle, row upon row of multi-storey hotels vying for a view of the seafront. And the weather was an even bigger disappointment. A tropical storm was brewing and the locals were warning it was going to get nasty.

At the youth hostel I met some other travellers and agreed to chip in towards hiring a car we could all use to explore the island. But first I went to the Australian consulate.

Again I submitted my application for a tourist visa, hoping details of my previous applications would not have reached Hawaii because of its relatively remote location. It was all in vain. The official rejected my application without a smile. My bike was bound for Sydney, but I was going to have to re-route to somewhere else. New Zealand, where I had relatives in Wellington, seemed a good option and there was a flight in four days.

For the next three days I travelled around the island with my hostel acquaintances. They were a pleasant bunch, but with each passing day the weather got worse. On the eve of my flight, the news channels and newspapers were reporting only one story: a hurricane was about to hit Hawaii.

That afternoon, my new friends and I decided to climb up a fire escape on the outside of a plush hotel near the youth hostel. From the roof of the hotel we could see for miles around. Waves were crashing over the sea front into the hotel's sea-front pool. In the distance we could see a huge swirling cloud system approaching the coastline very fast.

Battling against the wind, we ran back to the youth hostel, trees whipping in the storm, telephone wires already hanging to the ground where telegraph posts had snapped. When we arrived everyone was told to go down to the cellar where we huddled together, wrapped in blankets, shivering through the night as we listened to the wind whistle and roar above us. In the morning, we emerged from our temporary bunker. The wind was gone. In its place, silence and destruction.

Inevitably, my flight was cancelled. The storm having passed, idyllic tropical weather returned, so my new friends and I went exploring in our hire car, a huge black Oldsmobile limousine with blacked-out windows. Feeling like gangsters in a post-apocalyptic landscape, we cruised around the island. Trees had fallen in all directions, everywhere. Buildings had lost roofs and collapsed under the force of the hurricane. In many places we left the road to weave around the devastation left by the storm. I'd never seen anything like it.

For the next few days I had a fantastic time, swimming, surfing, driving off the well-worn tourist route miles up into the mountains to see how the locals lived while I waited for a replacement flight. I wasn't in a hurry. My bike was on a voyage to nowhere. Somehow I'd have to get it redirected to New Zealand.

As a British passport holder, I was allowed to work in New Zealand. Maybe I could get a job picking apples somewhere near Auckland or Wellington, but it wouldn't pay as much as an architecture position in Sydney and I needed to earn good money to finance the next leg of my journey.

When the airport reopened, I got myself onto a plane bound for New Zealand, still having not shaken off that nauseous, nervous feeling in my stomach. In spite of more than a week's rest in Hawaii, I didn't feel quite myself. Dog-tired, irritable with everyone and everything, over-emotional in my responses to the stresses of travelling, I wondered if it might all be a physical manifestation of my dread that my round-the-world plan was now going seriously wrong.

5

PART OF ME:

NEW ZEALAND

Auckland, 26 November 1982

New Zealand was a shock. Emerging from the plane was like stepping back thirty years into postwar Britain, a place I'd seen only in black-and-white films and family photos of England in the 1950s: rundown, poor, depressed. Few vehicles dotted the streets. A handful of Morris Minors, an occasional Australian Humber, some old motorbikes, but no European, American or Japanese cars or trucks.

Already anxious about my prospects of entering Australia to earn the money I needed to get me home, I worried about my chances of finding a job in New Zealand. Jobs were scarce and paid only the minimum wage. And there was little chance of finding employment in an architectural practice to fulfil my Part II architecture qualification if my visa troubles prevented me from working with Harry Seidler in Sydney.

I'd hoped to stay with Lester and Daniel, two Kiwi mechanics I knew from Gus Kuhn Motors, my local BMW shop in Clapham Road, in London, but there was no reply when I rang the number they'd given me, so I decided to move into a youth hostel for a few days until my appointment with the visa department at the Australian High Commission in Auckland.

My BMW was still at sea, somewhere between Los Angeles and Sydney. I'd made contingency plans for it arriving before me. If I wasn't able to get my Australian visa I'd ask the shipping company to redirect it from Sydney to Auckland, then I'd at least be reunited with my bike. But I was down to my last $500 and running out of money fast, so on my third day in New Zealand, I went to the Australian High Commission in Auckland. Desperate for a result, I asked to see 'the boss'. Several hours later, I was shown into a room where a middle-aged man was sitting behind an old mahogany leather-topped desk.

'A biker?' said the man behind the desk.

Fearing this immigration official was anti-biker and wishing I hadn't worn my leather biker jacket, I nodded hesitantly.

'What've you got?'

I pointed at the BMW badge on my lapel.

'Nice.'

I sensed he might be into motorbikes. 'And you?'

'A Triumph.' He started talking about his bike and we were away, two motorcycle fanatics sharing stories of machines and the road.

'So what are you doing here?' he said after a while.

'Trying to ride my bike around the world.'

His head dipped back, eyebrows raised. 'Around the world?'

'Yeah. And I've been trying to get a bloody Australian visa. I've been into every Australian High Commission and Consulate I could find in America, but none of them would give me a stamp.'

He nodded.

'I'm running out of money,' I said. 'And my bike's already on its way to Sydney.'

He looked down at my passport, leafed through the pages, his eyebrows lifting when he saw all the Australian visa refusal stamps. Then he turned to me, his eyes narrowing. 'So what's the problem?'

I shrugged. I didn't have an answer.

The official left the room. *Oh no*, I thought. *Here we go again. Another refusal, but this time it's the boss man, so it'll be terminal.* He returned about twenty minutes later with a rubber stamp in his hand, thumped it on an inkpad, opened my passport at a blank page and banged a visa onto it. 'There you go.'

'A visa?'

'Yeah.' He said it like it was the most natural, easy thing in the world. 'And a work permit.'

I didn't know what to say, other than 'Thanks!'

'Your trip sounds great. Good luck with it.'

As I left, I felt like hugging him. Instead, as I skipped down the steps of the High Commission, I rubbed my jacket and squeezed my lapel badge. If I hadn't worn them, it's unlikely I would ever have got an Aussie working visa. Maybe it took a biker to understand what I was trying to do, what it really meant.

Instead of hanging around at the youth hostel, waiting for Lester and Daniel to return to Auckland, I decided to take off on a sightseeing trip. Hitching along dirt roads, I travelled through unspoilt landscapes, past weather-beaten roadside shacks right up to Cape Reinga at the north-westernmost tip of the Aupouri Peninsula, at the top of the North Island. More than sixty miles north of the nearest small town, it was a beautiful spot. Staying in youth hostels because most of my camping kit was packed with my bike, I also stopped off at Karikari (although I failed to see what was meant to be special about it) and the Bay of Islands, which I found quiet, tranquil and beautiful. At stunning Ninety Mile Beach I found myself the only person on the sand for as far as I could see.

At night I lay on my hostel bunk and read through the stack of letters that had been sent to the poste restante in Auckland. Family and friends would send letters c/o the main post office up to a certain date at prearranged destinations. Picking up my letters every two or three months like this was always a highlight; I longed for news from home. Johnny had written to me from St Andrews in Scotland, telling me in intricate detail about the rebuild of his bike, various biking mishaps and a tea party to welcome freshers at his university at which the third years 'spiked the tea with a wodge of dope'. My brother Justy was 'still feeling pretty down about you going away', he wrote.

Having spent several months travelling to India, Johnny knew more than most people at home what I was going through. Nevertheless, he wrote:

It's very difficult for me to switch in to what you're doing. The scale of it (man!) means you have to have done it to know it. I hope you did not go too fast, so that you are not mentally saturated. When I reached India I was a wreck. I had seen so much that my head was about to explode – you know when one day you look in the mirror and see a stranger with crazed eyes.

Some of it resonated with me, but I didn't feel over-saturated at all. Maybe it would change when I reached Asia?

Mark's letter contained the surprising news that he intended to give up eating meat after discovering that 'dolphins cry when their friends are killed'. More pertinently, he also mentioned his campaign to persuade his engineering firm to post him to Sydney. Determined to meet me in Australia, he'd already bought a rucksack, customized it with a sewn-on Union flag, and had sold his beloved guitar to raise the funds for his trip. Lying on my hostel bed, I found it very difficult to imagine Mark in Australia or me travelling with him. I'd always intended doing my journey on my own, but now Mark was making his feelings quite clear: 'Through all this rubbish in the last couple of months, the one thing that remained constant was what I feel about you, you bum. Words fail me.'

Mark's clumsy words revealed a boyish keenness that I didn't find appealing, although I wondered if my hesitancy and anxiety were linked to my physical well-being. I still didn't feel right. That nauseous feeling I'd had in my stomach in Hawaii hadn't gone away and now I was getting painful stomach cramps and period pains. I'd started to bleed, heavier than usual, but I reassured myself this was because it was my first period in three months, which a doctor had forewarned me might initially be erratic when I came off the pill shortly before leaving home. Pressing on my stomach, I thought I could feel something, like a lump, but told myself that I was imagining it, that I was over-focusing because I was spending so much time alone.

I returned to Auckland, staying for a couple of days with Lester and Daniel, who took me to watch some sidecar racing one afternoon. Then I headed south towards Wellington to stay with Malcolm, a distant cousin.

After my rest in Auckland, I felt stronger. The nausea was less, although I now found myself frequently tired.

That night, asleep on a top bunk in a youth hostel, I was woken by extreme pain in my abdomen. You're not well, I told myself. You shouldn't be here.

I touched my tender belly, slipped my hand down between my legs, rubbed my fingers together. They felt wet. I looked at my hand. It was covered in blood. The sheets beneath me, I then realized, were soaking wet. I was lying in a pool of blood.

I was in trouble, but for a moment I stopped thinking of the pain and looked at all the mess I'd made. How was I going to get all this cleaned up so that no one would find out?

I tiptoed to the toilet, blood dripping down my legs, leaving a red trail behind me on the floor. Sitting on the toilet, doubled over with pain, flashing hot and cold, I wondered what I should do. I was in agony.

I opened my eyes: a small, austere room with white walls.

Vomit. Sweat. Pain. Two figures in medical scrubs: a doctor and a nurse, leaning over me, cleaning up my puke, asking me what's wrong. Was this a clinic? How did I get here? Did I call for an ambulance? Or did someone take me?

Soon it was obvious. Thankfully it was quick. Half an hour of contractions. All the pain of childbirth. But at the end of it, no child.

The doctor rushed out of the room with something in a metal dish. Behind him, the nurse was pale and couldn't look at me. The doctor returned a short while later.

'Do you want to see it?'

I knew what he meant: a foetus. *My child*.

'No.'

I couldn't face it. Or their stares. I turned my head away, towards the wall. 'We need to get you to hospital,' said the doctor, with a disapproving look. I knew what I wanted to say – 'I'm nothing like you think I am' – but instead I nodded and closed my eyes. When I woke, I was inside an ambulance, its sirens mercifully silent as the shock of it washed over me. I'd had another human being inside me. I'd been pregnant for three months and miscarrying for three weeks. *Pregnant. Why had I been so irresponsible?* I'd always wondered what I'd do if I ever got pregnant. This time I hadn't had to decide.

The hospital was in Wellington. After being cleaned up and checked for infection, I was left alone, a thin blanket covering me on a cold, hard trolley. There was a knock on the door. Malcolm and his wife walked in.

'How are you feeling?'

I smiled weakly. 'I've been better.'

They asked a few questions – caring, not prying – and I wondered if the doctors had briefed them, or if they'd worked out for themselves what had happened. Or if maybe they were too embarrassed to ask.

I stayed with Malcolm and his wife, but didn't feel I could talk to them. Struggling to make sense of my very mixed feelings about what had happened, I felt depressed, lonely, confused. Why had I miscarried? Were those long rides across America too strenuous? Had I not eaten enough? Now I wished I'd seen my baby. It had been part of me for such a long time and I didn't even know whether it was a boy or a girl. But at the moment I was given the opportunity to look, I was in too much shock. I simply couldn't face it.

A few days later, Malcolm's parents, Alan and Nan, picked me up from their son's home and drove me to their house in Nelson on the South Island. Still feeling very numb, I was relieved that Alan and Nan, like Malcolm, asked nothing. Welcoming and kind, they passed no judgement, but I still felt awkward, ashamed and embarrassed, particularly as they didn't even refer obliquely to my time at the hospital. Although I appreciated their tact and sensitivity, what was left unspoken almost made things worse.

I started to feel a loss, a grief for losing something that I hadn't even realized I'd had, but which I now missed nevertheless. I wondered what I would have done if I hadn't miscarried. Giving birth to a child fathered by Mark would have been very difficult. I wasn't in love with him; I didn't even know if I wanted to be with him. But I also knew that if the child had belonged to Alex, my feelings and thoughts might have been different.

Tiptoeing around the house, I realized I needed to get away from my extended family to allow my head to clear. I decided to do a small trip in the week before Christmas and set off for Christchurch.

Hitchhiking around the South Island proved to be much harder than on the North Island. Few cars passed me and I often found myself sitting or standing on the side of the road, thumb extended hopefully, for several hours at a time. It took me two days to travel 200 miles from Nelson to Greymouth, where I was offered a bed for the night by a woman who'd given me a lift in her Land Rover. Her home was full of crucifixes and religious books. It was a somewhat eerie experience, but her spiritual connections paid off the next morning, when she organized a lift for me all the way to Christchurch with a bishop and his family.

In Christchurch I found a quiet corner in a very dull youth hostel and settled down to write a long succession of letters and postcards to friends and family. Although I told my parents nothing about my time in hospital, it gave me a chance to reflect on my circumstances. Now that the shock of the miscarriage had subsided, I felt relieved. I was in the middle of my architecture training, halfway round a world trip, and a child would have been a massive complication. In my emotionally confused state, my mind was a mess of conflicting thoughts, but one thing I knew for certain: although fond of Mark I wasn't in love with him. That afternoon, I wrote to him. It was a very hard letter to write. I tried my best to word it carefully, but there was no easy way to tell Mark that he almost became a father.

'I don't want to spoil your Christmas,' I wrote. 'But the thing I had inside me was half yours. You lost something too.'

That night I noticed the front of my T-shirt was wet. I looked down and to my shock I realized I'd started producing milk, a reminder that although I was adjusting mentally to the events of the past fortnight, my body would take longer to recalibrate itself.

Day by day, as I toured the South Island, I felt stronger, determined not to let the recent events overshadow my journey. Returning to

Nelson to spend Christmas with Alan and Nan, I found a letter from Mark waiting for me. He made very little reference to the miscarriage until the end of the letter, when he announced he had resigned at work and bought a ticket to Auckland. He wanted to see me because, he wrote, 'I know you went through a hellish time with our baby.'

That night, I phoned my mother for the first time since the miscarriage.

'How are you?' she said.

Dozens of responses raced through my mind. How should I explain something that I suspected she already knew about? I kept it simple. 'Fine.'

In spite of more than 11,000 miles between us, we both knew what lay behind those anodyne words. I could imagine my mother's embarrassment at what she feared her New Zealand cousins might be thinking about my pregnancy – and by extension, what they thought of her and the rest of our family in London. Nothing more needed ever to be said.

'I think Mark is coming out to visit me,' I said.

'Good.' I heard the relief in my mother's voice. 'So what have you been up to?'

I passed on my news, steering well clear of the unmentionable, a subject that remained off-topic from that day onwards for ever – to my relief as much as my mother's.

Christmas with Alan and Nan was pleasant and quiet, a contrast to Christmas at Wimpole Street, which usually passed in a haze of my father's homemade fruit and vegetable wines.

On the 28th, I left Alan and Nan to travel to Christchurch, where I'd arranged to meet Mark. Stupidly, I'd let immature self-consciousness guide me. Instead of introducing Mark to Alan and Nan, I'd made sure my extended family didn't meet him because I worried that they would sense my true feelings for Mark and wonder why I'd let myself become pregnant.

With very mixed feelings, I waited for Mark to pass through customs at Christchurch airport, then watched as he walked straight past me through the terminal.

'Mark!'

He turned, did a double take as he matched my voice to my appearance. After we'd hugged, he took a step back, looked me up and down.

'I really didn't recognize you.'

Maybe it was losing more than a stone in weight, maybe it was the combined effect of long days, meagre meals and the miscarriage, but clearly my appearance had changed more than I'd realized. 'So how've you been?' he said.

'Oh.' I felt like looking at my shoes. 'You know . . . better, I suppose.'

Neither of us found it easy to talk about personal stuff, so instead of sitting down for an honest heart to heart, we skirted around the awkward subject. I still felt ashamed and stupid that I'd let it happen, particularly as I thought of myself as someone who didn't make silly mistakes. And now that Mark was standing in front of me, I felt even more embarrassed.

We decided to hire a car for three days, but after paying a fortune for it and sleeping for one night perched on top of a hill overlooking Lake Wanaka, we realized our mistake and returned it. Hitchhiking south via Queenstown, on New Year's Eve we arrived in Te Anau, a beautiful small town on a lake perched between steep-sided valleys in the Southern Alps. As a treat, we rented an A-framed hut and bought some wine to celebrate the New Year. Although simple, the hut was a luxury for us, a rare chance to have some private space. Maybe Mark relished the intimate setting, but having now travelled with him for several weeks, I wanted to be on my own again. Feeling very confused, I was again confronted by my eternal conundrum: travelling alone I felt lonely, slightly depressed, wishing I was with somebody. But when that person was Mark, it didn't work for me.

As midnight approached and the bottles emptied, I contemplated the previous twelve months. No question about it, 1982 had been a difficult year for me in many respects. Dumped by Alex, I'd got a third-class degree, then worked my arse off in a pub for four months. But I felt my journey across America had helped set some of my demons to rest. Although the miscarriage had been emotionally testing, I now somehow felt more confident and stronger. I was able to cope and deal with problems which I had not previously imagined I could do. I hoped 1983 would be better.

Three days later we were in Auckland and I was standing with Mark in the airport, about to fly to Sydney. Although I'd enjoyed New Zealand, I was relieved to be leaving the country. For me, it had always only been a stepping-stone to Australia, where employment, my bike and the beginning of the road home promised a better future. With very little remaining of my savings, I desperately needed to earn the money I required to get me back to London. And I always loved arriving in a new country. It wasn't just the excitement of seeing something different and new, but also the taking of another step towards achieving my goal. I was looking forward to having somewhere I could settle, unpack all my stuff and relax. Meanwhile, Mark would be staying in New Zealand, picking apples for the same farmer who'd employed Justin a couple of years earlier, and he seemed confident he'd find a way into Australia to work there.

Three months and many thousands of miles after leaving London, I now found myself halfway around the world, about to recreate the same set-up in Sydney that I'd worked so hard to escape from at home. Fearing Mark would still want to see more of me than I did of him, I hugged him and whispered something in his ear about not rushing to Sydney too quickly on my account, then turned away to board my flight.

PART 2

SYDNEY TO MADRAS

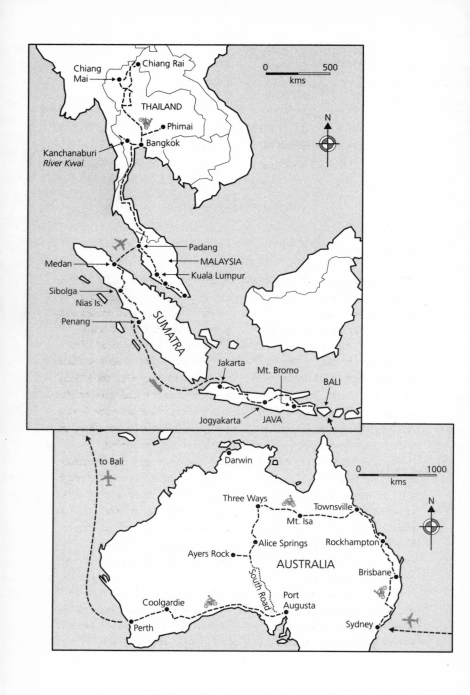

6

PIT STOP IN SYDNEY:

AUSTRALIA

Sydney, 8 January 1983

S tanding outside the airport, beaming a massive smile, Annie threw her arms around me, helped lug my blue rucksack to her car. 'Welcome to Oz!' she said over the roar of her car engine as we moved off. 'We'll be home in about half an hour.'

Home was Annie's mother's house in North Turramarra, a leafy suburb on the Upper North Shore of Sydney. As soon as I walked through the door, I felt at peace, pleased to be living with the family of an old friend. In London, where Annie and I had met at the crammer at which I'd studied for my A-levels, my parents' house in Upper Wimpole Street had been a second home to her. Now in Sydney, it felt like old times, albeit with our roles reversed.

For the first couple of days, I took my time, got my bearings. Australia seemed very much a mix of Britain and America. Although large, Sydney felt provincial, more like a town than a city, a bit run-down and seedy in areas, but likeable and characterful. On my third day in the country, a telegram arrived from Mark, telling me he'd be picking apples in New Zealand until April. Although I had enjoyed our six weeks travelling together it felt good to have my independence again.

When I finally managed to get hold of someone at the docks, I discovered it would cost me $600 to collect my bike, leaving me with only $50 to my name. Needing to get a job fast, I phoned Harry Seidler's office and was told to drop in the next day.

In a shirt borrowed from Annie and my best pair of trousers, I reported to Seidler's minimalist reception the following morning, then waited for the great man to arrive.

A Jew born in Vienna, Seidler had fled to England in the 1930s, then emigrated to Australia with his parents after the war. They commissioned him to build them a house, the first in Australia built in the Bauhaus style. The house immediately won a prestigious award, attracting other clients. By the time I came knocking on his door, Seidler was among Australia's most revered architects, several of his skyscrapers dotting the Sydney skyline.

'Ah . . . Elspeth.' A short, dark, balding, portly man wearing round glasses and a bow-tie held out his hand. 'I'm Harry Seidler. Come this way.'

I followed Seidler through his office, where his steady stream of orders, barked at his staff as he marched me to his office, made it absolutely clear he was very much in charge and not someone to be trifled with.

'So . . . what do you want?' Seidler pointed at a chair.

I sat down. 'A friend of my father suggested I contact you when I arrived in Sydney. I believe he wrote to you.'

Seidler nodded.

'I've got these.' I passed a letter of introduction from my father's friend and a photocopy of my lousy degree certificate across Seidler's desk. I had no other credentials.

'Tell me what you studied for your degree and what you think of Sydney architecture,' said Seidler.

By the time I'd finished bluffing my way through an answer, Seidler made it very obvious that he was not at all impressed by me. 'I suppose we can find you something to do,' he said with a sigh. A half-hearted sweep of his hand made it clear that he felt lumbered with me. 'We'll see you next Monday.'

I spent the weekend shopping in charity shops for office clothes and reading my post that had arrived at Annie's house. Johnny described Christmas at home. 'Went for drink at your mum's. Your dad sat with his back to everyone playing *Breakout* on the TV, while everyone discussed shoelaces in Brazil and careers, subjects which are pretty difficult to take seriously even when you haven't just emptied a bottle of best sherry down your gullet.'

A romantic card from Mark – 'I mumble and I stutter, but the day I met you was the greatest I ever had' – was followed by a letter that described his reluctant embrace of travelling. At last he appeared to be enjoying it. 'It seems a long way from the Devonshire, but I'm glad I went there that day in August,' he wrote, making only one reference to my miscarriage that had dragged him from London to the southern hemisphere: 'Sad about December.'

The following Monday I reported for work at Seidler's office, eager to get started on an architectural project that I could include in my portfolio for my Part II qualification. My first task was to make everyone a cup of tea. That done, I photocopied documents, duplicated architectural drawings on a dyeline machine, ran office errands. No job, it seemed, was too menial for me. By the third day, I was giving up hope of being given a task befitting an architecture graduate, when one of Seidler's staff called me over to an empty desk.

'Do you know how to draw up a window schedule for a building?' she said.

A relatively mundane architectural task, but at least it would involve the kind of drawing work for which I'd spent three years being trained. I was excited. At last something worthwhile.

'Elspeth . . .' Seidler was behind me, speaking loud enough for half the office to hear. 'No. I don't want you doing that. Can you go to the post office? We need some stamps.' I smiled weakly, realizing Seidler thought he'd done me a favour just by allowing me through the doors of his practice and that he would never let me do anything beyond the most humdrum tasks.

I felt a mug. My time was precious. I needed to get proper work experience for my architecture Part II qualification, but my Australian work permit was valid for only six months. I also needed to earn funds for my journey home, so I decided to look for an evening job in a pub or restaurant.

A few days later, walking home from Seidler's office, I walked into the North Sydney Hotel, a large former inn converted into a pub. It was a real spit-and-sawdust place, attracting a raucous, sport-obsessed crowd. Dressed in T-shirts and skimpy football shorts that they called stubbies, customers often marched straight into the bar after a match at the North Sydney Oval, an Australian Rules football ground on the opposite side of the road from the bar.

Darcy, the manager, offered me a trial the next evening. Once I'd got used to the different beers, and the customers asking for schooners or middies instead of pints and halves, it went like a dream. Darcy immediately offered me a string of shifts, including a couple at weekends that I lapped up when he told me he'd pay me time and a half on Saturdays and Sundays.

Gradually, things were starting to fall into place. Having arrived with no money, I now had a full-time job with Seidler, as well as several evenings a week at the pub, and often a double-shift on Saturday and an evening shift on Sunday. I had collected my bike from the docks and spent my spare time servicing it. When Seidler started paying me, I could start saving for my journey home.

By the end of January, I'd spent nearly three weeks at Seidler's office. We hadn't agreed a salary, or even a daily rate, but I'd done a lot of work for him. On the last day of the month, Penelope, his wife who handled the accounts, appeared in the office with a pile of pay cheques. Watching Penelope walk from desk to desk, I tried not to get too excited at the prospect of my first pay packet, but as she handed out the slips, I realized she was avoiding me.

'Penelope . . .' I tried to catch her eye. Maybe I wasn't going to get a proper pay packet for this first month? Maybe it would be just $50 a week, something to tide me over until I was put on the payroll?

Penelope glanced at me, then looked away. I tried to catch her eye again, but noticed her hands were now empty. All the pay slips had been distributed and I hadn't received one.

'Penelope . . .'

She shook her head, then left the office. It suddenly all made sense. I'd thought Seidler was keeping any proper architectural work from me because he didn't think I was capable, but perhaps it was to avoid having to pay me. He might have been a great revered architect but I didn't like him. Everyone in the office kept their heads down, rarely speaking as he marched up and down, snapping at anyone who caught his eye. It wasn't a nice place to work; I found the atmosphere cold and unfriendly.

I had also started to worry that I was outstaying my welcome at Annie's mother's house, where I was still sleeping in the living room. Towards the end of February, a letter arrived from Mark, saying he had saved enough money and would now be arriving in a couple of weeks from New Zealand. Not wanting to impose Mark on Annie and her mother, I agreed to housesit a flat belonging to Lillico, a friend of Annie's while she went on holiday just so I'd have somewhere suitable to live when Mark arrived.

Thoroughly bored at Seidler's office, I'd at last been assigned a more appropriate task, although the mind-numbing chore of counting the number of bricks in eleven town houses was usually the responsibility of a quantity surveyor, not an architect.

After spending a day and a half counting bricks, I reported to my supervisor. I'd counted just over a million bricks.

'That sounds right,' she said. 'They've already been counted twice.'

My heart pounded. I was being treated like an idiot. 'So why have I just counted them a third time?'

She shrugged. 'To check them.'

I tried to keep a smile on my face.

'Can you now break it down into facing bricks, common bricks and block work?' said my supervisor.

Working flat out, I finished the task early the next day, when I was told to copy 250 A1 architectural drawings. Each drawing had to be fed through a dyeline machine which stank of ammonia. Then each print had to be individually folded. It was a mind-numbing chore that would normally be given to a printing office, but which saved Seidler $90 that he would no doubt charge to the client. Like an idiot, I wanted to impress, so I stayed on until 7 p.m. to finish the job. I thought my diligence had paid off the next day, when I was assigned a proper architectural task, but Seidler soon intervened, telling me to sort and staple 800 sets of photocopies. Determined not to become despondent, I worked hard, finishing the job quickly.

'We don't have anything for you to do today, Elspeth,' said Seidler. 'Maybe you could read some of the architectural journals?'

The next day, I sat around doing nothing, then returned in a foul mood to Lillico's flat, where I found the fish tank, normally on top of the television, sitting on the floor. *Strange*, I thought, *I don't remember moving that.* I glanced outside and saw a ladder leaning against the balustrade of the balcony. *What's that doing there?* Then the penny dropped.

I went back into the living room. The television was gone. So was my Sony Walkman. I went into my room, delved into the bottom of a drawer and discovered that my father's beautiful handmade wallet, embossed with AWB in gold letters, was missing. It contained every penny I had earned. Thanks to Seidler's parsimony, I'd not amassed that much, only the $300 I had earned at the North Sydney Hotel, but to someone who had very little, it was a big blow. I reported it to the police, but nothing came of it.

I felt sick at the thought of someone rummaging through my belongings. Just as I'd started to get ahead, get my feet on the ground, make some money, someone had stolen it from me. Maybe it was time to take the hint that Australia and I weren't going to get along. Whichever way I turned, things didn't seem to work out.

By the next morning, I was in a better frame of mind, determined to make the best of my circumstances. The journey had made me more resilient. Every little defeat made me more determined to succeed and I got a kick from living on my wits. With my new resolve not to let setbacks grind me down, I decided not to turn up for work at Seidler's that morning. I had been working for him for six weeks and he hadn't paid me a penny and there was no point in sitting around his office reading journals. Mark had also arrived from New Zealand and I wanted us to have some time together. He had a few days before he started working at his company's Sydney office, so we did some sightseeing around Sydney and took a trip out to the Blue Mountains. The following week Mark started work and I walked the streets, looking for another job. Towards midday, Mark called. He had been told about McConnell Smith and Johnson, an architectural practice that needed someone to help out. I raced over there, willing even to do photocopying as long as I got paid for it.

As soon as I walked through MSJ's door, I could tell it was very different from Seidler's office. It was chaotic, noisy and friendly. I walked up to the receptionist. 'I hear you're looking for someone,' I said, 'and I'm looking for a job.'

A few minutes later, a tall, thin man appeared in reception. Casually dressed, Alan couldn't have been more different from Seidler. In his late forties, he was laid-back and incredibly easy-going. 'We can't offer you much,' said Alan, 'but if you want the job, it's yours.'

I started at MSJ the next Monday. On Thursday I decided to tell Seidler I had a new job. He looked surprised when I appeared at his office.

'Oh, hello,' he said. 'I wondered what had happened to you.'

I suppressed the urge to say that after being ignored for six weeks, I was surprised he'd even noticed I'd gone.

Away from work, my run of bad luck didn't end with the burglary. Three days later, a garbage truck reversed over my bike, smashing its headlight, fairing and mudguard. A quote for repairs came to $700. Although I immediately lodged a claim with the council, I knew it would take months to get a penny out of them.

I also needed to find somewhere permanent to live. Mark had moved into a place near Lillico's flat organized by his company and he suggested I moved in with him. Although financially it made sense I felt it would mean accepting that our relationship was becoming more serious. I wanted to keep my distance and maintain my independence, although it wasn't entirely about Mark. It felt wrong to commit to a relationship when I still had a long journey ahead of me.

Through my friend John back in London, I heard of an empty garage behind a house his sister was renting in the Sydney suburb of

Paddington. It was dirty, cold and damp, but I could have it for only $20 a week and, best of all, I could keep my bike inside with me.

Before moving in, I spent two weeks painting the garage, fumigating it to eliminate hundreds of two-inch cockroaches, and making furniture from junk thrown out every Thursday by Sydney residents. Using items found on the side of the road, I fashioned the top of a wardrobe into a table. I bolted one edge to a wall and suspended the front edge from two ropes attached to the ceiling because the floor was uneven and I didn't want to make legs. I painted and fixed three plastic milk crates to the wall as a wardrobe and found a jagged piece of broken mirror which I hung over the basin.

At last, after three months in Sydney, I had my own place, a refuge for my bike and two jobs. I was starting to save money and feel settled. Considerable progress, although not quite fast enough for me.

I wrote home, enclosing photographs of my new home.

'I'm sure you'll be pleased to hear that my bike is out of action,' I wrote. 'Please send my cardigan. I can't find any in Australia of that quality at any price.'

My beloved cardigan, bought second-hand in an Oxfam shop, was a particular bugbear of my mother.

'Having seen pictures of your primitive garage,' my mother replied, 'I'm now reassured that it's not a health risk, although I note the space for your beloved bike.

'Always a great relief to get a letter from you, especially when it includes news that your bike is hors de combat – a particular joy. But the very thought of sending that old cardigan precipitated an episode of *paralysis agitans*, i.e. uncontrollable shaking.'

Before I knew it, I was approaching six months in Sydney and my visa was about to expire. Justin wrote to ask about my plans:

> Whenever Mum refers to you, she does so in very dramatic terms, 'IF Elspeth returns . . .' being a favoured phrase. Mum also noted that you never mention Mark in your letters. M is really worried.

She wants to know what your plans are. Is Mark going to travel with you back to GB? I've been prompted to ask the question, but seriously: you really must consider it. It would be dangerous to travel back by yourself.

Mum's observation was a fair reflection on the state of my relationship. Although Mark and I were getting on well, our time together was sometimes limited. We both worked weekdays and I worked several evenings a week, so we would see each other whenever we could, which was often only at the weekends.

The arrangement suited me. Longer term I was on a solo mission that didn't include Mark, the first part of which was returning my BMW to her former glory after having received a compensation cheque from the council. Spotting financial opportunity in a setback, I decided to buy second-hand parts and do the repairs myself. I bought filler and fibreglass to repair the mudguard and fairing on the bike. By the time I finished, they looked like new. I attached my green rubber frog mascot in its home behind the fairing and admired my handiwork. The damage was invisible and both fairing and mudguard were stronger than before. Best of all, the repairs, including a new headlight glass, had cost me only $35 of the $400 compensation payment.

I had managed to save about $1,600. Although I had no idea how much money I would need for the journey home, I knew this wouldn't be anywhere near enough, so I applied for a visa extension. An immigration officer fired a series of questions at me – 'Why Australia? What have you achieved? Why a working visa?' – then told me a visa was to enable visitors to work as they travelled around Australia, not stay in one place.

'You can't work for one employer for more than three months,' he said. 'You can have a new visa, but only if your employer provides a letter stating they've fired you.'

That evening, I rode over to the pub to ask Darcy to write me a letter, and a few weeks later I got my visa extended without even mentioning my job at MSJ, where I was now designing buildings on a government-sponsored housing project as well as working on a new building at Sydney Cricket Ground and a hospital in the Far East. Architecture had finally clicked for me, I suddenly realized what it was all about, the breakthrough coming when I visited a building site and saw the foundations that I'd drawn rising out of the ground. Something that previously seemed remote and arcane suddenly fitted together and made sense.

Gradually I started to prepare for the next leg of my journey. I discovered I needed a Carnet de Passages to travel through India, Pakistan and several Far East countries. This was a customs document for my bike allowing temporary importation and was designed to ensure travellers with vehicles didn't sell them en route. It was issued on payment of a deposit based on the vehicle's value in its country of registration, and on the countries through which I intended passing, which I found impossible to answer as I needed to keep my options open. My father immediately set about obtaining the document from the AA in Basingstoke, no easy task as it required a current valuation of my bike from a certified valuer in Australia and a crystal ball.

The local BMW shop agreed to give me a valuation and while I was there they told me about someone in Sefton, west of Sydney, who had ridden his bike overland from Sydney to the UK five years earlier. Keen to get advice I rode out to meet him the following weekend through pouring rain that everyone told me was the worst weather in Sydney for years.

I was greeted by a quiet middle-aged man with fair hair and keen blue eyes behind his glasses. John Todd lived on his own in a suburban bungalow with a kitchen table crammed full of bike parts and DIY projects in progress. 'Do you want to see my bike?' he said after making me a cup of tea.

Of course I did. In his garage was a well-disguised 1961 R60/5, but apart from the trademark 'boxer' cylinders it bore very little resemblance to my 1974 R60/6. Battered, dusty and stained, it looked more like a two-wheeled metal workman's hut.

'Appearance doesn't matter to me in the slightest,' said John, patting the aluminium boxes he'd pop-riveted and attached all around his bike. 'What are you using for luggage?'

'I've got some soft bags. They were fine for America.'

Todd shook his head. 'They won't last five seconds where you're going; your luggage needs to be lockable, otherwise everything will get nicked.'

I made a mental note to look into buying something stronger. BMW made hard panniers, but they needed to be attached to a BMW rack, which alone cost $400 in Australia, much more than I could afford. The following weekend I was back at John's house.

'I think I'll make my panniers from fibreglass, using a mould,' I said.

John rested a hand on my arm. 'It took me six months to make mine,' he said. 'Why don't you have them. They're light and lockable.'

It was a kind offer, but I was reluctant to take something that had accompanied John halfway around the world. Instead, I returned to his garage the next weekend to start constructing my own panniers under his guidance. With John's help, I worked out a very simple design. The panniers consisted of aluminium sheets wrapped around and riveted onto aluminium angle. I didn't want to make a separate frame, then have to work out how to fasten the panniers and top box to it. Instead I fixed the bottom of each pannier to the pillion foot pegs, which supported their weight. The tops of the panniers were then bolted to the bottom of the top box, which simply sat on my pillion seat with a bracket at the back to secure it.

By early August, departure decisions were being forced upon me. Work was going very well at MSJ, which had put me in charge of designing 270 houses for a project north of Sydney, but the garage lease was running out and not renewable. Needing somewhere to live, I decided to bring my departure date forward to the end of October and kip on friends' sofas until then.

I'd planned a route: north from Sydney through Queensland to Townsville, then west to Mount Isa, south through the Northern Territory to Alice Springs and Ayers Rock, before a possible stopover in Adelaide to prepare for the 1,500 mile ride west to Perth. It was a long journey of more than 5,000 miles, but there was a lot to see.

If I left Sydney by the end of October, I could tour Queensland before the rainy season, which started in November and lasted until March. If I departed any later, I might be marooned in Queensland, waiting until the floods dispersed.

By the end of August, things in Sydney felt very similar to my last weeks in London as I ran through a procession of vaccinations, bike servicing, savings withdrawal, medical and dental checks, document organization, map collection and bag packing.

I wrote to my parents to suggest that we met in Kathmandu, which I thought would be less frantic and hot for them than somewhere in India or Southeast Asia. Throughout this time, my mother's letters continued to land on my doormat with the regularity of a metronome, their content often amusing.

'I've not heard a cheep from you for ages,' she wrote in one letter. It was a regular theme. Usually I smiled, particularly when Mum continued with one of her waspy observations. 'Justy blew in yesterday, then left very quickly,' she wrote. 'I wonder why? I think he has discovered sex.'

In September, Mark left Sydney and I moved temporarily into the flat he vacated until the end of the lease. His Australian visa having expired, he flew to Indonesia to backpack around the sights. I was sad to see him go but we made plans to meet up again somewhere in Southeast Asia after I had ridden across Australia.

Weekends became increasingly frantic as my departure time ticked ever closer. One late September Saturday, I rose at 6 a.m. to ride through torrential rain to a BMW garage in north Sydney to get the bevel drive in my rear hub replaced. I then rode to John Todd in west Sydney to work on my panniers until late afternoon, when I rode to the pub, where I worked until closing time, long past midnight. In early October, I rode to John Todd to finish my side panniers and top box. At last they were complete, but when I looked at my bike with its aluminium luggage system, which protruded about a foot either side of the bike with the top box eighteen inches above the rear seat, I wondered how on earth I was going to ride it. Normally I'd swing my leg over the seat, but the boxes made that impossible.

After several attempts, I realized the only way was to goosestep up onto the bike and then slide myself in between the tank and top box.

Even though the panniers were empty, my BMW felt very different; huge and unwieldy. My leg movement was limited and paddling forwards on the bike was difficult. But, in general terms, it worked well and the panniers felt very secure. Like me, John was a perfectionist and insisted on several final touches, including two aero-flaps that folded out from the side of the top box; an attempt to make the vast contraption more aerodynamic. We both stood back and admired our handiwork; pride was written all over his face. I asked John to sign his masterpiece, so he wrote 'Todds Special' in huge letters across the back of the top box.

For my last fortnight in Sydney I sofa-hopped around a succession of friends' flats, as much to eke out a few last shared moments with them as to avoid having to pay for a room in a hostel.

Meanwhile, a letter from Mark in Bali arrived. Unlike most of his previous letters, it contained no news.

I love you, Elspeth, and therefore the greatest thing I can give to you is the freedom you want so much.

I am writing this down so that if you need strength or encouragement at any time, you may read this and know that you have at least one good friend who is standing by you still.

Please come back safely.

Mark's sentiment touched me, but, as ever, it also left me uneasy about its implications, particularly as we would soon be seeing each other again. I had booked a flight from Perth to Bali on 30 December and a passage for my bike from Perth to Jakarta a few days earlier, so my course was set, not only for a reunion with Mark, but out of Sydney at last. I decided to leave on Wednesday 26 October, but the day came and went and I was still going into work every day at MSJ and spending nights at the pub. I always procrastinated when it was time to get back on the road and this time was no different. Part of me was itching to leave, but Sydney had started to feel like home.

The day after my intended departure, I took drastic action. For as long as I could remember I'd had long hair, which now reached halfway down my back. But since arriving in Sydney, it had annoyed me and I'd worn it tied back or in a plait. I realized that when I left Sydney, shorter hair would be far more practical and save me money on shampoo. My mind was set.

After a shift at the pub, sitting on a barstool, I mentioned to one of my colleagues that I wanted to chop off my tresses.

'My mate Danny will do it for you,' came the reply.

Danny turned out to be someone who also worked in the pub. 'Don't cut it too short,' he said. 'It'll be too much of a shock.'

Although I wanted it clipped short all over, I took his advice. Big mistake. Danny left it long on top and short at the sides and back. It looked awful.

The next morning, when I looked in a mirror, I didn't recognize myself. But practicality usurped vanity and, all things considered, I was pleased I'd done it. It felt incredibly free. There was no mistaking my intent. I was on a mission and didn't care what I looked like. The next day, my last Saturday in Sydney, I accepted an invitation from Alan, my boss at MSJ, to have dinner with him and his wife. We'd become great friends in the office, getting along really well even though I was half his age. After a lovely evening, they invited me to stay over. But I had a surprise when, in the middle of the night, there was a knock on the door of the spare bedroom where I was sleeping.

It was Alan. Completely naked.

Lonely and insecure, I could have sought comfort and human warmth in Alan's arms, but he was married and we were in his family home. If Buddy had taught me anything it was that casual sex left a bitter aftertaste. The next morning, there was a strange atmosphere and Alan's wife made a passing comment that led me to think she was aware of his movements in the middle of the night and that it wasn't entirely out of character for him.

Later that day, Ed and Sammy, friends I'd made at the North Sydney Hotel, held a party for me around the pool at their house. As each guest arrived, I noticed a look of shock on their faces when they saw my new haircut. Some said nothing, others simply 'Oh!', but one friend was more blunt.

'Your hair?' he said.

I smiled and shrugged.

'You look fucking awful.'

I wondered if maybe I should have paid to have it done professionally.

On Monday, I had yet another leaving party, this time with my colleagues at MSJ, who took me out for a farewell lunch that didn't end until late that night, when I stumbled into Annie's mother's house to spend my last night in the city in the same place I'd spent my first night.

Waking on Tuesday morning with a dry mouth and a hangover, I looked at the small pile of bags in the corner of Annie's mother's living room and felt as if I was back again in my little flat in Upper Wimpole Street, about to leave home for a solo life on the road. After seven months in Sydney, my days filled with stimulating work at MSJ, my evenings spent behind a bar or surrounded by friends, the thought of months on my bike with nothing but the road for company was daunting.

I looked out of the window. Rain was pouring over the edge of the gutter. I didn't feel like venturing off on a 20,000-mile trip back to London in the wet and decided to delay my departure by twenty-four hours. On Thursday, I pulled open the curtains. More rain. I checked the weather forecast and it was another two days of rain. Would it ever stop?

Again I glanced at my small pile of belongings, neatly stacked in the corner of the room. I knew the time for respectable procrastination had passed. What was I thinking? If a little rain was stopping me from leaving comfortable Sydney, what would I be like when I encountered far more treacherous conditions in the middle of nowhere? I pulled on my waterproofs and my motorcycle boots, went out to my bike, and loaded my gear into the aluminium panniers. I said my goodbyes to Annie and her mum, thanking them for all they had done. God knows how I would have managed without their help and support in the early months.

Suddenly I felt very alone. Just me, my BMW disguised as a motorized shed, and the open road. Maybe it would have felt different if the sun had been shining as I pulled out of Sydney. In the rain it seemed very bleak. But I couldn't do a solo trip without being on my own. I just hoped I wouldn't feel as lonely as I had in America.

Loneliness was a high price to pay for independence.

7

SURVIVING THE OUTBACK:
SYDNEY TO ALICE SPRINGS

Sydney, 3 November 1983

Once I got going, it felt good to be on the road at last, to have finished another chapter in my journey and to be starting a new one. I'd recuperated from the events of America and New Zealand, prepared myself and my BMW for the journey ahead and earned nearly US $6,000; enough – I hoped – to get myself home.

I assumed Australia would be easy: English speaking; empty sealed roads; petrol readily available; and I was looking forward to cruising around the country. But I decided not to set my sights too high. Just get out of Sydney, I told myself. Head for the national parks to the north, test the bike is running well so you can still turn back for repairs if necessary, find somewhere to sleep for the night. Tomorrow I would get some serious mileage under the old girl's tyres.

My first day on the bike with the panniers fully loaded was disconcerting. The front end felt very light, as if the wheel would lift up at times. By the end of the day, I was feeling uncomfortably wedged into the bike, my legs squeezed between the panniers and the cylinder heads. I wondered if I'd get used to it.

After a night in a youth hostel on the coast between Newcastle and Port Macquarie, I rode inland. The day started sunny, but by lunchtime it was pouring with rain. With my waterproofs on, I doubled back towards Apsley Gorge to see the impressive waterfalls, then via Armidale to another set of falls at Wollomombi, where I walked for half an hour along a ridge of the gorge.

Anxious to make up for the three days I'd lost slumming around before departing, I covered more than 500 miles on my second day, although the frequent diversions to view sights left me only 300 miles north of Sydney. The roads were better than expected, but I struggled on rough sections, jumpy and nervous about handling the bike on dirt with its bulky panniers and top box. And I hadn't reached the worst of it yet. Already the weather was playing tricks: muggy at 32°C when I woke, freezing cold and pouring with rain two hours later.

Waking with the sunrise, I kept riding north, the names on the signs – Black Mountain, Wandsworth, Llangothlin, Ben Lomond, Stonehenge, Dundee – a reminder of where the immigrants who established these little towns and villages originated. Only the sign for Bolivia was out of kilter.

Riding through a landscape of green rolling hills, little towns at the foot of long mountain climbs, the going was relatively easy until I reached Tenterfield and took a dirt road detour for sixty miles to see Bald Rock National Park, Australia's largest rock outcrop after Ayers Rock. I climbed to the top, a half-hour granite scramble in blistering heat, but well worth it. To the south lay New South Wales. To the north, Queensland. I could see all the way I'd come and as far as the coast ahead.

Compared with me, my bike was coping well with the hammering of the dirt roads. Nothing had fallen off, even after ploughing into God knows how many foot-deep potholes. I finally arrived in Warwick and, having promised my parents I'd phone every fortnight, I thought I'd make a quick call, then return swiftly to the hostel for an early night, ready for a long day in the saddle tomorrow. But Warwick had no payphones. After trudging for miles, I found one outside a convenience store, and tapped in the sequence of numbers required for a calling card connection to London.

Distant echoes and clicks passed down the line, then a ringtone. My parents' answering machine clicked into life and I heard a brief snatch of my father's voice asking callers to leave a short message.

I'd taken so long to find a payphone, I'd missed my parents before they left for work.

'It's Elspeth. I'm in Warwick and I'm fine,' I said. 'Sorry I missed you.'

Trudging for another hour back to the hostel, I planned my route ahead: towards Brisbane, then the coast road north. After four days riding over mountain passes, the novelty had worn off and I decided the coast road would be quicker. By Monday, I hoped to be in Rockhampton, and then I'd turn west towards the Carnarvon Gorge to see some wild kangaroos. It meant long days in the saddle, hard work after seven months pootling around Sydney, but I hoped the landscape would compensate.

Crossing into Queensland, the dirt roads were more frequent and as tough as any I'd encountered anywhere. Often only a single track, sometimes no more than dust, empty for hours until a road train approached.

I'd heard a lot about road trains, but until I came face to face with one of these snaking, articulated, motorized mammoths I didn't realize their dominance of the road. With up to four trailers, these marauding monsters were up to 150 feet long and took no prisoners. They carried everything from livestock and minerals to petrol and cars. The ones going in my direction were okay; I could stop and wait for them to pass, or overtake them if the road allowed. It was the buggers coming the other way that were the problem.

The first one I met head on, on a dirt road in Queensland, stormed straight towards me, making no attempt to slow down or move over, pushing me off the narrow tarmac track onto the dirt. Suffocated and blinded by dust, I jolted through the potholes along the side of the track, lucky not to lose control.

After the first few encounters with road trains, I decided it was safer to pull over to the side and allow them to pass rather than risk losing control of my bike. Soon I understood their *modus operandi*: at their normal cruise speed the rear trailer would swing from side to side, like a tail wagging behind a dog. When two road trains approached from opposing directions, they accelerated to prevent their rear trailers fishtailing, so they could pass without collision.

But when a lone motorcyclist was riding towards them, they kept going, as if the road belonged only to them.

Queensland was hard work. Large potholes frequently pockmarked the road. Recurrent roadworks enforced twenty-mile diversions along dust tracks and dried-out riverbeds. All I remember of it was the heat and dust, the mud, road trains and emptiness. It was exhausting, nearly 400 miles in one day to Maryborough, a few miles south of Bundaberg, just in time to escape a downpour that flooded a youth hostel run by a little old lady who seemed puzzled by me, but was very kind and polite.

Dodging thunderstorms all the next day, I passed through one-horse towns with few places to shelter and nothing worth seeing. Freedom on the road – the cliché of cruising into the sunset – simply didn't exist. Waypoints needed to be reached, schedules met, storms avoided, although I came to realize that most deadlines were no more than constraints of my own making. Routes could be changed and the tropical rains could be dodged simply by avoiding the hour or two of heavy downpour that fell every afternoon like clockwork.

Wanting to press ahead, I rode through the deluges, everything sodden within five seconds. I worried that the rainy season had started early this year. It would matter more when I began heading inland, where the dirt roads would turn into bogs until I got to Mount Isa, where climate and terrain would change again, becoming a hot desert.

It seemed Australia didn't do happy mediums, only extremes.

At the end of my fifth day on the road, I reached Rockhampton, where I met Tom and Ewan, two easy-going clean-cut guys. Tom was English, but looked quite Italian, and had bought a Honda CX500 in Sydney. Ewan, a Kiwi, had been hitching until picked up by Tom. Now he was riding pillion.

For three days we explored the area together, catching a boat to the Keppel Islands and snorkelling the southern reaches of the Great Barrier Reef. On 11 November we left Rockhampton side by side on a dirt road towards Mount Isa with a plan to camp together at the Carnarvon Gorge.

Loaded with water and petrol, my bike was really heavy and the road was terrible, the tarmac riddled with potholes, turning to dirt. Tom and Ewan dropped back until they were riding about a hundred yards behind me to allow the dust clouds behind my bike to disperse.

That's the last thing I can remember.

I woke in a bright, white room. A male doctor with dark hair was standing at the end of the bed.

'You've had an accident,' he said.

Waking up in hospital rooms was becoming something of a habit, only this time my belly didn't hurt, but I couldn't move my head. I glimpsed my motorcycle gear on a chair beside my bed, scuffed and covered in bull dust.

'You were lucky you had such a good helmet,' said the doctor. 'It saved your life.'

I looked at my full-face Bell helmet, cracked and missing a chunk of the outer 'skin' of fibreglass on the side above my temple. 'What happened?'

'You were brought here by ambulance from a dirt track in the outback about 180 miles away. It would be best if you slept now. Close your eyes.'

'Tell me again what happened,' I said to Tom, who was now standing at the end of my bed. It was the second time he and Ewan had visited me in hospital.

'We were travelling to the Gorge,' said Tom, looking to Ewan for confirmation.

'And then?' I said, unable to remember anything of this or of the week leading up to the accident. With only my injuries as evidence, it felt like it had all happened to someone else.

'The weather was good,' Tom continued. 'I was looking at the scenery and my dials. Then I looked up, saw you on your bike in the distance, about a hundred yards away. You were riding, then suddenly you seemed to lose control. Your handlebars wobbled. You and your BM cartwheeled several times. All I could see were bike parts flying off everywhere.'

Before I could ask any more questions, a nurse came into the room, asked Tom and Ewan to leave while she checked my dressings. By the time she'd finished, I'd fallen asleep.

A few days later and I was standing beside my BMW, next to a caravan on a campsite in Townsville. My bike's handlebars were twisted, its front brake lever snapped off. It was a lovely day, the sun warming my bruised hands, healing the cuts and scratches on my arms and shoulders. I wondered what had sent me cartwheeling down the road, a few hundred yards in front of Tom and Ewan, shattering my fairing, the one I'd reconstructed in Sydney after it was crushed by the garbage truck. Now it was gone and with it my frog mascot.

'It was bull dust that caused you to lose control,' said Tom. 'The road was partly sealed and pretty poor. Blinded by the dust, you hit a huge pothole, larger than the diameter of your wheels. And when the front wheel went down, all that weight at the back of your bike sent you arse over heels, cartwheeling down the track. When we got there, you were wandering around, concussed, dazed and muttering, incoherent.'

I knew about this last part. While recovering in hospital I'd discovered that the microcassette recorder I'd been carrying in my tank bag had switched itself on as my bike cartwheeled down the road. 'That's right,' I said. 'I could hear myself on the tape, wandering around, mumbling "Where's my money? Where's my passport?" Over and over again, more than fifty times.'

'It was like a mantra,' said Tom. 'You were obsessed.'

I nodded. Having Tom confirm what I knew only from hearing it on the tape made the events surrounding my accident feel slightly more real.

'It was lucky we were there with you,' said Tom. 'Ewan looked after your pulse and breathing rate, while I went for help, but there wasn't much traffic about. After a while a guy in a truck stopped. Luckily he had a radio-telephone and called the emergency services. Ewan discussed your condition with them as they decided whether to send a plane or an ambulance to pick you up. In the end they sent an ambulance and Ewan went with you.'

I'd heard the paramedics on my tape while I was in the ambulance, – still demanding to know where my money and passport were, my voice slurred, short of breath.

Tom explained that he and the guy with the truck lifted my bike onto the trucker's rig, dropped it off at a nearby farm. 'The farmer said I could use his workshop to fix the bike,' said Tom. 'I left it there and went to Moura, to the hospital where Ewan was with you.'

It all sounded unreal, simply because I couldn't remember any of it. And yet, surrounding me was the physical evidence of it all: my panniers, bashed and dented; my top box, buckled like a concertina.

'We hired a caravan for a few days,' said Tom, 'then Ewan and I rode to the farm the next day, about two hours away. We straightened your bike, then Ewan rode my bike to Moura, while I stayed at the farm, had supper with the farmer, then rode your bike back to the caravan. It was very late and kangaroos were all over the place.'

I don't know what I would have done without Tom and Ewan's help. They waited until I was discharged from Moura, then we rode back to Townsville where there was a BMW shop for spare parts. Tom and Ewan travelled north to Cairns while I repaired my bike. I bashed the top box back into a vaguely rectangular shape and reconstructed a connection between it and the panniers. I junked the bent handlebars; replaced them with higher, wider bars that I hoped would improve the handling, and fitted them with a new front brake lever.

Although I had recovered from my injuries, I was apprehensive about getting back onto the bike, partly because I had no memory of how I'd fallen off. But I wanted to continue on and, when Tom and Ewan returned three days later, we set off, heading inland, intending to cross Queensland to Mount Isa. Having always wanted to see kangaroos, now I couldn't escape from them. Appearing everywhere, they became a menace. Riding along, I'd spot one in a field, almost out of sight. Then, the kangaroo would make a beeline for me, jumping out into the road in front of my wheels, as if it had a death wish. It was bizarre.

Dead kangaroos littered the side of the road, riddled with maggots and flies that attacked us whenever we stopped, buzzing around us, invading my eyes, my nose, my mouth.

Riding through the outback was full-on contact with nature; not in all its glories, but at its most primal and basic, whether beast or human. The creatures were challenging and the people were rough, which was no surprise given the extreme lives that they led.

Even stranger to me than the roughnecks and exotic creatures that inhabited the outback were the many obscure and unnecessary rules and regulations. One-horse towns in the middle of nowhere would impose automatic fines on anyone who didn't park their vehicle with the tail pointing into the kerb. I'd always thought the only reason many people decided to live in the outback was to escape the mundanity of much of modern life, but the towns there turned out to be significantly more restrictive than many European cities.

We'd only ridden for about an hour out of Townsville when it started to rain. The road became very wet and slippery. A short distance further on, we came to a stop. Ahead of us, the first river crossing I'd ever encountered. A thick red-brown muddy soup flowed where the road should have been, not much of an obstacle in the grander scheme of things, but I'd never ridden through deep water before.

The three of us stood near the river, hoping another vehicle would come along and drive through so we could gauge the depth of the water. Nothing came, so I took a few steps closer to the water's edge, stared across the expanse of filthy water. Maybe thirty metres to the far bank, I reckoned.

I took a step into the water and felt it fill my boots. If I was going to cross this river on my bike, I wanted to check its depth across its entire width. After three steps the water was up to my knees. I kept pushing, the riverbed slipping beneath my boots. The current was too weak to knock me over, but strong and deep enough to make each step treacherous. I got to the other side, turned around immediately and returned to my bike.

'What's it like?' said Tom.

'No more than knee deep. There are no rocks, just slippery sand on the riverbed. As long as our tyres don't lose their grip, we should make it across.'

Slowly I edged the BMW down a shallow bank, the weight of the panniers and top box threatening to pull the rear wheel around on the slippery mud. I entered the water, tried to use my feet to stabilize my bike, but realized the best thing was to maintain forward momentum. It turned out to be easier than I'd anticipated.

It didn't stop raining, so we made it only as far as Charters Towers that evening, less than ninety miles from Townsville. As we struck camp on a concrete-floored shelter, the rain bouncing off its corrugated iron roof, Tom turned to me.

'I don't know if this is a good idea,' he said.

'Sleeping here?'

'No. Riding to Mount Isa.'

I was disappointed, but not that surprised.

'If the roads are this bad,' said Tom. 'Maybe I'll try it again, later. When the rains have stopped.'

I didn't have a choice. 'I've got to be in Perth by the end of the month.'

The next morning Tom turned back, leaving Ewan to hitch on to Mount Isa, as there was no way he could ride pillion on my bike with the top box on the back seat. 'If I try it again, I might sell my bike,' said Tom, 'and take the bus.'

It was a much better idea. Unfortunately I had no choice.

It took me one day to ride nearly 500 miles of dirt tracks from Charters Towers to Mount Isa. Travelling alone, I found it hard going. Bumping over mile after mile of corrugations on dusty single-lane roads in the forty-degree heat was physically crippling. I'd ridden similar distances in America, but that was tarmac from coast to coast. By comparison, every inch of the road to Mount Isa was a battle. And when I got there I wondered why I'd bothered. Two elderly Aussies living in an old car at the edge of town set the scene. Flies, roadworks and a vast mineral mine summed up the rest of the town.

I stayed the night at Mount Isa, then visited the mine in the morning, where one of their public relations team interviewed me. A week later a short story appeared in *ISA News*, the mine's weekly newspaper, the first publicity I'd managed to get for my trip. It felt good to have some interest in what I was doing.

Mount Isa was only the stepping-stone to my ultimate goal, Ayers Rock. After the mine visit, I set off for Tennant Creek, more than 400 miles further west. About a quarter of the way, near the state border between Queensland and the Northern Territory, I ran into Ewan. He'd done well; his first hitch, a German guy on a bike, took him 100 miles in one hit. Since then he'd been riding with a Swiss brother and sister in a Holden car.

We travelled towards Three Ways, which as the name suggests was the junction of three roads: the main road west meeting the great north–south highway that connected Darwin on the north coast to Adelaide in the south, right through the centre of Australia. At some point, I lost touch with the Holden and was back on my own, lonely in the vast expanses, wishing I had company for moral support and to help combat the environment.

Each day the riding seemed to get harder. In the heat, I needed to stop every half-hour to drink water. On an average day, I'd get through three to four litres. Physically I found it exhausting, but mentally it was even tougher. Never knowing where I might find water or fuel, I'd stop to refill whenever there was an opportunity, then ride on, always on edge, unable to relax, anxious and tense about running out of fuel, water, daylight and energy.

In most cases, the places I'd stop would be roadhouses, often little more than a shack in the middle of nowhere that happened to have some petrol. No more sophisticated than farm outhouses, these were rough-and-ready buildings made of breezeblocks and corrugated iron. Outside them stood a row of old cars and dogs, docile in the heat. Inside, the clientele convened – truckers and sweaty, dirty, sheep farmers in a bare room, the walls and floors sometimes fully tiled so the management could hose them down at the end of the evening, washing all the dirt, puke and broken glass out into the street.

Invariably, the roadhouse would be the only place for hundreds of miles that I could get petrol and a drink, so I'd have no choice but to walk in and face a scene like something from a film. Lined along the bar would be a row of drunks, all men. Sometimes the staff wouldn't even serve me, no matter how long I waited. I felt their hostility wasn't because of the bike, but because I was a woman. And, as quite a few of the clientele made very clear in the remarks they made as I waited for a drink, my cropped short hair plus riding a motorbike meant I had to be 'a dyke'. I'd often end up outside the roadhouse, filling up my water from an external tap and drinking it in peace, sitting under a tree.

At Three Ways, there was only a single building beside the junction, the imaginatively titled Three Ways Roadhouse. I ran inside, drank water for more than a minute, then looked around, hoping to spot a face that wasn't scowling at me. At the other end of the bar were three bikers, one of them on a BMW R60/6, just like mine, the other two on a newer BMW.

'I saw you earlier, on the road to Mount Isa,' said the guy with the R60/6. 'It's difficult to miss you.'

'You mean the shed?'

He nodded and smiled.

I held out my hand. 'Elspeth.'

'Glenn.' Fair-haired and tanned, Glenn had an easy manner and, as I later found out, told good stories that made me laugh.

As we were talking, Ewan and the Swiss couple arrived in the Holden. We all decided to continue together in convoy towards Tennant Creek. When we got there, we continued beyond the town into the outback. That night, I camped with them all, swimming together in a water-hole as the sun went down, cherishing every moment of their company.

My first night under clear heavens in the outback, the sky was extraordinary. I lay on the ground, staring at more stars than I'd ever imagined existed. I'd never seen anything like it. Among the shooting stars, the only sign of human life came from satellite specks, twinkling as they slowly crossed the grainy sky.

*

At 4 a.m. I got up, eager to get on the road to cover as much ground as possible before the heat of the day beat me into submission. I shook the others awake and made my goodbyes, arranging to meet Glenn and Ewan in Alice Springs that night.

I wasn't looking forward to the day at all. Several hundred miles of awful road lay in front of me. Knowing it would be a slog, I wished I'd bussed it or hitched, like Ewan. And it was made worse by the knowledge that at the end of it all, there'd be nowhere decent to rest except my tent or a bare-boned hostel with hostile staff and clientele. I'd be glad when I got to Alice Springs and even gladder when I reached Port Augusta.

Taking down my tent, I jumped back in surprise as a snake scurried off from beneath my groundsheet. I'd obviously slept directly on top of it; maybe it had sought my body heat. I was beginning to get used to the sight of these venomous creatures. The previous day, near where I'd stopped to sip some water by the side of the road, I'd seen a brown snake, the second most poisonous land snake of all. I had also recently encountered a redback and a funnel-web spider, the venom of both powerful enough to seriously incapacitate humans.

Until about 9 a.m., when the heat started to rise, the climate was almost pleasurable, although the road still shook me to bits. Now south of the tropics, the terrain was bone dry in spite of the heavy rains, bereft of vegetation other than scrub for as far as I could see. On the dirt sections I didn't average more than 30 mph. It was tiring and I worried about what it was doing to my bike. My poor old girl was taking a beating. And when the roads weren't rattling us to pieces, they were trying to mire us in their waters.

By noon, the heat was too much to bear and I hibernated under a tree, waking at about four o'clock to eat, then climbed back on my bike for another three hours of riding before it got dark. Looking around me, I wondered why anyone chose to live in this God-forsaken place. I loved the endless skies, but the heat, dust, flies and the climate combined with the laconic Aussie characters were too much for me. As for the towns, they were so small and empty they barely qualified as settlements. I'd sweat all day, riding like hell to get to somewhere marked on my map, and when I arrived I'd find nothing apart from a few corrugated shacks.

By early evening I was standing outside Alice Springs youth hostel, 300 bone-jarring miles from Tennant Creek with the passing of each mile feeling like a small victory. Not long after I arrived, Glenn pulled up.

'Let's keep going,' said Glenn. 'We can make Ayers Rock by midnight, then see the sunrise there.'

I wasn't convinced. 'I've heard a really bad cyclone's hitting Australia. All of west and central Australia's going to get it.'

Glenn gave me a sceptical look and I could guess what he was thinking: Alice Springs was yet another Aussie outback dump and there was little point in hanging around.

'Wait for Ewan,' I suggested. 'Then we can do Ayers Rock together – tomorrow.'

Ewan stepped off a bus two hours later and, as I hoped would happen, he wasn't inclined to head for Ayers Rock that night. Instead he persuaded Glenn to take him on the back of his bike the next day.

The ride to Ayers Rock, a 300-mile detour from the main highway south, was as uneventful as any in central Australia, which is to say it was long, hard, dusty and dotted with dingoes and kangaroos, but at least I arrived in one piece at a place I'd always wanted to visit.

From a distance the rock, known now by its aboriginal name of Uluru, looked gentle and quite easy to climb, but it was a lot steeper, bigger and higher than I had ever imagined. It was a one-mile climb. Using chains to pull ourselves up on some parts, we reached the top of the sandstone monolith with a real sense of achievement, took in the view, explored the summit, then returned to camp. With dark clouds gathering on the horizon, we went to bed early, ready to greet the rock at sunrise.

By morning the storm had arrived. The rock, which I had remembered from photos as a dramatic dark red outcrop set against a clear blue sky, had been turned into a sludgy brown hulk under the dark grey sky.

'Told you we should have come the night before,' said Glenn. 'If we'd come here yesterday morning, we would have seen a proper sunrise.'

Glenn was right, but I wasn't going to concede. Riding at night was too dangerous with all the kangaroos. Not seeing the rock in its full photogenic glory was a price I was prepared to pay for caution. What I hadn't anticipated was that we wouldn't be seeing the sun for another two weeks, an extraordinarily long period in central Australia.

Rain started before we'd finished packing up our camp, flooding the only road out and making it impossible for us to visit the Olgas, another rock formation nearby, so instead we decided to head for Alice Springs. The rain became torrential. I was itching to get going, but Ewan and Glenn were dragging their feet, pottering around our camp with no sense of urgency.

In pouring rain and on flooded roads, we rode all day until dusk. It was a nightmare. Cows wandered randomly all over the road. Road trains hacked past at 70 mph, their drivers probably with a six-pack inside them. Then, as darkness fell, an electrical storm started. For me, that was the final straw.

'I'm not riding any further,' I told Glenn.

He looked at me with weary eyes. 'Why?'

'Isn't it obvious? Electric storm plus metal top box equals trouble. And I can't see the mud in the dark.'

Glenn wrinkled his nose, considered things. 'Okay.'

I was pleased. I didn't care where we stopped, where we camped, as long as it happened very soon, but I noticed Ewan getting fidgety.

'You're not serious, are you?' said Ewan, addressing Glenn as much as me.

'Els wants to stop,' said Glenn. 'Why do you want to press on?'

'I want to get a bus first thing tomorrow morning from Alice,' said Ewan.

'No way,' I said. 'It's too dangerous.'

'What's wrong with riding in the dark?' said Ewan. 'You must have done it thousands of times.'

'Not in torrential rain, mud and floods,' I countered. 'And not with cows and kangaroos wandering all over the road.'

Ewan narrowed his eyes and lifted his eyebrows.

'You think I'm exaggerating?' I said.

Ewan didn't answer. Instead he pointed at Glenn. 'He could lead.'

'No way.' Glenn shook his head. 'No way at all.'

'This is so stupid. You're both paranoid,' said Ewan.

I said nothing. Glenn was looking at the ground.

'You lead then, Elspeth,' said Ewan. 'Take it slowly. We'll be okay.'

'It isn't your bike or your neck that I'll be risking.'

Finally Glen agreed to lead and so we set off, with me riding behind him, travelling at no more than 30 mph for 100 miles. Even so, I almost hit several cows. Four hours later, shortly before midnight, we rode into Alice. I was absolutely knackered. My arse was sore. My shoulders ached. I was soaked.

Ewan looked sheepish. 'I think I owe you an apology,' he said.

'That was so unnecessary,' I answered. 'If you two had got yourselves organized quicker this morning we wouldn't have needed to do that. The whole thing was a risk we shouldn't have had to take.'

Before Ewan could respond, Glenn emerged from the youth hostel, looking dejected. 'They're fully booked.'

'We could camp,' said Ewan.

'In this weather?' I said. 'Really?'

We found a guesthouse. As I lay in bed that night, listening to the rain hammer against the roof and windows, I was very glad not to be in my tent.

8

LAYING DEMONS TO REST:
ALICE SPRINGS TO PERTH

Alice Springs, 25 November 1983

We woke to the news that six inches of rain had fallen overnight. More than the entire previous three years' rainfall, locals feared the roads would be impassable as there had been no sight of any traffic coming from the opposite direction.

'I'll see you in Port Augusta,' said Ewan, leaving to catch the bus. As I watched him run down the street, his bag on his head providing some shelter, I wondered how he was going to get there, but still wished I was in his shoes rather than in my sodden motorcycle boots.

Within minutes of leaving the guesthouse, Glenn and I discovered that six inches of overnight rain equated to three feet of thick, sticky mud. Roads had become canals, with the water trapped between the gravel dykes that lined each side of the road, formed when the surfaces were graded.

'Let's try the station,' said Glenn. 'See if the trains are getting through.'

Having set off from Sydney with the intent of riding right across Australia, I was reluctant to load my bike on the rails. At the station, Glenn booked his bike on a goods wagon leaving later that day for $40. I shook my head. It wasn't for me.

'You could be in Adelaide by tomorrow,' said Glenn.

'I know.' I shrugged. 'Maybe I'm making a mistake, but I'm going to try to ride as much as possible.'

We said goodbye and I rode to a petrol station at the edge of town. I filled up the old girl, asked around about conditions on the road south. The south road was notorious at the best of times, 300 miles of dirt and corrugations and the only highway running from the north to the south of Australia. Most of the truckers told me to forget riding for at least the next few days. One of them, a thin man in stubby shorts and a shirt with its arms torn off, warned me strongly against leaving Alice Springs.

'I've been driving road trains for more than thirty years,' he said. 'The road will be bad, I've never seen so much rain.'

Something about this man's quiet authority and his craggy weather-beaten face made me trust his advice. He was quieter, older and seemed more considered than most of the other truckers.

'What do you suggest I do?' I said.

We were standing under an awning. The trucker looked out at the floods and smiled. 'I can give you a lift. It might be better further along the road.'

I felt I didn't have a choice. It was impossible even to walk on the road without sinking up to my knees, let alone ride on it. 'Okay,' I said. 'That's very kind. But I'm only hitching a lift until the floods clear.'

The trucker held out a hand. 'Name's Des.'

I shook his hand. 'Elspeth.'

Some of the other truckers helped us haul my bike up into the rear of Des's third and last trailer, then strap it to the side before we set off. Des was an amazing driver with a real feel for his rig. Slipping and sliding his truck from one side of the road to the other, he maintained momentum because, he said, 'if we slow down or stop we've had it. Then we'll be digging ourselves out.'

Unlike some truckers, Des didn't drink alcohol when driving, but he did keep a cool box beside him in the cab. He offered me a drink, but we didn't talk much. Driving his rig through the mud and flooded roads required Des's full concentration.

The truck's windscreen was covered in mud. I looked out of the side window, saw the rear trailer fishtailing, spraying water and mud either side behind it. Then, about an hour out of Alice, the road turned into one huge lake for as far as we could see. Unable to see where the road emerged across the far side of the water, Des stopped his rig, climbed onto the top of its cab to get a better look. Having worked out roughly which direction to go we set off again, but soon we were stuck and going nowhere.

'Time to dig,' said Des.

I took my shoes off and stepped down into thick, glutinous mud – it was like cake mixture. Des handed down shovels from his cab and climbed out. While he waded around the flood, sinking down to his knees in mud, I scratched around for bits of bushes and brush. Beyond the water, the terrain was very barren, so it took a long time, but I found a few and shoved them under the road train's wheels to give them some grip. Des climbed back into the cab, tried to move his truck.

'This isn't working. We need racks or ladders.' Des shook his head. 'But I got none.' He looked around, pointed at a shack in the distance. 'I'll be back soon.'

Des returned with a local farmer who stank of sweat and alcohol. Leaning against the back of his van in a chopped-off shirt over a T-shirt, stubbies and boots, he smirked under his Aussie hat. 'What do you want me to do?'

Between them, Des and the farmer unhitched Des's truck from its trailers, laid down racks and pulled each of his three trailers out of the mud separately onto firmer ground. Once all the trailers had been pulled out and re-hitched we were soon back on the road, passing a succession of stranded cars and vans, some with people sleeping in them, the mud up to the top of their wheels in some cases.

We drove on through a devastated landscape, the road littered with abandoned trucks and debris. At the third lake, our luck and skills ran out and we joined the crowd, sharing spades and chains, all clubbing in together to free ourselves from the mud's sticky grip.

By early evening, news reached us that the police had officially closed all roads. Although they didn't actually stop anyone they just didn't want to be responsible for rescuing people. Ewan's bus, we heard, had been stuck for nine hours further along the road, even though it had low-ratio four-wheel drive. By the time darkness fell, Des had pulled his rig free of the lake and we were back in motion, driving through the night, keeping going until he couldn't drive any further, when we stopped and slept in his trailer until Des was ready to drive again.

Arriving in Coober Pedy very early the next morning, we were the first vehicle the locals said they'd seen come through in days. As I climbed out of the air-conditioned cab, I almost fainted. It was 52°C and the first time I'd seen the sun in weeks. Filthy, covered from head to toe in mud, the pair of us looked a sight.

Coober Pedy was where the dirt road ended and the sealed road started, so we stopped at the first road stop for fuel and asked some truckers to help us lift my bike out of the rear trailer.

Relieved that my bike had survived the ride undamaged, I turned towards Des and held out my hand.

'Thank you so much,' I said. 'I don't know what I would have done without your lift.'

I couldn't thank him enough. It had certainly been an adventure and Des had been a true gentleman throughout our three days spent together.

Des smiled and looked me up and down. I'd sensed when he first picked me up that he'd been reluctant to have a 'Sheila' in tow, but now he was glad to have had the company.

'No, thank *you*,' he said and shook my hand. Des was a man of few words, but we'd been a good team and by working hard digging, helping free his rig time after time, I felt I'd earned his respect. 'I've been driving the same route from Darwin to Port Augusta for nearly thirty years and I've never seen the road so bad. Thank you.'

It was nearly 1,500 miles from Port Augusta to Perth. In between lay the Nullarbor Plain, 75,000 square miles of virtually uninhabitable scrubby desert along the south Australian coast. Crossing the Nullarbor was one of those quintessential traveller experiences celebrated on bumper stickers and backpack patches, and now it was my turn. I'd been told that over a distance of 500 miles or more, I'd see no sign of human life at all. No water, no roadhouses, no petrol stations. Nothing.

The next morning, I started the long ride west, laden with extra petrol canisters in my top box because I'd been told that roadhouses across the Nullarbor were spaced far further apart than in other parts of the outback. With a full tank I could do around 300 miles before going onto reserve, which gave me another 30 miles. The extra gallon I was carrying would give me another 60 miles. With a range of nearly 400 miles I should be fine, provided I took it steady and didn't ride too fast. A couple of hours later, I was fully enveloped in the climatic challenges of the infamous desert, but instead of dehydrating in the stifling heat as I had expected, I was shivering with cold beneath my full winter gear.

Whipped by the wind, drenched by rain and frozen by the cold, I pressed on, wishing there was something to distract me from the grim weather. But there was nothing to occupy my attention at all, just miles and miles of flat scrub. Even the most barren parts of America, such as the plains of Texas or the New Mexico desert, had a few hills to interrupt the monotony. But here: nothing at all. And the worst of it was that after riding through several hundred miles of emptiness, I had nothing to look forward to the next day except for another few hundred miles of barren scrub. The highlight of the first day was seeing a road sign saying 'Police Air Patrols in Force', which someone had defaced and written 'Pigs in Space' underneath it. It kept me amused for hours.

After a while, the complete absence of any discernible features played with my head. Along one section, the road was as straight as an arrow for more than ninety miles. I'd heard stories of people falling asleep at the wheel, spinning their car around and not knowing from which direction they had come. The only solution was to wait for the sunset to show them which way was west.

Occasionally, a small sign of civilization arose on the horizon. I'd ride towards it, almost excited at the prospect of contact with another living creature, but when I got there, having ridden for hours in blistering heat or crushing cold, I got a reception like I was the last person on earth they wanted to see.

It was hard going, not helped by my bike, which kept misfiring intermittently. I pulled into a sheep station and the owner offered me the use of his garage to repair my bike and a bed for the night. I felt bad about turning down his kind offer, a seemingly rare display of human kindness in these parts, but I'd heard there was a petrol station further down the road that might have the tools I needed.

At the petrol station, the owner was just as generous as the guy at the sheep station. I got out my Haynes manual and removed the tank to get to the electrics. 'Any idea what the problem is?' said the petrol station owner. I shook my head. By the time we had worked out that my starter relay was faulty, the petrol station owner had called over all his mates to give a hand. Between us, we put my bike back together. I turned the key. She fired up immediately. The petrol station owner very kindly let me stay there overnight and the next day I rode further along the coast to Coolgardie, an old mining town where I found a good youth hostel, then continued on to Perth via Wave Rock.

Perth felt very remote and isolated. At the end of a very long railway line, it had become a destination simply because it was the largest town in Western Australia. Even though it was the first port for ships coming across the Indian Ocean it wasn't easy to find any information for the next stage of my journey. This was a problem as I had to work out what I needed to do about getting to Indonesia. My quest for information in the pre-internet era wasn't helped by the absence of an Indonesian embassy, consulate or tourist information bureau, so in search of enlightenment, I wrote to Mark, care of a poste restante in Singapore. About a week later a letter arrived at my $6-a-week hostel.

'Sorry to hear about the bonk on your bonce,' he wrote, 'although you sounded more concerned about the state of your fairing. The rest of your trip sounds relatively normal for a Beard expedition.'

His letter provided the information I needed. 'It is possible to ride through Bali and Jakarta in the rainy season but it will be very hard to make it through Sumatra unless time is unlimited. The roads are very boggy. I met some Swiss riders on BMWs who said the roads in Indonesia were the worst they'd seen anywhere – and that was in the dry season.'

After such a tough crossing of Australia, the promise of a rest from riding the bike was very appealing, particularly as the weather was likely to be extremely wet and humid. After making some more enquiries, I decided the islands, such as Java and Bali, were too small for island hopping. It didn't make sense to ship my bike to Bali only to piddle around the island for a week before shipping it to Java and doing the same again. I'd ship my bike directly to Singapore, which was much cheaper, and arrange to meet Mark in Bali. But a ship didn't leave for three weeks, so I decided to do a tour of Western Australia, south from Perth.

At the hostel, I'd met a wholesome, jolly German woman with a beaming smile called Simone. We'd shared a room and got on well, so I asked if she would like to join me on my tour south.

I spent a couple of days servicing my bike, removing the panniers so Simone could ride pillion, fitting a new tyre, changing the oils, repairing the headlight at a welder's workshop and giving it a general service. Then we rode down the coast road from Perth to Albany, along the south coast to the Valley of the Giants, famous for its incredible Karri and Tingle trees. Celebrated as some of the tallest trees in the world, these towering giants grew to a height of more than eighty metres.

Continuing along the south-western coast of Australia, Simone and I were riding along a deserted highway, having seen no sign of life for more than 100 miles, when a plume of white smoke rose in front of the handlebars.

I stopped the bike immediately.

'What's the matter?' said Simone.

I pointed at the smoke curling around the petrol tank. 'That.'

Simone jumped off the bike. I followed and stood back, beside Simone. 'Should I try to put it out?' I said.

'It's your bike,' said Simone. 'It's your decision.'

'It could blow up. The smoke's coming from under the tank.'

Crouching down, I couldn't see any flames, but the smoke was getting worse. The clear lens of the headlight was milky white.

'I can't just stand here, watching my bike burn.' I pulled off the jumper I was wearing under my leather jacket. 'I've got to do something.'

Now, thick clouds of white smoke were coming from under the seat as well. My bike looked as if it was about to burst into flames. I was going to lose it and I was just standing watching it.

Panic set in, but having never seen a bike fire before, I didn't know what to do, how to douse the fire safely. I grabbed my jumper, jammed it into the space beneath the tank, hoping it would smother the flames. To my surprise, the smoke died down, almost as quickly as it had appeared, then stopped altogether, leaving a nasty stench of burnt plastic and rubber.

I crouched down to see if I could work out what had happened under the petrol tank. Hoping the flames wouldn't reignite if I pulled out my jumper, I tugged the singed material out of the gap and peered into the space beneath the tank and the seat. No flames. No smoke. Just a messy congealed mess of matted plastic.

'Oh shit.'

'Bad?'

'It doesn't look good,' I said. 'I think all the wiring completely burnt out and melted itself into one big lump.'

'But you know what to do, don't you?'

'I can fix just about anything on this bike, but I'm not much good when it comes to electrics.'

Simone's eyes were big. 'What are we going to do?'

We hadn't passed anything for more than 100 miles; I didn't have a clue. Gazing forlornly down the road, my eyes focused on a small shack about quarter of a mile away. Behind it was a bungalow; in front of it was a blue sign. I could just about read it. I squinted into the sun. *Auto-electrician.*

'I don't bloody believe it.' I pointed at the sign.

Beside me, Simone gazed into the distance, turned towards me and caught my eye, starting to laugh. 'No . . . ?'

'Yes!' I began to laugh too. It seemed ridiculous, farcical even. Of all the places my bike could have had an electrical fire, she had chosen to do it within shouting distance of possibly the only auto-electrician for maybe 100 miles or more.

When Simone and I managed to stop laughing, we wheeled my bike up the road to the shack, where a short man with cropped hair and overalls was leaning over the uncovered engine of a large estate car. He looked up.

'Hello.' He had a slight Welsh accent. 'What can I do for you two ladies?'

When I heard his accent, I almost had a second fit of giggles. But I kept my cool, saying simply: 'I've got a bit of a problem.'

'What kind of problem?'

'You any good with bike electrics?'

'No.'

'I've had a bit of an electrical fire.' I said. 'But I do have a Haynes manual with a wiring diagram in it.'

I got out the manual and showed him the diagram, which was covered in my oily fingerprints from previous electrical repairs I'd attempted.

'I could have a go . . .'

We wheeled my bike into his garage and I removed the petrol tank, revealing a solid block of charred plastic and rubber interspersed with a few metal strands.

The mechanic, who introduced himself as John, told me he knew how to wire a BMW car. 'And when I look at your bike,' he said, 'it doesn't appear to be that different – the same parts, but in different places.'

Tracing the trail of melted gunk, we worked out what had happened. A wire under the petrol tank had been rubbing against the frame, which had probably exposed its insulation. It had shorted out and burnt out most of my wiring harness.

'The fire must have started under your tank,' said John, 'spread up to your headlight, then down to your alternator, rectifier and starter motor. Only the wires to the taillight and rear indicators are still intact.'

'That explains the electrical fault in the Nullarbor,' I said.

John raised his eyebrows.

'It kept shorting.'

'And you did nothing?'

'I thought I'd fixed it,' I said. 'And the electrics are the only part I don't really understand.'

We stripped down the entire electrical system, removed everything that remained of the wiring, then started to make a new wiring loom from scratch. John had only two colours of wire: brown and black. Armed with my Haynes manual and a reel of each coloured wire, John and I threaded our homemade loom onto my BMW. Other than a few relays, the fire hadn't damaged any components, so we only replaced the wires from the middle of the bike to the front, which to this day are simply black and brown, making tracing any electrical fault at the front of the bike very difficult.

John was really kind, letting us stay with him in his home. He had never seen a BMW bike, let alone worked on one. We worked from eight in the morning until eight at night for two days. John did an amazing job.

On the second night, a bunch of John's friends arrived at his house in a pick-up truck. We shared a few beers, then Simone and I joined them in the back of their pick-up truck, standing behind the cab, our knuckles white around a steadying bar as we hurtled into the night. After bouncing along a dirt road for a few miles, the driver veered off the track into the scrub, flicking on a bank of huge floodlights. Ahead of us, pinpointed in the beams, was a kangaroo, its huge eyes like lumps of coal. Having heard that Aussies liked to go 'roo huntin', I hoped no one had a gun. Fortunately, they wanted to do nothing more than have a bit of fun chasing it for a mile or two through the night.

On the morning of the third day, we got ready to leave. Having worked with John, I now had an intimate knowledge of my bike's electrics, of which I'd always had a rather vague understanding. Since leaving home, all the problems I'd had with the bike – rusty terminals, loose wires – had been electrical, so it was a relief to have a whole new electrical system that I understood better and was confident would now get me home.

Gingerly I inserted my key in the old girl's ignition and turned it on. Ever the reliable trooper, she started first time. No flames, no smoke, just the quiet purr of her engine. I could have hugged her – and John too, especially when he asked me for a very reasonable $200. Considering he'd made the harness himself, when a new

BMW harness cost $150 plus the same amount again for labour, John's fee for installing a homemade harness seemed like a real bargain.

After the repairs, we rode to Bunbury, where we spent a night, then to a very small village about fifty miles south of Perth, where we'd arranged to meet some travellers that Simone and I had met at the youth hostel. It was a quiet, beautiful place in a forest with a river flowing through it, a perfect venue for Christmas Day, which we spent paddling kayaks up the river, eating fruit and drinking Champagne. It was lovely, even if in the midsummer heat the river had run almost dry in places.

The day after Boxing Day, I needed to return to Perth to have my vaccinations and pack my bike for shipping. Wanting to stay longer, Simone arranged to get a lift back with one of the other travellers. As I attempted to ride away, I discovered that my throttle cable didn't work – one of the teeth on the throttle's cog mechanism had worn out – so I was now stuck in a forest, unable to ride. I couldn't bodge a repair, so I persuaded a guy who was also camping in the woods to give me and my bike a lift to Perth in his pick-up truck.

With two days remaining before I had to ship my bike to Singapore, I raced around Perth, gathering the parts I needed to repair my worn-out throttle; another $60 unexpected expense. The bike was reaching that age when more and more parts were wearing out and I was worried that it would grind to a halt somewhere and I'd not be able to get a replacement for a fairly mundane component. At least my throttle had failed in Australia, not somewhere in Southeast Asia, where replacement parts might be impossible to get. As my last days in the relative civilization of a first-world economy were ticking away, I felt a rising panic that they were passing too fast for me to prepare my body, my mind and my bike for the rigours of the road ahead. I still had a long way to go and reckoned that so far I had done the easy bit.

Reinforced with cholera and typhoid boosters, a gamma globulin injection and various malaria tablets, I wrote to my parents to ask them to send me some clean needles and syringes in case I needed medical attention in India, where I had heard of travellers picking up hepatitis from infected equipment.

At the end of the day, I posted my tent home. With cheap hostels ahead of me, I wouldn't be camping again, but I was sorry to see my tent go. It had served me well, making it possible for me not only to visit places far from civilization, but also to save money in America and Australia.

Somewhat sooner than I felt ready for it, I found myself at the docks in Perth, knocking on the door of the shipping company I'd booked for my BMW's voyage to the tropics of Southeast Asia. Exporting anything from Australia was a rip-off because the government had a complete monopoly, as I found out when they tried to charge me twice as much as quoted on the grounds that my panniers doubled the size of the shipment. Removing the panniers and top box from my bike, I squeezed them into the same crate as the bike and proved them wrong – not that it stopped the authorities from trying to charge me double. I stormed out and eventually they relented, probably to get rid of me, charging me only an extra 10 per cent, but it was still more than I wanted to spend when I had less than US $4,000 dollars left to get me home, most of it stuffed into a money belt holding up my jeans.

After fifty-one weeks in Australia, I was relieved to be leaving. Before arriving, I'd assumed it was going to be an easy country in which to work and travel but it had been really tough. The weather, the floods, the roads, the dust, the mud, the road trains, the flies everywhere, the kangaroos and the accident had conspired to test me to my limits. It was the harshest, most unforgiving country I'd ever experienced. I loved my time in Sydney and I had some good times on the road, but I found it incredibly hard work both mentally and physically. I was apprehensive about what lay ahead in Southeast Asia, but it was exciting. I was looking forward to the change.

Although bruised and battered by Australia, stepping onto the plane to Bali I felt proud of what I'd achieved. Penniless and jobless on arrival, I'd ended my time in Sydney in charge of a project to build 270 houses. I'd prospered and earned enough, I hoped, to finance the rest of my journey, halfway round the globe back to London. Now every mile I rode would be a mile closer to home.

Australia put my demons to rest. Crossing the continent had been so tough that I'd not thought of Alex for a second. And now I was actually looking forward to seeing Mark's familiar face. Surviving a life-threatening accident taught me to worry less about what lay ahead. I couldn't anticipate the future, which paradoxically made me relax. Instead of obsessing over details, I'd eased into the rhythm of the journey, living in the moment, taking each day as it came. Whatever was going to happen, would happen.

And I'd be fine.

9

ALL IS LOST:

BALI TO SINGAPORE

Denpasar, 30 January 1983

Sitting on the plane to Denpasar, reading through a stack of letters sent by family and friends to Perth, I wondered if Mark would again fail to recognize me at the airport. Running my fingers through my cropped hair, I laughed at a cartoon Justin had sketched of me riding an old bike that he'd captioned 'Dingo 900 running on kangaroo piss and Foster's pre-mix', then turned to Johnny's letter from St Andrews.

'Your bike looks like a mobile kebab kitchen,' he wrote. 'If you haven't shaved your head by now, you never will. Or to rephrase it: if you haven't, you are probably not on the way to complete mental illness.'

Maybe he had a point.

Letters from home, containing news of relatives and my father's delight at his new electronic typewriter, seemed like missives from another planet.

'I'm relieved to hear you've recovered from your accident,' my mother wrote, adding that she had stuck a map of Australia on her fridge. 'I hope you and Mark will meet in Indonesia to share all your experiences.'

Another letter, written a few days later, revealed my mother's mood. 'Christmas is going to be very bleak without you here.'

I wished I could assure her that I might be home by next Christmas, but in truth I hadn't the faintest idea when I'd next set foot in my family home.

*

Mark and I did recognize each other at the airport, but this time it was my turn to nearly miss him. He had lost a lot of weight and had grown a beard. Although I had never particularly fancied men with beards, somehow it really suited Mark. Ten weeks solo travelling through Indonesia had transformed him. Travelling on his own had clearly done him a power of good.

We caught a bus direct to Ubud, a town in the centre of Bali, chatting all the way, trading tales from the road.

'What's with the Aussie accent?' said Mark, in a bad imitation of one.

'What d'you mean?' I replied.

'See – there it is again.'

I couldn't hear it, but according to Mark I had picked up a very noticeable Australian twang, which he didn't like at all and mercilessly teased me about.

Surrounded by gently rolling rice paddies and dense forest, dotted with tombs and museums, Ubud was a very pleasant contrast to Australia and a much less frenetic introduction to the Far East than Denpasar, the crowded, smelly, charmless capital of Bali, through which the bus had carried us to the central foothills of the island. Having seen the dense, chaotic traffic in Denpasar, I was reassured that shipping my bike straight to Singapore had been a sensible decision. My BMW was due to dock in seven weeks. Until then I could enjoy the luxury of public transport. And after months travelling alone on a bike, I really enjoyed not having the responsibility of looking after it. No worrying about breaking down or where to find the next petrol station. It gave me a sense of freedom, which felt odd as I had always thought my bike gave me the independence and freedom I needed. But after a few days of travelling on public transport and being squeezed between locals, their rice and their animals, on a bench in the back of an open-air pick-up truck bus called a *bemo*, I did start to miss the isolation of travelling solo on a motorcycle.

The public transport system looked chaotic but seemed to work. Hailed simply with a wave from anywhere on the side of the street, each minibus appeared to be individually owned and often raced to beat competitors for custom. Arguments broke out between drivers as they claimed passengers and there was no schedule or timetable because the drivers would wait until their vehicle was crammed to capacity before departing. If they weren't full, they drove tirelessly around town, shouting their destination as they touted for passengers.

As for Mark, he had changed, not just physically but also in spirit. Solo travel had made him far more relaxed and laid-back. He appeared to have lost his awkward boyishness, the quietly confident, self-assured, streetwise person sitting beside me in the *bemo* very different from the shy, nervous, naive, gullible engineer to whom I'd waved goodbye at Sydney airport only a couple of months earlier. Indonesia was the making of Mark and I immediately felt more attracted to him. After the physical demands and mental stresses of Australia – the constant worrying whether I'd make it across a river or to the end of a dirt road – it was very comforting to switch off and not worry about these things. As Mark was retracing the route he had already travelled he knew where to sleep, where to eat, where to go. I loved it. I didn't have to think at all.

That night, as we shared a meal and some celebratory beers in a restaurant in Ubud, I listened intently to everything Mark had to say, feeling very different about him, but I was worried about his health. Alcohol and acidic fruit made Mark very ill. Having not had a gamma globulin vaccination in Sydney, Mark feared he had picked up hepatitis. He'd spent Christmas Day in bed with a fever. Extreme tiredness had lingered for about a week, but it had taken him about a month fully to recover.

'What did it feel like?' I was really worried.

'Muscle pains across my shoulders, up my neck, across my skull at the front.'

'Anything else?'

'Severe pain here.' Mark pointed at the right side of his ribcage, above his liver.

'You've lost a lot of weight.'

'I couldn't hold down food or water.'

I suggested we ask my parents for medical advice. Maybe a change of diet would be a benefit? Perhaps gamma globulin would help?

That evening we went to a chant-dancing event at a village fifteen miles from where Mark and I were staying. To my untrained ear, it sounded like a bloody row, but when seen combined with the dancing, it was beautiful. Unfortunately a bunch of drunken Aussies kept shouting 'it's a barbie' when the dancers lit a fire, which spoilt it for me.

After visiting three temples overrun by huge lizards and encased by the noise of the jungle, we left Ubud for a tour of Bali. Our route took us down to the coast at Kuta, where we rented an entire wooden Batak house for fifty cents. That night, we discovered why it was so cheap. The bed crawled with bed bugs and there were hundreds of mosquitoes. Mark, cold in the night, covered himself with a blanket. By morning, he was in agony, bare skin almost hidden by bites, his ears so badly attacked they were bright red, hot and throbbing with pain.

From the sticky heat of Kuta we took a bus through pouring rain to Bedugul, where the lakeside mountain air was cool and still, then bussed to the west of the island, where we caught a boat to Java.

Crowded, filthy and hostile to women, Muslim Java felt very different from Hindu Bali. Men leered at me, a shock after Bali, which had been very laid-back. I was pleased to be with Mark, particularly on buses, which felt edgy and tense, but they were the only way we could travel to the sights. At Bromo, we rose before dawn and walked up the volcano to see the sunrise. Sitting on the edge of the rim, looking out over the crater, was an unforgettable experience. Volcano smoke rising on one side, the sun rising on the other, it was a lunar landscape that stank of sulphur.

We travelled on to Jogjakarta in a bus driven with reckless abandon by a driver who routinely overtook other vehicles on blind bends or approaching the brows of hills. It was all quite scary, almost on a par with my battle with road trains and dust across Australia, when at least I'd been in control. In Jogjakarta, we stayed three days and made a day-trip to Borobudur, where we visited an intricately carved five-tiered ninth-century temple that was preserved for 900 years under volcanic ash.

Jakarta was another bus ride from Jogjakarta. With filthy slums, a stinking river and unbelievably primitive living conditions, it was a shock. I'd been to other dirty, hot, ramshackle third-world cities, but compared even to Cairo, Jakarta was a cesspit. Six hours spent there were six hours too many, but we needed to get the boat to Padang on Sumatra, from where we took a bus straight to Bukittinggi. It turned out to be a great place to stay, with delicious street food and beautiful temples.

Before leaving, we stocked up on malaria pills for our visit to the island of Nias, where we'd heard an Aussie surfer had been bitten by mosquitoes, developed fever, but kept surfing because the swell was so good. By the time he collapsed and was rushed to hospital in Padang it was too late for treatment.

After riding a bus across the equator, we arrived in Sibolga, a port town on the Sumatran coast, where we had been told we could catch a boat to Nias, a remote island with a reputation for a cannibalistic past, that was worth visiting and rarely reached by tourists. Only cargo boats sailed to Nias and a chain of smaller islands off the west coast of Sumatra. Seeking adventure and wanting to put our intrepid spirits to the test, we tracked down a captain of a boat that took rice to the island and brought back coconuts.

'Why do you want to go to Nias?' said the captain as we slipped away from a decrepit jetty in Sibolga's little harbour.

'Because it's there,' said Mark, 'and it's meant to be beautiful.'

'Beautiful? Maybe. But also strange.'

'Strange?' I said. 'What do you mean?'

The captain explained that there were lots of stories of Portuguese colonists and German explorers reaching the islands and never being seen again because the islanders were head-hunters.

'When was that?' I asked, thinking it would be ancient history.

'A long time ago. In the 1930s.'

'The thirties!' It felt quite recent.

Twelve hours later we jumped off the side of the captain's small cargo boat, waded through the surf and arrived on an island on which some of the inhabitants of its more remote villages had apparently never encountered Westerners.

In some parts of Indonesia, I'd had the feeling that I had stepped back fifty years, but Nias was like going back several centuries. Compared to the mainland, it was a different country in a different era.

Mark and I climbed a hill to one of the villages, all of which were situated on hilltops. Walking through the village, I was speechless at the beauty of the wooden thatched houses. With extraordinarily detailed woodwork on their fronts, they were modelled on Portuguese galleons, but built on stilts and joined to each other in rows and open at ground level, where the animals lived. After being beckoned into one of the houses by a villager, we found ourselves walking through a succession of homes, connected end to end, like a long corridor.

The village had only two rows of houses, which faced each other. Between them was a wide stone-paved central area, like a street where everyone met. On a remote island with a tiny population and, until recently, no traffic, there seemed to be no reason to pave the space, so I asked one of the islanders, who seemed to understand a little English, why stones had been put down. He responded with a shrug.

'What did he say?' said Mark.

'I don't think he knows why it's paved.'

'What about the bigger slabs, over there.'

Turning to the islander, I pointed at a large slab shaped like a throne and some even larger stones covered in washing that was drying in the sun. 'Are those for people to sit on?'

The islander smiled and leant towards me. Pointing at a large flat slab and miming cutting his throat, he said, 'human sacrifice'. The islander gestured towards the throne-shaped stone. 'Chief chair.'

Suspicious that he was kidding me, I smiled awkwardly. If true, it seemed a strange place to dry washing now.

'Do human sacrifices still take place?'

The islander smiled gently and shook his head.

I didn't know whether to believe his denial. I'd been told that cannibalistic societies believed eating outsiders was the only way to get rid of bad spirits brought into their community, but I wondered if in the past it had simply been expedient, a way of dealing with hunger.

That night, Mark and I stayed in a hut beside a beach.

'Check the door's well locked,' I said, not entirely joking.

We whiled away the next few days, swimming, snorkelling, fishing and exploring the incredibly humid island while waiting for a boat back to the mainland. With time running out, we eventually took the first boat available, a tiny vessel loaded to its gunnels with raw rubber and waves splashing onto the deck of our minuscule craft. In relatively calm waters, the top of the gunnel was less than a foot above water. Then it started to rain.

The captain piloted our little boat through squally seas with all the sense of urgency of a leisure cruise on the Norfolk Broads. After eight hours, we called in at a port, but it didn't look anything like Sibolga. Half an hour later, having unloaded some cargo, we set off again, sailing back the way we'd come.

'Oh no,' said Mark. 'We sailed away from Sibolga. It's going to take us twice as long to get back now.'

In all, we spent twenty-four hours on that boat, sleeping above the hold, on a space on the open deck. By the time we got off, all our clothes reeked of raw rubber and diesel, a thoroughly revolting smell that still lingered days later, but it had been a sacrifice worth making to stay on a truly extraordinary island that for a few days felt like the furthest place on the planet from civilization.

After alighting in Sibolga, we continued our slow trek north, along the coast of Sumatra to Lake Toba. Eighty miles in length, the lake was so vast it could accommodate a massive island, on which we hired an old Batak house on stilts and spent four days gazing out over the water.

With Mark deciding the itinerary, we continued on to Jakarta, trekking through a jungle to climb Mount Sibayak, a volcano, and visiting some Karo villages, home to a small clan of the Batak people.

Having originated in the Philippines, the Bataks dispersed around northern Sumatra, forming separate tribes. The Toba Bataks settled around Lake Toba, the Karo Bataks lived around Mount Sinabung and Mount Sibayak and near the city of Medan. I was fascinated by the way the dispersal of these people to different areas had resulted in their architecture evolving in very different ways because of local foods and climatic conditions. Whereas Toba Batak houses were smaller and thinner, usually occupied by one family, the Karo Bataks lived in huge houses, populated by six to eight families who shared three or four fireplaces for cooking and heating. Their entire roof was one massive chimney with all the roof timbers covered in soot. Fascinated by their buildings and culture, I took lots of photographs, again realizing that my trip was bringing architecture to life for me. A few years later I actually returned to north Sumatra to study the different designs of Batak houses for my dissertation.

At Medan we tried to get seats on the next day's plane to Penang, but it was fully booked, so we reserved seats for the next week and took a bus to Bukit Lawang, an orang-utan rehabilitation centre in the jungle of northern Sumatra. It was an extraordinary, inspiring place. Wealthy Indonesians liked to keep baby orang-utans as pets but when they grew to become 'difficult' adults, the apes were thrown out onto the streets. This centre taught abandoned orang-utans how to live in the jungle and find food. We watched and helped with the feeding at meal times, when the orang-utans would come in from the jungle.

Seven weeks after crating up my BMW in Perth, I was reunited with my beloved bike in the Singapore docks. Two days earlier we'd flown into Penang, then bussed it from Penang to Singapore to be reunited with my girl. While bouncing along in the bus, I read through the pile of letters that had been waiting for me in Penang, most of them from my mother, describing in great detail the build-up and drama of my cousin Richard's forthcoming marriage to Caroline, an event which I struggled to take an interest in from a distance of nearly 7,000 miles.

I ripped open Justin's letter next, the letter I really wanted to read, but had kept as a treat.

You have, no doubt, had various reports of Christmas from Mum and possibly Poppy, if she has written. Well here's my report . . . yup, that's about it. Seriously, apart from a few brief moments, it was pretty boring. We had this video camera thing that Dad had bought, which was quite fun, and the usual over-indulgence of food and booze. I also managed to get some work done on my dissertation – shock horror. My bike is going really well at the moment, although it fell over last night in a very strong gale.

I missed Justin more than anyone in my family, particularly as his university studies meant he was committed to England and I wouldn't see him until I got home. Meanwhile my mother, who had tried and failed to get my father to spare enough time to visit me in Australia or Malaysia, had now finally secured his agreement to a trip to India that would culminate in a long-awaited rendezvous with me in Kathmandu. After all that had happened on the road and in various hospitals, I was slightly apprehensive about meeting up with my parents. How could I begin to explain everything I'd experienced and its multitude of effects on me?

Singapore was everything that Indonesia wasn't – spotlessly clean, highly efficient, totally soulless. Buses actually ran and they left within fifteen minutes of their published departure times. Toilets flushed, even if they were still crouch jobs. Showers actually spurted water, even if it was a single cold stream through a spout. After six weeks of washing in water scooped by a hand bucket from a blue plastic drum cut in half, it felt a luxury to stand under something that could semi-legitimately call itself a shower.

Mark and I had a great time, wandering around the shops, eating and snacking, killing time by simply relaxing. The food was tasty, filling and very cheap. The only problem was the accommodation, which was ruinously expensive. After spending two days searching for a cheap hostel, we stumbled on Sim's Place. Located on the tenth floor of a half-built building, it was operated by Sim, a small, balding, sweaty guy with a smile that could soften the toughest hearts. It was a huge room with a concrete floor, windows, some interior walls, some basic plumbing and some hastily fitted fluorescent lights, but nothing more. For $10 a night we were allocated some space on the hard concrete floor with a little foam mattress and access to one shower shared between twenty people. It was a grim place, but relatively clean and cheap. There was no security at all, so I packed all my valuables into my money belt, carrying them everywhere I went.

Singapore appeared to be one big shopping centre. But given that it was always either raining or so humid it might as well be raining, the air-conditioned malls were a blessing. Other than wandering around shops, we found very little to do in Singapore, a strangely sanitized society.

Back at Sim's Place, I started to plan my route ahead, but soon discovered that the rain clouds that had plagued my journey across Australia had also wrought havoc in Malaysia.

'Every sixty years . . .' – Mr Sim punctuated every sentence with his charming smile – '. . . it rains over the Chinese New Year.'

'Yes?' I waited while Mr Sim smiled again.

'And this is the sixtieth year.'

'Yes . . .' I knew not to press Mr Sim into speaking faster.

'All Malaysia is flooded.'

Although Mr Sim was correct, I discovered the floods weren't quite as bad as he claimed. The east coast was shut, floods and landslides blocking many roads and the railway. But the west coast was mostly open. I hoped that by the time I was ready to leave Singapore I'd be able to ride up the west coast to Thailand, which presented its own problems. Every scrap of information I was given about Thailand contradicted the previous advice. Some people said it was impossible to ride a foreign bike into the country. Others said that Thai customs officers were sharp-eyed when collecting duties on bikes and I'd have to pay a small fortune. Yet more claimed that Thai officials weren't interested if the bike was more than three years old. Unable to make sense of what I suspected was mainly conjecture, I decided to take my chances. After all, who would be interested in a ten-year-old BMW with almost 60,000 miles on the clock?

While I continued my ride home, Mark was going to make his own way to Bangkok, then to Burma for a week before flying from Rangoon to Calcutta. If all went to plan, we'd meet in Kathmandu for some trekking before he left for Delhi and a flight home.

Wandering through yet another shopping mall, we stumbled upon a large food court with noodle stalls and a central eating area.

'What about a fruit juice?' said Mark.

Sticky in the heat, I agreed.

'Why don't you just take that off and put it in my bag,' said Mark, referring to my money belt, as we sat down at a nearby table.

Relieved to be freed of the heavy belt around my waist, I wrapped it into a small bundle and put it in Mark's bag while we cast a thirsty gaze across the row of stalls selling fruit juices. 'What do you fancy?' said Mark.

I pointed at one of the stalls. 'Maybe that.'

I bought two drinks and a snack, carried them back to the table.

The drinks were good, the snacks even better. I relished the cool liquid slipping down my throat, almost ignoring the shouting coming from a table across the other side of the room.

Mark rose to his feet. 'I think they're having a fight.'

I craned my neck, peered at two men pushing each other. It seemed little more than a small disagreement, not a proper fight.

Drinks and snacks finished, we prepared to leave. Mark reached under the table for his bag that he'd carefully placed between his feet.

It was gone.

'What?' My pulse was beating faster, harder. 'Are you sure?'

Everything I owned – passport, travellers' cheques, a small amount of cash, BMW key, bike documents and all my shipping papers – was in the bag.

Dropping to hands and knees, we scoured the floor. I jumped back up, stood tall, scanned the room. Nothing stood out. Just a room full of shoppers, eating, drinking, chatting.

'I feel sick,' I said.

Like me, Mark was in a panic. We were thousands of miles from home and all our most valuable possessions were gone.

10

IT'S A DOG'S LIFE:
SINGAPORE TO INDIA

For weeks I'd not let anything of value out of my sight, but Singapore with its glitzy shopping malls and squeaky clean streets, gave me the sense I was in a Western country – not that pickpockets and thieves didn't roam the streets of Europe – but my delusions of security in a familiar environment had made me relax too much.

To make matters worse, it was Valentine's Day. Oh, the irony of it – the second anniversary of my split from Alex, the day that at the time felt like the worst of my life, but which this morning I'd realized I'd finally disassociated from the past. I'd felt liberated, renewed. But now I had a new reason to associate this damned day with another bloody disaster.

'That fight across the food hall must have been a decoy,' said Mark. 'They must have crawled under the table, pulled the bag from between my feet and walked off with it.'

Mark was in shock and felt guilty that he'd encouraged me to put my money belt in his bag.

'It's not your fault.' I touched Mark's arm.

Of course no one was at fault, but that didn't mean we hadn't been very foolish and needed to learn some basic lessons: if we couldn't see it, we had to feel it. I felt so angry: two passports; two money stashes; two sets of documents. What were we thinking?

We scoured the backstreets behind the food hall, checking to see if the thief had discarded Mark's bag, maybe taking only the money and leaving our documents behind. In an alley we found a few scraps of paper that looked familiar, but nothing more than that.

'What are we going to do?'

Mark looked blankly at me. 'Go back to Sim's Place?'

'Maybe we should report it to the police?'

Mark nodded. 'Good idea. And then?'

'What about the British Embassy?'

We found a police station quickly, but were assigned a policeman who could not speak or write English. He passed us a piece of paper, a pen and pointed at us.

'I think he wants us to write our own report,' I said.

'You're not serious?' said Mark.

But I was serious. And it was ridiculous.

I sat down to write. Half an hour later I had described the incident, listed the missing documents and valuables, explained our circumstances. When I'd finished, the police officer looked at my statement, gave me a look that indicated he hadn't a clue what I'd written, then signed it.

The British Embassy was closed, so we returned the next day.

'So what's happened to you?' sighed an official with a resigned look.

As I explained our sorry circumstances, the official's disdainful, disinterested vacant gaze immediately made me wonder why we'd bothered wasting time and the tiny amount of money we still possessed crossing the city to the embassy.

'It happens a lot.' The official's tone gave the impression he resented our intrusion. 'You're not the first British tourists to fall victim to petty thievery. And you won't be the last.'

'We've got no money,' I said.

The official gave us a well-rehearsed look of insincere sympathy. 'You'd better take more care next time.'

Shocked by the lack of assistance at the embassy, we walked to the offices of American Express. Fortunately, my diary, in which I'd noted the numbers of all my travellers' cheques, wasn't in Mark's stolen bag, but at the hostel. I pushed a scribbled list of the numbers and the police report over the desk of an Amex employee.

'No trouble, miss,' said the Amex employee. 'We'll get you replacements by tomorrow – if you can get your passports reissued.'

At last we were getting some help. 'We've got absolutely nothing,' I said. 'Can you lend us some money?'

The employee nodded. 'Fifty dollars each. That's all I can give you, I'm afraid.'

It was much more than we'd expected, particularly as we weren't able to prove our identities. Now we could eat. Back at our digs, Sim was also helpful.

'No need to pay,' he said with his trademark grin, 'until you get some money.'

Of course he knew that we couldn't leave Singapore without passports, but Sim also offered to lend us some money until we were back on our feet.

Setting off in search of somewhere that produced passport photos, we soon discovered that Singapore's shops were geared to satisfying tourists' retail fantasies, but not their essential travel requirements. Several hours later, hidden down an obscure back alley, we at last found a photographer who produced passport photos, but by then the British High Commission had closed. The next afternoon we stood in line with a bunch of other hapless British subjects, pushed our photographs, $50 and several multi-page forms across a counter to an official in a booth, then waited for new passports to be issued. Unexpectedly, the High Commission proved to be very efficient. A few hours later I had a new passport, although it was only valid for a year, leaving me with the daunting prospect of getting it extended in India or Pakistan. But I couldn't worry about that now. With our new passports in hand, the following day our travellers' cheques were replaced at American Express.

Four days after we'd been robbed, I had my money back and new identity documents. It should have been the end of my hassles, but it turned out to be only the start.

For the next month, I traipsed around sticky Singapore, organizing replacements for my stolen keys and documents, including new visas for the countries I hoped to visit on my journey home. I even had to repeat vaccinations I'd already had in order to get a new international health card.

Replacing my bike documents turned out to be the hardest task. The DVLA officials in Swansea acted as if it was the first time they'd been asked to reissue a vehicle's papers lost or stolen overseas. In an age before email and mobile phones, it wasn't made easier by the seven-hour time difference. Eventually my father came to the rescue, writing a series of increasingly exasperated letters on my behalf until the desk jockeys in Swansea sent me a new registration document.

When we weren't battling bureaucracy, we spent most of our time at Sim's Place or in the National Library, the only cool place I found for writing letters. Singapore was expensive for an enforced extended stay. With little money to spare, I passed long days on my mattress in the concrete-floored dorm, dreaming of returning to the road.

By the time I had obtained replacements for all my essential belongings, it was already mid-March and I was behind schedule. My plans for a leisurely two-month tour of Malaysia and Thailand were in tatters, not least because I was now behind budget after paying for new documents, extended accommodation and a new bike key. To recoup some of my costs, I persuaded customs officials at the docks to change the wording describing my bike on my shipping documents so that I didn't need a forklift. Deleting two words – 'in crate' – saved me $50.

That afternoon, I wrote to my mother from a desk in the Singapore National Library, explaining my proposed itinerary. After riding up the west coast of the peninsula via Malacca, Kuala Lumpur, the Cameron Highlands and Penang, I planned to spend three weeks in Thailand, returning to Penang by 18 April to catch a freighter across the Andaman Sea to Madras (now Chennai). If all went to plan, I'd arrive in Kathmandu at the beginning of May. 'These plans are definite,' I wrote to my mother, 'unless something drastic happens – which it WON'T.'

Finding it quite difficult to move on after so long spent stationary in Singapore, it took me a long time to depart. I had been travelling with Mark now for eight weeks and for the first time I was sad we were going our separate ways. We had become close during our travels through Indonesia and our enforced stay in Singapore. My feelings for him had completely changed and I realized for the first time that I was really going to miss him. This took me completely by surprise. I had never imagined I would feel the way I did; falling in love with Mark was so unexpected. I suggested meeting up in Malacca, which was about 150 miles up the west coast, so we could spend a few more days together before Mark went straight to Bangkok and I started my gentle ride up the coast.

I'd almost reached Malacca, when my streak of bad luck reared its ugly head yet again. Having stopped for fuel and food, I was walking back to the bike when I noticed the rear tyre was flat. I had a puncture, surprisingly only the second of my entire trip. On a good day I could change a tyre in less than an hour.

But not this time.

Attempting to lever the tyre off the wheel rim, the lever slipped and I fell awkwardly onto my hand. I found it hard to move my left wrist without it being painful. Fortunately it was my left wrist, so I could finish repairing the tyre, but when I attempted to squeeze the clutch and engage first gear, I yelped with pain. I had sprained my wrist. Riding my bike, I limped on to Malacca and met Mark who was waiting for me.

We found a cheap room. The next morning I waved Mark goodbye on the bus to Bangkok. Still in pain I stayed in the hotel for the next week, waiting for my wrist to recover. At least Malacca was a pleasant town with an old Portuguese port, some old red colonial buildings and nice churches that I explored, but I was soon restless and keen to get back on my bike.

Bit by bit events were steadily chipping away at my plan of riding around Thailand. The end of March was nearing and I needed to be back in Penang by about 14 April to catch the boat to India on 18 April. Even with good roads and short distances compared to Australia, I needed to recalibrate my expectations and my itinerary. If I limited myself to one more week in Malaysia, I could spend two and a half weeks in Thailand.

Good roads meant fast progress, but also recklessly fast drivers. At times I wondered if half of Malaysia's drivers had that morning bought unexpectedly powerful cars after years of driving old bangers. They drove flat out, as if the power and speed of their vehicles was a thrilling novelty. Terrified, I spent most of my time dodging random vehicles hurtling towards me on the wrong side of the carriageway, so I decided to keep off the main roads. The BMW was running reasonably well, although it didn't seem to like the heat too much or the low-octane petrol, which made the bike slow and sluggish.

At the end of my first day back on the road, I arrived in Kuala Lumpur, fortunately one of the few places in Southeast Asia I'd been told I could buy Continental tyres. Even if they weren't completely worn out, I would have considered replacing my tyres here before departing for India, where I'd need to buy the last set of tyres I'd need to get me home. I tried the BMW dealership, but they appeared to be unaware that their company made motorcycles and thought I'd stuck a BMW badge on some random bike.

Eventually I found a shop run by a short, fat, sweaty Chinese man. Talking ten to the dozen about big bikes, he was a motorcycle fanatic, a bit of an oddity in a country in which the only two-wheeled form of transport appeared to be bicycles, scooters and mopeds. Eager to talk biking, he invited me out to lunch with his wife, chatting for ages about the best way to take corners at speed and the merits of tuning engines. And at the end of a long meal, he announced I could have the tyre at below cost price. Back at his shop, he kept to his word, writing out a $90 invoice for a $140 tyre.

'I'll have the tyre tomorrow morning,' he said. 'You come back then.'

I nodded. 'That's very kind. Thanks.'

'I have many contacts in the newspapers. I can get publicity for your trip.' I hadn't really thought about getting any publicity, but it sounded interesting. But I was already behind schedule and reluctant to waste more time. 'Only if it's a national newspaper,' I said.

'Okay . . . okay . . . you come tomorrow morning.'

The tyre was sitting on the counter when I walked into the shop the next morning. And beside it was a woman from the *New Straits Times*. Agreeing to an interview while the shop owner put the new tyre on my bike's rear wheel, I was impressed with her angle of questioning, which focused on the peculiar difficulties faced by a female motorcyclist riding around the world, an enterprise that at that time was reserved entirely for the boys.

From Kuala Lumpur, I rode towards Penang, stopping off in the Cameron Highlands, where I spent a few days exploring and hiking. Much cooler at altitude, the empty roads were a welcome and beautiful respite from the busy coast road. The vegetation was different, ferns predominating instead of rubber plants, and there were fewer people. I was coming to realize I much preferred the countryside to cities.

At Penang I bought a copy of the *New Straits Times* and cringed when I read the article, which claimed I 'used to zoom around London at the neck-breaking speed of 130 to 150kph.' I had never told the journalist I rode at nearly 100 mph.

'Her huge BMW looks intimidating to the non-biking enthusiast, but isn't to her,' it continued. 'With one swing of those long, powerful legs, the lanky blonde adventurer mounts the monster easily.'

This didn't correspond with the angle the journalist had taken during the interview. I checked the byline. The article was written by a man. So much for the journalist's feminist credentials – she had done the donkey-work of interviewing me, then a man got the glory for writing it up. I was disappointed.

Like many border towns, Penang was very busy and a good place to stop, with lots of Chinese people and lots of cheap street food. Having stopped here with Mark on our way down to Singapore, it all felt familiar and I checked into the same hostel we'd stayed in before. I went down to the docks, where I was assured by the shipping company that the freighter to Madras would be leaving punctually on 18 April. Very early the next morning I rode from Penang up to the Thai border. After the many warnings about the difficulties of taking a motorcycle into Thailand, my passage into the country was exceptionally easy. Examining my carnet, the Thai

Me and my first bike, a Yamaha YB100, parked outside my home in central London, in 1979.

Above: My family home from 1968 to 1991 in Upper Wimpole Street, London.

Right: Working on my bike before my departure in 1982.

Below: Me with my dad, 1978.

Above: September 1982, on the day I rode to Dartford in Kent to get my bike crated and shipped to New York.

Below: White Sands National Monument in New Mexico.

Above: Making my aluminium panniers in John Todd's garage in Sefton, Sydney.

Left: My home in Paddington, Sydney; the converted garage where I lived for six months with my bike.

Below: After working every weekend for three months, my bespoke aluminium panniers were finally finished.

Above: The desolate road from Mount Isa to Tennant Creek in the Northern Territory, Australia.

Below: Flooded roads in South Australia; Des's road train stuck in the mud on the road to Coober Pedy.

Above left: Road trains, used all over the Australian outback to transport goods. Travelling at speed and at over 150ft long, they gave way to no one.

Above right: The '90-Mile Straight' on the Eyre Highway in Western Australia, one of the longest straight stretches of road in the world.

Left: Me with Simone, spending Christmas Day together near Bunbury in Western Australia.

Below: Sacrificial stones outside the chief's house on the island of Nias (me in the middle).

Above: Travelling through the Cameron Highlands, Malaysia's most extensive hill station.

Above right: Leaving Singapore and entering Malaysia.

Right: Getting lost in Thailand; road signs in Thai script.

Below: The Golden Triangle; the northern-most point of Thailand.

Above: The Thai family helping me repair my bashed-up panniers after my accident.

Right: My bike being offloaded at the port of Madras, India.

border officials were more familiar with the procedure than the officials in Singapore. It took them a few minutes to go through it all, stamp the relevant sections and hand it back to me with a smile and a wave. Welcome to Thailand.

Two long days of riding brought me to within 100 miles of Bangkok. I might have got closer, but it was impossible to ride after dark. As dusk approached, there was a mad rush by vehicles to get to their destinations or off the road before darkness fell at 7.30 p.m. It was almost like a curfew, strange because the roads were the best yet, reacquainting me with the concept of double lanes and even occasional white lines down the middle of the road. The only problem was the weather. Yet more torrential rain soaked me and turned stretches of roadworks into huge bogs.

Approaching Bangkok the next day, I stopped off at the River Kwai to see the old metal railway bridge built by allied prisoners captured by the Japanese during the Second World War. I found the bridge, and the 7,000 gravestones of soldiers who died building it, interesting and moving. Next stop was Nakhon Pathom to see a huge *chedi*, supposedly the tallest Buddhist stupa in the world, before heading into the city. I'd wanted to avoid Bangkok, but all roads appeared to lead to the capital, so realizing I'd have to pass through, I decided to make the most of it.

Bangkok was just as frenetic and noisy as Jakarta, but much cleaner, more organized and friendlier. Arriving during rush hour on a highway in the midst of extensive roadworks, I found the traffic overwhelming. Four lanes of the highway were squeezed into a single lane – like every major road into the city, it seemed – and I crawled into Bangkok in extreme heat, grumpy and ready to drop.

I found a cheap room in a guesthouse in Banglamphu, the old centre of Bangkok, then set out to explore the historic palaces nearby. Stepping out into the street, I spotted a familiar figure emerging from a guesthouse directly opposite mine. It was Mark. I was so pleased to see him.

Out of all the thousands of guesthouses in Bangkok, we'd ended up staying in two that were directly opposite each other, thanks no doubt to Lonely Planet, which had recently published the first edition of *South East Asia on a Shoestring.*

In Bangkok to get a visa, Mark had time to kill, so we spent two days wandering around together, a lot of it in my pursuit of a map of northern Thailand. Walking fourteen miles in one day, we traipsed from bookshop to bookshop. After hours, trying tourist information centres, travel agents and bookshops, eventually the best I could find was a photocopied scrap of a schematic map of the roads in northern Thailand. Crucially, it included the place names in both English and Thai script – essential if I was to have any chance of finding my way around the rest of country.

The next morning we said our goodbyes and I rode north to Ayutthaya, the old capital of Thailand. This ruined town of temples and *wats* was immense and deserted, not a single other person there. I rode on to Pak Chong, east of Bangkok, stopping only to replace a burnt-out condenser above the alternator that brought my BMW to a temporary stop.

After the repair I headed for Phimai to see one of the most significant Khmer temples in Thailand. Like other tourist destinations outside Bangkok, it was deserted and I realized I hadn't seen a single Western face since leaving the capital. While it was a relief to get away from the well-worn travellers' path prescribed by guidebooks and travel companies, it had its downsides.

On the road, some signs showed directions in both Thai and English but this was only for Bangkok and occasionally Chiang Mai. Most of the time I'd pull up in front of a sign that appeared to me to be a series of hieroglyphics. Matching the squiggles with my map I managed to work out which way I had to go. In time, I learnt to recognize the Thai script for larger cities such as Chiang Mai and Chiang Rai, but until then, it was a laborious process at every roundabout or junction.

On 2 April I reached Sukhothai, the first capital of Thailand, or Siam as it was then, and the first place I stayed for more than one night since Bangkok.

Sukhothai was surrounded by ruins, many of them so far apart that it took me five hours to ride the dust roads around just to see the highlights. I loved any ruins, especially if I got there early and could have the place to myself. Years of being dragged around European ruins and churches by my father had clearly paid off. I was now just as obsessed with not leaving any archaeological stone unturned.

Drinking a cold drink in a café that evening, I got talking to the owner, who asked where was next on my itinerary.

'Chiang Mai,' I said.

'And then?'

'Maybe further north to the golden triangle.'

A serious look of concern flashed across the owner's face. 'You must be careful.'

I reassured him I always rode carefully.

'But there are bandits in the hills,' said the owner. 'Marxist bandits.'

I'd heard rumours, but I'd dismissed them as scaremongering.

'Many roadblocks. Maybe the police stop you.'

I'd already passed through two roadblocks, but they had taken no interest in me.

'I'll be okay,' I said.

The owner held up one finger. 'When you get to Chiang Mai, there will be many more.'

Instead of worrying me, roadblocks reassured me that the authorities had things under control. I thanked the owner for his advice and left to return to my hotel. As I walked along a side road to my hotel, a group of Thai teenagers called out to me in the universal greeting I'd come to recognize from almost any young people in Southeast Asia.

'Hello, what's your name?'

'Elspeth.'

'Where you from?' It was always the second question.

'England.'

'England! Look!' They thrust their English homework books in front of me. 'Help us.'

I struggled to explain to them that I was dyslexic and found their English homework really quite difficult, but they didn't care.

'Look . . . look . . . English. You help.'

Crouching by the side of a dusty side street, the Thai kids huddled around me while I helped as much as I could, although I worried I'd spelt a lot of it wrong. After an hour and a half helping them with their English, they bought me a can of Coke, convinced it was a worthwhile investment.

Riding on towards Chiang Mai the next day, the roads were great, although I wondered why the government had spent a lot of money building a dual-carriageway when it still let dogs, sheep, chickens and cows roam freely over it and drivers could routinely perform U-turns over the central reservation. The closer I got to Chiang Mai, the more remote it felt, and the greater the number of roadblocks, which for me had the fortunate side effect of scaring away Western tourist hordes. Northern Thailand was a place of fantastic roads, lovely people and police everywhere. All in all, it was great.

Chiang Mai turned out to be a tourist trap with tour operators vying to entice the few tourists onto treks to visit remote hill tribes for a few days. Fed up with the hassle, I decided to do it my way by riding a bike into the hills and up to the Burmese border. I loved it; cooler, less sweaty than Bangkok and southern Thailand, the north of the country was much more relaxed. After two days in Chiang Rai and two days in Lampang, I began the long ride south towards Penang, where I had an appointment with a ship to India.

I was riding south, feeling good, relaxed and at ease, needing only to reach Penang to catch the boat to Madras, confident that I'd make it in time. Glancing down, I checked my bike's dials. The alternator light was on. Oh shit.

I had to stop. If I continued riding, my battery would die before the end of the day. At the edge of a small town, I pulled over to the side of the road, got out my Haynes manual, sat in the shade of a tree, had a think about it and tried to work out what could possibly be wrong.

Footsteps. A middle-aged Thai man approached, a smile on his face. He spread his hands, raised his eyebrows, the universal sign language for 'What's up?'

I smiled back, pointed at the alternator.

Confusion flashed across his face.

I turned on the ignition and pointed at the red alternator light, which was on. I started my bike, opened the throttle, pointed at the red light, which was still on. It should have gone out, so I waved my hands, palms pointed downwards, hoping he'd understand what I was trying to convey: 'That shouldn't happen.' We hadn't spoken a word, but the Thai man seemed to understand and turned to walk away, beckoning me with his finger. With nothing to lose, I climbed on my bike, rode it slowly behind him, around a corner and down a street for about 300 metres to a garage that was open to the street.

He pointed at my bike, then at the garage, so I rode inside and watched as he explained my problem in Thai to two overalled men in the workshop. Head scratches, pointed fingers, shrugged shoulders all followed. Eventually, working together, we figured out that one of the diodes no longer functioned correctly.

If I'd been at home, I would have replaced the whole diode board, but in a tiny Thai town there were no BMW spare parts. Instead we unsoldered the faulty one, soldered a new diode in place and reconnected the board above my alternator.

I twisted the BMW's key, started her up. The red light went out. He'd repaired the fault and saved my skin. And still not a single word exchanged between us. His cobbled-together diode board is still working on my BMW today.

I tried to push some Thai banknotes into his hand, but he shook his head, almost turning his back on me to make it clear he wouldn't accept my money, so I left his workshop, bought six cans of beer and put them on his workshop bench with a decisive gesture to indicate I wouldn't accept refusal from him.

Riding away, I patted the old girl's tank. Apart from the clothes on my back, she was all I had in the world and, yet again, she'd not let me down. We were like a dog and its owner, although I wasn't quite sure which of us was the master. But I was also becoming aware of the toll of the rough roads and many miles on my companion. She was starting to tire and I hoped she'd not expire before I reached home.

For the first time on my trip, I was in a hurry. Having spent a leisurely couple of weeks stopping off at every ruined temple and sight I wanted to visit on the way up to the Burmese border in the far north of Thailand, I was now on a deadline to get to Penang with enough time spare to make all the arrangements for my passage to India. Adherence to tight itineraries was a Western way of thinking that I'd already discovered didn't work in Southeast Asia, where it was foolish to rely on ever being anywhere at any particular time. Fortunately, the smooth roads of Thailand were among some of the best I'd encountered so far. It was the wildlife wandering randomly across them that was the problem. But with the good roads and my time limited, I increased my speed, riding faster as I became more carefree.

That's when I hit the dog.

It ran out from behind a truck travelling in the opposite direction and was under my front wheel before I even had a chance to brake. Within seconds I was sliding up the road watching my bike as it disappeared out of sight into a ditch. It all happened so suddenly and unexpectedly, there was nothing I could do.

When everything had stopped moving I staggered to my feet. I looked around but the dog was gone. I limped over to my BMW, which had hit a tree and now had its front wheel and exhaust wedged against its trunk. My metal pannier boxes had been ripped off the back of my bike and the mirrors, indicators and other parts were scattered all over the road. As I tried to pull my bike free I noticed my bloody handprints all over the front wheel. I stopped and assessed my injuries. I was battered and bruised all over, a total mess. But I didn't care. All that mattered to me, all I could think about, was getting my bike back on the road and reaching Penang in time to catch my boat to India.

While I'd been contemplating my predicament, five men had appeared from a small farm on the side of the road. I got them to help me pull the bike off the tree, out of the ditch and up onto the side of the road.

She was a sorry sight.

We'd taken a hammering, my bike and I, although it was not as bad as previous injuries. This time at least we were both still standing, each of us vaguely in one piece. But that cargo ship wasn't going to wait for us, so I immediately set about getting us back on the road. First the BMW. Then me.

Eyes on the ground, limping as I kicked through the long grass along the road's edge, I searched the surrounding area for my bike's missing parts. Beside me, the farmers tapped my shoulder, attempted to make me sit in the shade and rest. After a few minutes they gave up and joined me. Within ten minutes we'd located everything and I was sitting, as they'd instructed, on a wooden platform in the shade of a large tree at the side of the road, surrounded by a large crowd of Thais.

They came in every combination of age, generation and height. Women with babies clamped to their hips, men with stubby cigarettes between their lips. I guessed they were all one big family, staring at me while I clenched my teeth as the mother of the farm dabbed at my wounds with alcohol and poured Mercurochrome, a bright pink antiseptic they called *curo*, all over my hands, legs and knees. When she was finished I removed a pair of flimsy shoes I'd bought in Australia. Wishing I'd worn my protective motorcycle boots, I looked at my swollen toes. At least two of them appeared to be broken.

Examining my injuries made them really hurt and my head spin. I felt faint and queasy, not least because of the thought of the mammoth task required to sort out the bike and get back on the road. I sat under the tree, thinking it all through. Having not seen my parents for nearly two years, I dearly wanted to meet them in Kathmandu. But it was going to be a close-run thing. The Penang boat was the last to Madras for at least three weeks. If I made it and it docked on schedule in Madras, I'd have two weeks to ride north through India to Calcutta, and on to Nepal, a distance of about 1,500 miles to Kathmandu. And I had no idea what horrors the Indian roads might offer.

After about an hour, I decided I'd had enough of the Thai family's insistence to keep still. If I did nothing, I'd achieve nothing. I needed to check the damage on my bike. Walking around her, examining her more closely, I found her looks had taken a severe battering. Her silencers were dented, her headlight smashed. There was a large dent in her tank and scratches all over. But these were just cosmetic injuries. The physical state of her exhaust pipes and cylinders concerned me more. Having taken the brunt of the collision with the tree, one of the exhaust pipes now emerged from its cylinder at an acute angle which would allow the exhaust gases to escape. Her other cylinder had a crash bar pushed hard against it and looked as if it might be bent.

The keys were still in her ignition, so I twisted them. She fired up immediately, and didn't sound too bad. Not for the first time, I thanked solid German engineering. Behind me, the family cheered, clapped, talked excitedly. I could guess that they were saying something like 'What's the problem? Everything's fine,' but I frowned and pointed at the base of one cylinder. Oil was pouring out. I suspected a broken gasket.

A young man, who I guessed was one of the sons of the woman who'd dressed my wounds, shrugged, handed me a dirty rag, then smiled. He seemed to be suggesting that this was all that was required to deal with the problem.

I shook my head. It wouldn't do. Not all the way to Penang, it wouldn't.

A pick-up truck drew up and the eldest son jumped down, bare-chested, his hand held out with a smile. He pointed with his thumb at the truck.

'Doctor.' The first word of English I'd heard in several days.

For a moment I considered refusing his offer, then I gave in. It made sense. He helped me into the truck and sat beside me, explaining that he'd learnt English at school. He had more English than I had Thai, but not enough to keep up a conversation all the way to the small clinic he drove me to, where a nurse looked at my cuts, wrote *tetanus* on a card, raised her eyebrows.

I nodded.

The nurse smiled, beckoned me into a treatment room, bandaged my hands and injured foot, sent me off with a concerned look in her eyes and a wave. On the way back to the farm, passing through a village, I spied a shack with a row of scooters and motorbikes outside it. I pointed at it and yelled 'stop!'

The workshop had everything I needed, including a vice to straighten my bike's bent exhaust pipes. I explained in sign language what I needed to do and returned with my bike a short while later, chugging and trailing oil.

I started work with the owner of the shop helping me, but he soon realized that I knew more about my bike than he did and left me to it, only helping me when I couldn't hold a particular tool in my bandaged hands. Struggling at times to grasp even a spanner, I stripped down the cylinder, taking two hours to do what I would normally do in one.

As I worked, an entirely male audience built up around me. I guessed they'd seen very few tourists and probably none that were female motorcyclists. Standing in a semi-circle around me, they pointed, exchanged comments, clearly not knowing what to make of me or my bike. I ignored them, concentrated on nursing my bike to health until the mood suddenly changed.

A Thai woman had arrived.

Slowly, other women joined the crowd and started talking. As the women's voices started to match, then drown out the men, I wondered what was going on. Then, as I was loosening a bolt, I felt a slap on my back. I turned around slowly and was greeted by the sight of a young Thai woman with a raised thumb and a broad smile.

Unable to share a single word, I knew exactly what she wanted me to understand. Our lives and circumstances were very different, but from the glint in her eyes I knew exactly what she wanted to convey.

'You and me, we're the same,' she was saying.

Something flashed between us and I realized we were united in our common cause. I knew that she wanted to prove to the men standing idly around, watching and talking about a woman doing something that was traditionally associated more with them than with women, that we were just as capable as any man, if only given the chance.

Smiling and nodding conspiratorially with the Thai woman, I turned back to my cylinder. It appeared undamaged, but as I'd suspected, the base gasket was damaged. I found a spare in one of my bashed-in metal panniers, fitted it, then bent the exhaust back into shape as far as I dared without risking a crack in it. I fitted the exhaust to the cylinder, filling the gaps around it with asbestos fibre to seal any gaps.

By now, I'd been working on my bike for more than two hours. It was even longer since the dog had knocked me off it. The sun was blisteringly hot and just as I was starting to lose strength an old man on a Honda scooter pulled up beside me in the other bay of the workshop. He mimed drinking from a can and eating a bowl of noodles, then pointed at the pillion on his scooter. I climbed on and rode for a few hundred metres to the village centre, where we stopped beside a food stall. He showed me to a plastic chair as a bottle of cold Coke was pressed into my hand. Small kids surrounded me, poking my skin as if I was oblivious to it. A woman passed me a plate of food and a spoon. The kids pressed closer, their eyes following every spoonful of food from the plate to my mouth, fascinated, I guessed, to see how Westerners ate. Giggling as they stared, they obviously found me very amusing.

When I'd finished, I patted my trousers for my wallet, but the man and woman immediately tensed. I mimed paying them, but they shook their heads. I was their guest, they explained in gestures. Any attempt to pay them would be refused.

Grateful and touched by their generosity when they clearly had so little, I rode pillion on the little Honda back to my big BMW, humbled by the awareness that it was worth many times what any of my hosts would earn in a year. It took me another hour to finish my engine repairs, by which time most of the men had wandered off, although the women were still watching closely.

With a smile and what I hoped my audience of ladies would take as an ironic flourish, I started the engine. It roared into life. No oil leak. No escaping exhaust smoke. I was back on track. Now I just had to hope my injuries would repair as easily.

I thanked the shop owner, offered him some money, but he simply shook my hand and his head. He wouldn't let me pay for anything.

I rode back to the farm where the family had kindly offered to look after my bashed up metal boxes while I'd been at the bike shop. I started to rebuild my metal pannier boxes, but my hand injuries made drilling and riveting very difficult. The three sons had never seen a pop rivet gun before and were very happy to help. I pointed where I needed them to drill and rivet. They did the rest, all of them cheering every time they popped one. By the hundredth rivet, the novelty had worn off for me, but not for the three brothers, who continued repairing my boxes. By dusk, we had fixed them back onto my bike and I was ready to leave.

Bats were swooping in the failing light as, gesturing towards the farmhouse, the three brothers insisted I should stay with their family until I had fully recovered. In no mental or physical condition to ride, I gratefully accepted and was shown into a small room next to the kitchen. It had a wooden floor and no furniture except for a twenty-four-inch television, huge by the standards of the day. Sitting on the floor, next to the sons, watching television for the first time since I'd left Sydney six months earlier was utter bliss. Unable to understand a single word, I enjoyed every minute of it, my mind zoning out, my body relaxing properly for the first time in ages. I was starting to drift off when the mother of the house beckoned us to dinner and we shuffled out of the room to eat rice, vegetables and meat, sitting outside on benches around a long table under a corrugated iron roof.

After dinner, we went back to watching television until the programmes ended, when the mother brought in a pile of blankets. Taking one each, we lay down beside each other: father, mother, grandmother, the sons and me and went to sleep. Or in my case, tried to go to sleep.

Bruised all over, aching in every muscle and limb, I found it impossible to get comfortable on the hard floor, tossing and turning through the night. It was hot and sticky, but if I removed the blanket, the mosquitoes descended and I got bitten all over. Eventually, delirious with exhaustion, I drifted off into a fitful sleep.

And so it continued for two days and three nights, a simple routine of lazing around, sleeping and watching television, eating rice, meat and vegetables, while my body healed itself. At times I wondered if it might be marginally less painful to ride my bike to somewhere with a comfortable bed but I enjoyed being part of a family again. Watching them go about their daily routine not only gave me an insight into the life of a typical Thai family, but also made me realize how much I missed being in the bosom of my own clan.

On 17 April, the day before the Madras boat was due to sail from Penang, I felt ready to leave. I packed up my things, then went to say goodbye to all the family. I found the mother in the kitchen and wandered over to thank her for her extraordinary hospitality. Clutching her small bottle of *curo*, she extended a creased hand and offered me the antiseptic. I was very touched and leant towards her, intending to hug her, but my eyes were drawn to something extraordinary behind the woman, on the table.

The dog I'd run over.

Most of the animal was missing, but it was unmistakable. The knife marks were straight and clean, the work of a skilled butcher. Well, that explained the generous portions of meat with every meal.

For a few moments, not knowing what to say or do, I hesitated. Then I accepted the offer of the *curo*, clasping my hands together in front of my chest and bowing my head with a smile to show my thanks. Once I'd got over the thought of what I'd been eating for the last week, I realized I felt comforted to know what had happened to the dog. I had killed it and provided food for the family. No wonder they were so welcoming to me.

I was determined to make up for lost time, and although I had abandoned any hope of catching the cargo boat to Madras as planned, I hoped I could find another way. I was spurred on by a deep desire to get to Kathmandu by any means so that I could be reunited for a short time with my parents. Eighteen months had passed since they waved off a rather reluctant traveller from Heathrow. It was a long time and I really needed to see them.

Getting back on my bike was not easy. The wrist I'd sprained in Malaysia had still not fully healed, but in addition to that injury

I now had my cut hands and arms, which made squeezing the clutch lever even more painful and twisting the throttle sheer agony. That night, after riding 250 miles to Chumphon, I spent two hours looking for a chemist shop to buy painkillers and more bandages to re-dress the wounds on my hands and my foot. The next day I made it to Hat Yai, about twenty miles from the Malaysian border, and about 100 miles to Penang. Knowing it would take about four to five hours to get across the border, I set off early the following morning, reaching the border before 10 a.m. Already it was busy, the crowds of people moving slowly through the checks. For hours I waited in queues to get various papers and my carnet signed and stamped. Shortly after 2 p.m., I was away, and I arrived in Penang shortly before dusk.

Penang almost felt like home. Visiting the city for the third time in less than two months, I quickly settled back into the same hostel, recognizing some of the locals in the surrounding streets and pleased to see a few Western faces again. That evening, I listened to some other travellers chatting around a table in the hostel. Desperate to talk to anyone about anything, I found myself tongue-tied after such a long period spent entirely on my own or with non-English speakers.

'What happened there?' One of the travellers pointed at my bandaged hands and the wounds on my arm.

'I hit a dog . . .' I noticed the shock on their faces. They thought I was some kind of animal-hating brute. 'I mean, this dog ran out into the road in front of me and I collided with it.'

'Wow.'

I described what had happened and my subsequent recovery among the Thai farmers. When I finished, the table was silent, nervous glances flitting between the travellers.

No one said anything.

I shrugged. 'It was nothing,' I said. 'It just happened.'

By relating my tales of the road, I had unintentionally trumped all of their stories. Any chance of making friends with this small band of fellow travellers was now ruined. Travelling solo and by bike seemed to set me apart from every other traveller I'd met, and I didn't enjoy feeling like an outsider.

First thing the next morning, I visited the shipping company's office at the docks, where I was told my ship's departure had been delayed by five days. I couldn't believe my luck, maybe now I would be able to reach Kathmandu in time to see my parents after all.

One of the officials handed me a sheaf of paper and pointed at a pen. I leafed through them. They were identical. Six facsimiles of the same three-paged forms.

'Eighteen pages?' I asked one of the officials. 'Do you really need all of these?'

He smiled. 'Eighteen. Yes. Need.'

'But why eighteen?'

'Yes. Need.'

Realizing I was not going to get a coherent answer, I began to work my way through the most tedious paperwork I had ever encountered. A couple of hours later, I presented the eighteen identical pages, fully filled out, to the official.

'Good.' The official glanced at my forms. 'Need stamp.'

'Stamp?'

He pointed out of the office and crooked his finger to indicate that I needed to go down the corridor.

Following the official's directions, I found myself in a large room with rows of desks, overloaded with piles of paper, behind which men toiled, like a scene from Dickens.

'I need these stamped,' I announced to the room. No one looked up, so I went over to one of the desks. 'Excuse me, I need these stamped.'

The official behind the desk glanced at my sheaf of forms. 'Yes.'

'Can you stamp them?' Hoping for a positive answer, I beamed a smile.

'Yes.'

Greatly relieved, I presented my forms to the official.

'Sign first.'

There was an empty space at the bottom of the form. I pointed at it. 'Here?'

'No!' The official looked exasperated. He pointed out of a window. 'There.'

For the rest of the day and all of the following day, I traipsed from office to office, seeking the correct combination of signatures and stamps. It was farcical. One official could not stamp or sign one of the forms until another official had stamped one of the others. At one point, I was sent from Penang Island to the mainland five times, the officials being unable to agree who should sign one of my forms next. Stuck in the middle of their dispute, I was losing my patience and could envisage the ship to Madras leaving before I'd even completed the formalities. By the end of the second day, I started yelling at them.

'This is bloody ridiculous! I've had enough.'

My outburst was met by a wall of blank expressions.

'I'm not going back to the main customs building until you phone them up . . .' – I pointed at the phone on the desk of one of the officials – '. . . and sort yourselves out.'

Most of the officials looked away, but one of them caught my eye. 'Phones not working,' he said very calmly.

I couldn't believe it. If this continued, I would be stuck in Penang for ever. I walked over to a small man who was concentrating on a piece of paper in his hand.

'What can I do?' I asked.

He smiled, asked for my documents, read them. 'I can do nothing.' He pulled a long face. 'It will take a week.'

'A week?'

'Yes, for all the forms.'

I felt like screaming. Then I remembered the article in the *New Straits Times*. I whipped it out, showed it to the official.

'Come this way, please,' he said, leading me out of the door and into the office of the chief manager. I made my case, explaining that I needed to catch a boat to Madras in the next few days. I showed him the newspaper clipping.

'Round the world?' The chief manager looked impressed. He called over one of his underlings and all of a sudden they were scrambling around like ants, racing around various departments. It was ridiculous. In an hour and a half I got all the paperwork filled out, signed and stamped, a task they had previously warned me would take at least a week. Now I could prepare myself for India.

The evening before the ship sailed, I rode my bike down to the docks and sat for hours on the dockside, watching stevedores load everything else onto the ship. My bike, I had been told, would be the last cargo to be loaded.

Finally, at midnight I was summoned to the quayside. Two stevedores unrolled a net, wheeled my bike onto it.

'Careful,' I said.

John Todd in Australia had told me that when his bike was hoisted, the net caught the side of his panniers and broke the brackets, something I wanted to avoid. I made sure my bike was enveloped in the net, slowly, with care and attention, then ran towards the gangplank to the ship to supervise my bike's arrival on deck.

A guard stepped out in front of me, started to raise his hand to stop me, but I pushed him aside and walked quickly up onto the deck. Nothing was going to stop me; I was determined to see my bike safely onto the boat. By the time the port authorities arrived on deck and insisted that I remove myself from the ship instantly, I had managed to secure my BMW to the gunnel, ready to sail.

According to the Shipping Corporation of India, which operated the M.V. *Chidambaram*, a rusting passenger liner that had seen much better days, my passage to India was supposed to leave early the next morning. At the appointed hour, everyone was aboard, but maybe we shouldn't have been surprised that it took until mid-afternoon before we were ready to sail.

The timetable, I realized, was largely irrelevant. The only mystery was why they bothered to issue one at all. The *Chidambaram* sailed slowly between Singapore, Penang and Madras according to a schedule that was entirely at the captain's fancy.

Sailing out of Penang, I gazed back at the Malaysian coastline and felt a weight lift from my shoulders. Southeast Asia had been very enjoyable, but I was pleased to be putting it behind me. With a sense of triumph that I'd survived the penultimate leg of my journey, I knew that once I arrived in India, it would be overland all the way home.

PART 3

MADRAS TO KATHMANDU

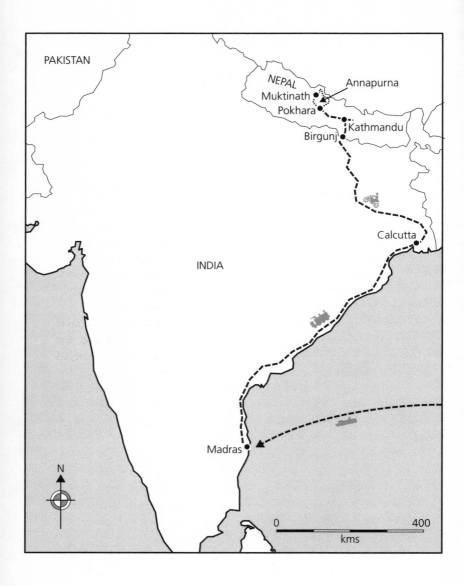

11

WELCOME TO INDIA!:
MADRAS TO CALCUTTA

Madras, 25 April 1984

We arrived in Madras at dawn, our first glimpse of India emerging through the mist: a flotilla of tiny multi-coloured fishing boats floating out to meet the big liner easing into port. It was exactly how I'd always imagined India would be: crumbling, colourful, chaotic and charming, enveloped in a mystic haze that was probably more smog than fog.

For four days I had been travelling second class, the lowest class that Westerners were permitted to use, on an ugly, stinking rust bucket of a liner, overrun with rats and cockroaches, reeking of grease and filth. Everything I touched felt sticky.

I had imagined a nice peaceful boat trip, sitting in a recliner, watching the ocean slip past the deck rails while I waited for the next meal to be served. This vision of civilized gentility, I soon realized, was not to be fulfilled.

Advised to travel first class, I'd opted for second, which put me in a filthy cabin that I was expected to share with three Indian men. Cockroaches crawled all over the floor and walls. One toilet, which didn't work and which emitted a stench that pervaded the entire deck, was shared with a neighbouring cabin. Risking a glance behind the toilet door, I gagged at the sight of the toilet full to the brim with human excrement that had spilled onto the floor. And this was before we'd even set sail. It was impossible to find a clean foothold, let alone breathe in the toilet. There was no way I was sleeping here for five nights. I went to find the person in charge and, in a corridor, I bumped into a young German couple, absolutely livid because they'd thought the voyage would be akin to a romantic cruise.

The man was tall, with an angular face and brown hair. 'This is disgusting,' he said. 'They can't expect us to sleep here.'

I shook my head. His partner looked close to tears and said, 'We had the choice to fly for the same price, but chose to go by ship because we thought it would be nice, more fun.'

The Germans upgraded to first class, which was beyond my budget, so I persuaded the Indian steward to give me a second-class cabin to myself. While moving my bags, I passed an Australian girl with frizzy hair and a humourless expression on her face.

'You aren't staying here?' she said.

I explained I was remaining in second class, but in a cabin on my own.

'If you don't travel with the locals, you're not really experiencing the country.' She gave me a withering look. 'You have to immerse yourself in the culture, you have to really feel the country to understand it.'

I left her to it and headed off to my own cabin. Needless to say, after one night sharing with the natives, the Australian idealist came knocking on my door, sheepishly asking if she could share my cabin. I didn't have the heart to turn her down or to tell her that I'd done my fair share of living with locals, but I really didn't care what she thought; India was going to be difficult enough anyway without making it harder.

I spent as much time as possible in first class, trying to persuade the kitchen staff to give me some decent food whenever the friendly German couple I'd met managed to sneak me into their dining room. With white tablecloths, china plates, silver cutlery and three courses served for every meal, it was a world apart from second-class dining, where the dining room had rows of Formica tables with bench seats and the food's only virtue was its consistency: rice and dhal for three meals a day, served with all the grace of a prison kitchen.

When I couldn't slip into first class, I spent most of my time asleep, avoiding the Australian girl, or on deck, where I spent a few hours each day trying to read while the diesel engine thrummed deep beneath decks and the stench of the toilets wafted on the breeze. Surrounded by dirt and rust, I picked my way through a stack of letters I'd collected in Penang. My father's letter was typically obsessive: a minute-by-minute itinerary of his and my mother's visit to India before our rendezvous in Nepal and intricate details of how much he'd saved by bulk-buying nearly a thousand blank videotapes. Mark wrote an uncharacteristically light-hearted letter full of breezy news and amusing anecdotes from his travels. John Todd offered commiserations for the theft of my belongings in Singapore and asked how I was intending to pass through '*the tricky spots*' of war-torn Afghanistan and Iran.

Reading John's letter, I realized I didn't have a plan, not because I'd been remiss, but because the journey had taught me that making plans was pointless. The only way to survive was to take one mile at a time.

On the last day of the voyage, I got talking to an Indian man in his sixties.

'You are travelling on your own?' He pointed at my bike keys hanging from a belt hook on my shorts. 'In a car?'

'I'm on a bike,' I said. 'A BMW.'

'A BMW? Do they make bikes?'

I showed him my bike, tied up on deck. When he'd recovered from the shock that I owned a motorcycle larger than any he'd ever encountered, my new Indian friend invited me to stay with him and his family in Madras. Knowing that accommodation in Madras would be expensive and difficult to find immediately after the ship's arrival, I accepted his kind offer.

When the ship docked the next day, I tagged along with first class, entering the customs hall ahead of most other passengers to find a row of smartly dressed customs officials seated behind wooden desks in a massive warehouse, eagerly awaiting our arrival. Presenting myself at one of the desks, I explained I had a motorbike and was told I'd have to wait for the official in charge of the carnets to arrive. Apparently he was the only one who could stamp it.

I settled down for a long wait, watched the other passengers arrive. Within a few minutes, I was open-mouthed. The *Chidambaram* was full of bootleggers.

At that time, India forbade the importation of foreign goods, which of course put them in great demand. I watched as a succession of Indian men and women presented themselves to the customs officials, laden down with watches, televisions and many other consumer goods, including even washing machines. Bought when the *Chidambaram* docked in Singapore before its arrival in Penang, these goods were imported simply by bribing the customs officials. It was so blatant, I ended up laughing. The passengers all appeared to have a pre-arranged deal with a particular customs official. A staggering amount of money, watches and calculators passed under the tables as the officials pocketed what must have been the equivalent of several months' salary in a single day.

From what I could see, there wasn't an honest official in the hall. I began to fear I would have to bribe someone to get my bike into India. For Indian officials it was obviously a way of life, but I was determined it wasn't going to be part of mine.

Shortly after midday, the carnet official arrived.

'Yes?' He seemed annoyed at my presence; he had some work to do now. I explained my situation. 'Get your motorcycle off the ship.' He waved dismissively. 'Wait for me on the quayside.'

I returned to the ship. On deck, the stevedores were unloading some cargo. I approached a gang of five deckhands. 'Can you help me with this?' I pointed at my bike. 'We need a net.'

They nodded, then started to tie a single rope to the frame under the seat.

'No, stop! That's not going to work.' I drew a picture of a net; one of the deckhands indicated with a smile and a nod that he understood. A few minutes later, he returned with a net less than one metre square in size. Absolutely useless. I decided to look for one myself. I found my way down to the cargo hold, rummaged around in some cases and finally found a net big enough for my bike.

Back upstairs, on the top deck, I laid the net out, wheeled my BMW onto it, waved and shouted to the crane driver. I hooked up the four corners, got him to lift the net slowly. The moment the bike lifted off the ship's deck, one of the deckhands appeared at my side, his hand extended.

'*Baksheesh . . . baksheesh . . .*'

'You must be joking.' I absolutely refused, trying to explain that I had done all the work.

'*Baksheesh!*' Now they all had their hands out and they were angry, shouting at me.

I walked away. All the deckhands followed me, the calls for *baksheesh* escalating in volume and frequency until they realized I was no fool and left me in peace.

In the customs hall, the carnet official had disappeared and no one could tell me where to find him, so I went outside, sat by my bike and waited. About an hour later, he ambled back into view. I pointed at my bike and showed him my papers.

The official pursed his lips, sighed. 'Okay.'

I almost couldn't believe it. The paperwork was relatively little. I paid some port duties, which went straight into his pocket. He checked the bike over, wrote some notes in my passport, stamped my carnet. I was free to go.

I rode out of the port feeling very apprehensive, as I often did when first setting off in a new country. That sense of being unsure, feeling my way, discovering how much things should cost, always unnerved me.

Riding through the dusty industrial streets of Madras, rickshaws buzzing around me, I was pleasantly surprised by the roads and the traffic. Not quite the completely chaotic mayhem I'd anticipated; the roads were all sealed and in reasonable condition. Before long, I'd found the address given to me by the old man on the ship and was being made very welcome by his son and his family, who owned the house there. Very well off even by Western standards, they had several colour televisions, every conceivable electrical appliance and a couple of servants, one of whom showed me to my room, then left me to shower.

Over a delicious dinner of vegetables, curry and rice, I got an insight into the family dynamics. Speaking little English, their conversation with me was limited, making me wonder why the old man had invited me at all, but I could tell that the son was very much the master of the house, his wife only speaking when directly addressed.

After dinner, they invited me to watch television, a Bollywood film that was not my thing. Making my excuses, I explained I'd had a long day and headed for bed. On my way up to my room, I met the father.

'Come here.' He beckoned me towards him, like he had something important to tell me.

'I'm afraid I don't understand,' I said.

The old man spoke so quietly and with such a strong accent I had to listen intently to decipher what he was saying. As I leant in closer, he grabbed me, pushed me up against the wall, breathed heavily down my neck.

'Get off me!' I pushed the old man away. Taller and stronger than him, I wasn't scared.

The old man looked at me, muttered something under his breath – I guessed it was something about me being a 'loose' Western woman – and walked off. With the rest of the family downstairs, I didn't feel in any danger and continued up to my room, where I sat down on my bed and thought it through.

It was very strange. On the ship, the old man had been a perfect gentleman – respectable, polite, educated, decent. But in the sanctity of his family's home, he was a pest. I felt angry more than afraid.

I stood up, started to undress. There was a knock at the door. Hoping it wasn't the old man pestering me again, I opened the door cautiously in a long T-shirt, ready to slam it shut.

It was the old man's son, a towel in his hand. Impressed by his concern for my comfort, I opened the door. Before I could step back, the son pushed his way into room, his hands running all over my body.

'Get off!' I yelled and within seconds he was gone.

I caught sight of myself in a mirror. I looked tired, and with my short hair and baggy T-shirt, I hardly looked as if I was inviting attention.

I locked the door and climbed into bed. Strangely, I didn't feel at all threatened. The father and son's fumbled attempts to feel me up were very brazen, but also extremely naive, and as soon as I'd started to fight back I'd seen the fear in both their eyes. It seemed to be more about clumsily taking advantage of what was to them a very unusual opportunity.

I was short of time: four days to ride more than 1,600 miles to Kathmandu in order to arrive before my parents was a tall order, but I was determined not to be late. At breakfast, I asked the family how long they thought it would take me to ride to Nepal. 'At least four days to Calcutta,' said the son, 'then at least the same again to Kathmandu, maybe more. Or if you take the train, one day and one night to Calcutta.'

I'd heard all about Indian trains and their infamous unreliability. Some trains arrived days or even weeks late. But I was also apprehensive about riding in India. I had heard so many awful stories about the crazy drivers and the very crowded roads. It was also unbelievably hot, about 45°C during the day, not much cooler at night. I really didn't fancy riding, but I was trying to make excuses for avoiding it because I felt that putting my bike on a train was a cop-out. In Australia I'd had no choice, but this time I was simply daunted by India, a place I'd always wanted to see, but also a place about which I'd heard some of the worst stories. In the end, I told myself that because my parents were coming, it was better to arrive safely and punctually in Kathmandu than not to arrive at all.

I was taken to the station in the family's chauffeur-driven Hindustan Ambassador, a charming copy of a 1955 Morris Oxford, accompanied by their male secretary. The station was full of people, hundreds of them in every direction, pushing their way through to wherever they were destined. And all but a very few of them were male.

The secretary and I fought our way through the marauding mass of men until we were in sight of the ticket booths, when the secretary started shouting, pushing me to the front of the queue.

'Women,' he shouted, 'especially if white, have priority.'

I smiled with gritted teeth. Already the focus of attention, being given priority was just what I didn't need.

Hundreds of pairs of dark brown eyes, showing little emotion, were following me everywhere I went. I could cope with furtive glances, even when they were lascivious, but these expressionless gazes were very unnerving. In other countries I found that if I stared back at intrusive men, they looked away or smiled. But here my experience was very different. The men didn't look away, instead continuing to stare, with their hands in their pockets, scratching their balls and fondling themselves.

Eventually we were sent to an office to wait for the ticket supervisor.

'All trains to Calcutta fully booked,' said the supervisor, when he arrived.

'And how many trains go to Calcutta?' I asked.

'All trains booked for this week and next week. But for Western ladies,' said the supervisor, 'we keep a small number of special tickets.'

It sounded suspicious to me, something that would require a bribe, but before I could say anything, the supervisor stood up and left.

'What's going on?' I said to the secretary.

'Don't worry,' he said. 'I have a friend who works here. The supervisor will get you a ticket somehow.'

'But what about the bike?'

'That's never a problem, there is always room for freight. It's getting seats that's difficult.'

I laughed to myself. How ridiculous that there was room for my bike, which took up twice as much space, and no seat for me. The supervisor finally returned and told us he'd booked me a seat, but the ticket had to be collected from a different building that could only be entered if we had a pass, which was issued somewhere else entirely. Indian bureaucracy was living up to its infamous reputation.

We set off in a rickshaw to the 'pass' building, which was about a mile away. It was a huge Victorian building with vast rooms, each full of Indian men sitting behind desks, almost hidden by the piles of paperwork around them. I suspected that the paperwork – covered in the same thick patina of dust that was everywhere – had been lying on those desks for years.

After being sent to three different offices, we stumbled upon the right one, where we were given a pass to enter the building that issued tickets, but first the pass had to be stamped in yet another building. By this stage, having seen so many different people in different offices in different buildings, I was beginning to forget what I had come for in the first place.

We left with the pass and continued onto the next stage: yet another Victorian building with more piles of paper surrounding hundreds more Indian officials. Eventually, having collected all the requisite passes and stamps and found the correct office, a clerk handed over my train ticket with a caveat.

'This ticket isn't definite,' he said. 'You will have to confirm it.'

'Confirm it?' I was reaching the end of my patience now. 'Why can't you do that for me here?'

'I can't do that,' said the clerk with a hapless, ingratiating smile. 'You will have to go back to the main station.'

'The main station?' I said. 'Where we started?'

He looked at his watch. 'Tomorrow.'

'Tomorrow?' I was on the point of losing my cool.

'They are closed for today.'

'But the train leaves at seven in the morning and I have to get my bike on the train as well.'

He raised his shoulders. 'There is nothing I can do.'

The secretary assured me there would be no problems in the morning, but I'd already worked out that telling people exactly what they wanted to hear was a national pastime. So, with no other choice but to spend another night with the Indian family and its multi-generational gropers, I returned with the secretary to the house.

After a thankfully non-eventful night with the family, absolute panic reigned when I arrived at the station before dawn. I got my bike weighed, stuck labels all over it, then wheeled it up the platform, the station porters insisting on loading it on the train.

'Stop!' I tried to make the porters understand I didn't have a confirmed seat for myself, but they looked at me as if I was stupid.

Ten minutes before the train was due to depart, the secretary arrived with my confirmed ticket and I realized how fortunate I was to have him helping me. Without him, it would have taken me days to obtain a ticket, if I'd got one at all.

I looked around but now the porters were nowhere to be seen. Enlisting a bunch of Indian men hanging around the station, we lifted my BMW two feet up onto the goods wagon. Climbing aboard, I started tying it down, but was stopped by a hand on my shoulder. I looked around. The hand belonged to a guard.

'No . . .' The guard shouted a stream of words at me, but beyond the first one, I understood nothing.

Gesticulating wildly, I tried to make clear I needed to secure my bike to the side of the goods wagon. But the guard pushed me out of the carriage onto the platform, slammed the door shut and locked it. My bike would definitely fall over, but at least it was on board.

Of course my reserved seat was already occupied, but the train was a surprise: cleanish and reasonably comfortable, which was fortunate as it would take at least thirty hours to reach Calcutta. Having reclaimed my seat, I found myself sitting opposite a bald, obese man dressed in a floor-length white tunic and baggy white trousers. He was so enormous he occupied two seats, leaving his servant to sit on the floor while he munched his way through a succession of pastries, sweets and other snacks, all of them intricately packaged in banana leaves and other wrappings.

The train started to move, only half an hour later than time-tabled. For the next few hours, we crawled through a succession of slums, the train's whistle blowing almost permanently. By the side of the track, rows of people squatted along what had become a continuous public toilet, some of them even holding magazines to read while they vacated their bowels.

Next to me, my fellow passengers introduced themselves, then asked a stream of questions: Where was I from? Where was I going? Was I married? Did I have children?

Mentally and physically exhausted, I answered as briefly as politeness allowed. Fortunately, they soon ran out of things to say and the compartment became silent, my mind wandering as I stared out of the window.

All in all, I was quite pleased with myself. I couldn't believe that I was going to be in Calcutta the next day. At $40 for the bike and $9 for me, it was ridiculously cheap for a train journey of more than 1,000 miles. The petrol alone would have cost me $55 and I'd also have needed oil and three nights' accommodation. I felt sure I had made the right decision. And all I had to do was just sit and watch India pass by the window. I got out my Walkman. For the first time on my trip, I felt the need to withdraw from my surroundings. Two days in India had done that to me. Looking at all the poverty and hardship slide past the window, listening to Mozart's *Requiem*, alienating myself from it all, was almost like watching a television programme. The day passed incredibly slowly, the train stopping every few minutes, never ambling along at more than 20 mph. Closing my eyes, I tried to pretend I was somewhere else.

As darkness fell, the daytime seats were transformed into night-time bunks and passengers started to organize their sleeping places. Ending up with a top bunk, I had an incredibly hot night, but at least it was above the staring gazes of my fellow passengers. I slept badly, worried about having my gear stolen, and was glad when the morning eventually came.

We arrived only about four hours late, a triumph by Indian Railways standards. I stared out of the door at Calcutta (now Kolkata). Its name alone conjuring up images of squalor and poverty, I wanted to put Calcutta behind me as soon as possible. Pushing my way through the crowds on the platform, I was relieved to find the carriage carrying my bike was still attached to the train. Better still, it was locked. After hassling several train guards, I got the door opened, climbed into the wagon. My bike had fallen over, fortunately without damage.

Several porters surrounded my bike, eager to help, if only in expectation of a large *baksheesh*.

'Stop! Slow down,' I yelled, concerned that they might damage it.

Ignoring me, they hauled my bike upright, lowered it to the platform, their fingers rubbing against their palms in anticipation of *baksheesh*. Instead of money, I offered them a can of beer given to me by the Indian family in Madras. Shared between six of them, they seemed delighted by it.

Arriving at the platform exit with my bike, I was stopped by yet another Indian Railways official and told to exit through the goods depot, where another official demanded a customs form.

'I've come from Madras,' I said. 'I don't have a customs form.'

The official shook his head, held out his hand. 'Customs form.'

I showed him my carnet, the only customs documentation I had. He refused it, waved his hand in the vague direction of a building. 'Customs form.'

'I came on the train from Madras. I don't need a customs form.'

Another shake of his head: 'Customs form.'

I trudged over to the building. In a dark filthy room packed with people, I queued for hours until another official called me to his desk. I explained my case.

'Customs form?' The official looked blankly at me. 'Not here.' He pointed me back to the gate.

I wanted to scream. Back at the gate, I explained to the first official that I'd been told I didn't need a customs form. While we were arguing, a young Indian man rode up on an old Royal Enfield.

'Can I help?' he said.

With short hair and a friendly face, Sanatan spoke good English. 'Let me speak to the official,' he said.

For a few minutes I watched Sanatan and the official converse in Hindu, their voices becoming louder, their gestures more animated.

'We need to go to the office,' said Sanatan.

'I've been there already. They said I didn't need a customs form.'

I could see by the look in Sanatan's eyes that it was more complicated than that.

'Do they want *baksheesh*?' I said.

'I don't think so.'

We returned to the office. After a long wait followed by a long conversation with Indian officialdom, we didn't get any further than I had done alone. We were sent to a different office, where we queued and made our case again. At the end of it: no customs form, no way of leaving the station.

We sat down. 'I don't know what to do,' said Sanatan.

'I'm losing hope of ever leaving Calcutta station,' I said.

'You could just push it through the front entrance. There are only five steps.'

I felt as if anything was worth a try at this point. I climbed onto my BMW and started pushing it through the station. Within seconds someone was behind me, tapping my shoulder. Expecting to be told to go back and get a customs form, I turned around.

'No sitting on the bike,' said a scruffily dressed official.

I raised my eyebrows.

'You must stand beside and push it.'

The official's insistence that I conform to an approved way of pushing my bike was so ridiculous, I started to laugh. I was about to ask if he was joking, but I had learnt that confronting Indian officialdom was futile. I would never understand their logic.

I climbed off my bike, wheeled it to the entrance, bumped it down the steps, across a forecourt and onto the street. No one stopped me. No one mentioned a customs form. At last I was free to go wherever I wanted.

'Do you need somewhere to stay?' said Sanatan. 'I can help you find somewhere.'

Not relishing the prospect of finding my way around Calcutta looking for a room, I followed Sanatan on his bike, down crowded streets, weaving in and out of people, cyclists, rickshaws, cows and carts. Fortunately, everything moved incredibly slowly, so there was little chance of a serious collision.

After trying a few hotels that were too expensive or full, we arrived at the IAA, the Indian Automobile Association. I followed Sanatan up a flight of steps into an extraordinary colonial building in which I immediately felt at home. The foyer was shabby, dirty and in need of a lick of paint, but the familiar Victorian architecture gave me a sense of security as I approached the reception desk.

'Do you have a room available?'

Behind the desk, an elderly man shook his head. 'Only to members of the Indian Automobile Association.'

'I'm a member of the Automobile Association in London,' I said. It was a worth a try, I thought.

'Oh.' The receptionist looked impressed. 'That will be fine.'

I arranged to meet Sanatan later and went up to my room. Although large and quite pleasant, it looked as though it hadn't been cleaned or painted since the days of the Raj. Downstairs, the restaurant was very impressive, almost like a museum, but just as dilapidated as my bedroom. Its walls were festooned with AA badges and shields from all over the world, all of them carrying about an inch of dust. There were far too many waiters, especially as I appeared to be the only guest. They were all dressed in very smart uniforms that, like the rooms, looked as if they'd last been washed in colonial days. But they did appear to have a problem with their shoes, as all of them were wearing flip-flops.

When I had signed the register, I noticed the date, 28 April. It was my birthday and it had completely passed my notice. I wrinkled my nose. It felt a bit strange to be on my own on my birthday, so I decided I would treat myself to a rare bottle of beer at dinner.

After dinner, Sanatan returned to take me to the airport to cash some travellers' cheques. News of my arrival in the city had clearly got around; Sanatan was now accompanied by ten bikers and we picked up many more along the route. Riding pillion on Sanatan's bike was the first time I'd been on a Royal Enfield. We bumped along potholed streets through slums and backstreets. The old decrepit houses, once handsome, fascinated me. The streets, alive with huge crowds of people, let bikes move freely through the throngs. It was the first time I'd really seen India and it was a great way to spend my birthday evening. But once we reached the edge of Calcutta, the mood changed.

Accelerating to 60 mph in total darkness, I realized Sanatan and his two dozen mates regarded themselves as the Calcutta equivalent of Hell's Angels, giving every impression of having little interest in surviving the night. Buses and trucks were passed on blind corners.

Above left: Welcome to Nepal! After crossing the Miteri bridge from India into Nepal.

Above right: Trekking the Annapurna Circuit, Nepal, with Mark.

Below: Climbing up the foothills of the Himalayas on the road to Kathmandu from the Indian border.

Above: Outside the Cosy Corner Lodge in Kathmandu, Nepal, just after cutting my top box down.

Below: Riding out of Kathmandu, Nepal.

Above: Buying food at a roadside stall in Rajasthan, India.

Right: Ancient and modern transport; our bikes parked on the side of the road in Rajasthan.

Below: Robert trying to fix a puncture in Rajasthan. I had to push the crowd back so he was able to breathe.

Above left: Sikh bikers, who stopped to help us after hitting a cow near Palampur, Himachal Pradesh, India.

Above right: One of the many landslides we encountered on the road from Srinagar to Leh in Ladakh, northern India.

Below: With Robert on the road to Leh in Ladakh, northern India.

Above: A road sign a few miles outside Quetta in Pakistan; the first I'd seen showing the distance to London in over two years.

Right: The open road; Robert on his bike.

Below: Riding through the province of Baluchistan, western Pakistan.

Above: Mending a puncture in the middle of the desert in Baluchistan, before realizing both our pumps were broken.

Left: Covering up in Iran.

Below: The 'NO WESTERN' sign at the border between Iran and Turkey.

Above: Getting bogged down after a night free-camping on the beach in southern Turkey.

Below left: Robert in Turkey, recovering from hepatitis.

Below right: Back home, completely stripping down my bike before the rebuild.

Outside my parents' garage in central London in 1984, after 35,000 miles and over two years on the road.

Cows and cyclists were missed by inches. It was too terrifying to be exciting. Convinced I would never reach the airport alive, I implored them to stop and let me off, but they refused even to cut their speed. Not wanting my last living moments to be unhappy ones, I tried not to think about it, although it did occur to me how strangely chronologically neat it would be to die on my birthday.

Eventually a glow appeared on the horizon. The airport at last. A few minutes later, we arrived, twenty to thirty bikers making a terrible noise. The airport staff appeared to think they were being attacked and ran inside, peering nervously through glass doors at us as I made my way into the terminal. Travellers' cheques exchanged quickly for cash, I was soon trying to think of a way to avoid getting back onto Sanatan's bike. Without leaving myself stranded, there was no escape and I pleaded with him to ride back slowly, but he seemed to think I was joking, and we set off again at breakneck speed. Mercifully, however, a few minutes into the return journey, Sanatan's throttle cable jammed.

Grinning at my good luck, I prayed that Sanatan wouldn't be able to fix it. To my delight, it was beyond him. We completed the journey at a stately 20 mph, arriving back at the hotel quite late.

'Stay another day,' pleaded Sanatan. 'We'll show you Calcutta.'

Only four days remained until I was due to meet my parents and I had little idea how long it would take to ride to Kathmandu. 'I can't,' I said. 'I have to get back on the road.'

12

DOUBLE ENGINE, SELFIE START:
CALCUTTA TO KATHMANDU

Calcutta, 29 April 1984

Keen to get out of Calcutta before the roads became crowded, I left early. Relying on a very sketchy map of the city centre with three roads marked, I opted for the road heading north and hoped for the best, knowing I had to cross the River Ganges.

Eventually I came upon the Ganges, following it until I reached a bridge, dodging through a convoy of heavily laden trucks spewing out thick black diesel fumes. Even early in the morning, the heat in the side streets was stifling. Wedged between trucks, it was unbearable. Sweat dripping into my eyes, my T-shirt already a filthy dust-sodden sweat sponge, I made my way across the bridge. Any semblance of traffic order or road discipline had long been abandoned. The bridge was like a dodgem car track where bikes were simply ignored. I made it across only after twice being shunted from behind. If riding through India was going to be like this, I wouldn't enjoy it or stay alive for very long.

For three hours I crawled at walking pace along a single-track road. Two truck convoys going in opposing directions made overtaking impossible or pointless; when a space appeared, I replaced the back end of one lorry with another. And this was the main road north out of one of India's largest cities. Only slightly wider than a single car and with dirt either side, the sealed part of the road contained enough traffic to overwhelm a six-lane motorway. Putting my bike on the train from Madras to Calcutta had definitely been the right decision.

After four hours with not a single road sign, I didn't know if I was going in the right direction and no longer cared. My main objective was to get out of Calcutta as soon as possible, then worry about finding the road north.

Slowly the roadside buildings spread out, fields appeared and the truck convoy came to a complete standstill. Pulling out to overtake at least 100 trucks, I reached the front of the queue, where a broken-down truck sat at the side of the road. Stretching into the distance, an opposing column of trucks faced towards me, backed up behind a single truck parked nose-to-nose with the truck at the head of the column I'd just overtaken.

Standing in the middle of the road, a group of Indian men gesticulated wildly and argued. If it wasn't so ridiculous, I would have laughed out loud: a deadlock because they couldn't agree who should reverse first.

It was good to get the bike over 50 mph. Sitting in traffic for four hours in temperatures above 40°C hadn't been good for her engine, even if I had turned it off several times to try to cool it down, so after putting a decent distance between myself and Calcutta, I stopped under a tree in a deserted spot to allow us both to recover. I'd been there for less than a minute when a small group of Indian men appeared. I looked around. The landscape was empty, yet somehow they'd appeared from somewhere. More people arrived and soon I was surrounded by about thirty Indian men, all of them staring and pushing closer for a better look.

I wondered if maybe they'd never seen a bike like mine before and guessed they'd never imagined one being ridden by a woman. After a few minutes I realized I wasn't going to be left alone, so I dipped my eyes and ignored them until a faint murmuring started to spread through the crowd. Looking up, I noticed one of the men pointing at the two large cylinders that stuck out from the sides of the BMW engine.

'Oooh . . . double engine . . . double engine,' the man was saying. A second man, his head poking over the speaker's shoulder for a closer look, took up the chant.

'Oooh . . . double engine. . . double engine,' said the second Indian, turning to a third man at his side. 'Double engine . . .'

Spreading quickly through the crowd, the double-engine mantra was repeated from man to man, with all the authority of the truly clueless suddenly considering themselves experts. Aware that thirty pairs of eyes were watching my every move, I put on my helmet and gloves, slid myself onto my bike and pressed the starter motor. When the engine burst into life, the entire crowd gasped and jumped back.

'Oooh . . . selfie start . . . selfie start.'

Again a mantra rippled through the crowd, but this time it was less sure, as if they couldn't quite believe what they were seeing. Riding off, I wondered what they would tell their friends and family that evening – and whether anyone would ever believe them.

I rode on through flat barren land crawling with people, individual villages difficult to distinguish because they merged into one continual village lining the road. As the sun dipped towards the horizon, I checked my watch. Riding for ten hours, I'd covered less than 100 miles. India was certainly going to be a slow process.

Time to seek a hotel. Searching for accommodation was hard enough in daylight; I didn't want to be looking for somewhere in the dark. Eventually I spotted a small sign by the side of the road. *Hotel.* A big arrow pointed down a track. Two miles later I came to an empty field. I backtracked, rode towards a small building I'd noticed. When I arrived, a woman came out.

'Hotel?' I said.

A puzzled frown creased the woman's features. She ran inside, slammed the door. I took it as a 'no'.

Back on the main road, I finally reached a town called Asansol, which had only one hotel, making my job of choosing a bed for the night very simple. The owner wanted thirty rupees for a filthy room so small that I could step onto the bed from the door. With no other option, I took it on the condition I could wheel my bike into the front reception area for safekeeping. The owner agreed and we returned to the foyer, where a huge crowd now enveloped my bike, eager to stare at it and a stranger.

Pushing my way through the people, I found my BMW, started it up. 'Ooh . . . double engine . . . ooh . . . selfie start' rippled through the crowd. As I rode up three steps into the reception area, I underestimated the crowd's enthusiastic assistance. Pushing me and my BMW from behind, they broke the rear bracket that attached my top box to the bike. Just what I didn't need when knackered after a long day's ride.

I went upstairs, had a shower and lay on my bed, trying to muster up the energy to go down and fix my bike. An hour later, I returned to the foyer, expecting the crowd to have dispersed. They were still there, eagerly awaiting my return.

Ignoring my audience, I sorted through odd pieces of aluminium I carried with me, reconstructed a new bracket, the crowd pushing forwards to get a closer look until some of them were inside the lobby. Entirely male, there was no way of knowing if they were there to stare at my bike or at me. To my relief, the hotel owner shouted at them, pushed them out and pulled a metal safety grill across the entrance door. I looked at them all, pressed against the bars. I felt as if I was an animal in a zoo.

The next morning the crowds returned to see me off. After another 'double engine . . . selfie start' departure, I left the town, very relieved to see it fade in my rearview mirror. An hour down the road, my bike started to misfire, eventually firing entirely on one cylinder. I stopped, checked the plugs, cleaned the points. It seemed okay. Ten miles further, it did the same again. And so it continued: 150 miles that day, stopping every ten miles to clean the points. I couldn't understand what the problem was.

At Patna I found a hotel easily, one that allowed me to park my bike outside my room. Had the door been any wider, I would have taken the bike inside. After a cold shower, I lay on my bed under the fan, listened to some music. It was bliss, the first time that day I hadn't been hot and sweaty. Closing my eyes, I could have been anywhere.

'Hello.' A knock from a young Indian lad who worked at the hotel.

I found it difficult to contain my irritation. 'Yes?'

'The manager wants to see you.'

'Why?' I sighed. 'I was trying to sleep.'

The young lad bobbed his head. 'Yes.'

Realizing I wasn't going to be left in peace, I followed him downstairs, where he told me to wait. A short while later, the manager appeared, fat and sweaty, with a big smile on his face.

'Hello,' he shouted. 'I'm sorry I wasn't here to welcome you.'

I smiled. 'You weren't expecting me.'

'We get very few Westerners here. I always like to give them special treatment.'

I wondered what exactly 'special treatment' entailed, but nodded and smiled politely, answering questions about where I was from and where I was going.

'You pay for nothing,' he said. 'Your meals are free and I'll give back the money for your room.'

'Really?' I felt very uneasy. 'Why is it free?'

The manager smiled, shrugged his shoulders, said nothing.

'What do you want?' I said.

Another silent shrug.

'It's really not necessary. I prefer to pay.'

'Why don't you come to my house and meet my wife and family?'

It seemed innocent enough. In the light of his generosity, I felt I should agree.

We walked across a field, arrived at a lovely old house with a series of rooms set around a courtyard lined with intricate framework.

'My wife,' said the hotel manager, gesturing at a short, round woman who'd appeared from inside the house.

'Hello.' I held out my hand, but she didn't take it. Her eyes darted from her husband to me and back again. I sensed I was not the first Western female he'd brought home.

'Get some tea,' said the manager to his wife. 'And some food.'

I felt uncomfortable at the way the hotel manager ordered his wife around, like a servant. 'Thank you,' I said, 'but I'm not hungry. Or thirsty.'

'Then let me show you around my house,' said the manager.

Even though I was uncomfortable, I was intrigued because his house looked interesting. To my relief, his wife accompanied us, but his home was disappointing, a series of small, dark, empty rooms, all of which we rushed through until we got to a larger, brighter room.

'This is my bedroom,' he said, with great emphasis on *bed*.

'Very nice.' I turned to leave.

'Please stay. I have something to show you.' He opened a wardrobe. The shelves were stacked with boxes of Charlie perfume. 'This is very special,' he said. 'You can't buy this in India, but I have a friend who works in customs.' *Yes*, I thought to myself, *I know all about that*.

'Your wife is very lucky.' I felt it was appropriate to draw attention to his wife, who was also standing in the room.

'My wife?' He looked confused, as if he'd forgotten she existed. 'No. No. No. This is for me.'

Grabbing a bottle, the hotel manager sprayed himself copiously, then told his wife to dress me in a sari. Fearing they'd be insulted, I obliged.

'Keep it,' said the manager. 'It's a gift.'

Again I felt uncomfortable, but worried that refusing their national dress would be rude. 'Thank you. Now I must get back to my room.'

The respite back at the hotel was short-lived. Another knock at the door.

'The manager would like to see you.' I followed the same flunky who'd knocked on my door earlier. In his office, the manager was eating a huge meal.

'Sit. Sit.' The manager sucked a chicken leg, pointed at a chair. 'I have always wanted a Western woman.' He sucked the chicken leg. 'I have plenty of money. Just say your price.'

My heart sank. I wasn't angry, just sad that I was seen as a commodity by him. 'I am not for sale,' I said calmly, getting up to leave.

The manager moved quickly to the door, locked it, opened a desk drawer, withdrew a thick bundle of dollar notes.

'Take as much as you want.'

I looked at the money on the desk and found my mind racing. I could travel for months on the hundreds of dollars he was offering me. But one look at his face and I knew there was no way I could do it.

'I just want to go,' I said.

The manager pursed his lips, his breath whistling through his nostrils. I thought he was losing patience, determined to get what he wanted, money or not.

'I'm going to leave,' I said.

Snapping his hands around my wrists, the manager grabbed me, slammed me against a wall. I struggled, cried out.

A knock at the door.

'Go away!' The manager's spit flecked my face.

Another knock at the door, more urgent this time.

'Go. Away.'

Urgent, heavy thuds on the door. The manager released his grip on my wrists, unlocked the door.

Seeing a shocked face appear in the gap, I didn't wait for the manager to explain himself to his employee. I slipped through the open door while I had the chance, ran to my room and bolted the door behind me.

Desperate to depart without encountering anyone at the hotel, I rose before dawn, leaving when the first glow of light coloured the sky. My parents would arrive in Kathmandu in two days and I was determined to be there before them. Nineteen months after Heathrow, I was desperate for another round of hugs and tears. And, tired of travelling, the prospect of a five-star hotel and conversation with someone other than myself was very exciting.

After only a few miles the bike started to play up again with a general loss of power, mistiming and uneven running, but this time I decided to push ahead and stop every twenty-five miles to clean the points. I'd fix things properly in Kathmandu.

By four o'clock I was at the Nepalese border, muttering under my breath that none of the ten Indian officials who were lazing around would stamp my carnet when the carnet official had gone for tea. I considered remaining in India for the night, but I'd already had enough and decided to stick it out and wait.

Eventually the carnet guy returned, wrote my name and the BMW's registration number in my passport and half a dozen different books and pieces of paper, then gave me the go-ahead to leave India. With a sense of relief I rode onto Miteri Bridge, officially no-man's land between the two countries. But it was more than just a symbolic divide; in travelling only a few yards everything changed and suddenly the multitudes of people disappeared.

I rode down a short section of road and passed through a large, ornate gate with three towers into Nepal, where a short man in a neat uniform greeted me with a huge smile on his face. 'Come in,' he said enthusiastically. 'Come in.'

He was so nice and friendly, I felt suspicious as we entered his small border guard hut.

'Please sit down. Do you have a visa?'

'No.' Having heard conflicting advice, I was worried that I'd be sent back to India to get a visa first, but instead I was given a form to fill out. Five minutes later, I emerged from the hut, visa issued and passport stamped. No multiple forms, stamps and signatures. Just a single form, stamped once. What a relief.

'Welcome to Nepal,' said the guard.

Continuing to a customs building a quarter of a mile further along the road, I received a similar reception. Processing of the paperwork was calm, methodical and straightforward. The officials were polite, friendly and helpful. I'd moved only half a mile, but it felt as if it was a different planet from India, not simply a neighbouring country. I was sure I was going to like Nepal.

By the time I had passed through customs, it was dark, so I rode a few miles up the road to Birgunj in search of a hotel. After finding none along the main street, I was considering riding to the next town when a young Nepalese kid pulled alongside me on a Honda trail bike and smiled.

'What have you got there?' said the kid, looking my bike up and down, as if he was trying to work out what the aluminium contraption on the back was all about.

We exchanged a few words about bikes and I mentioned I was looking for a hotel.

'My father owns a hotel down the road and your bike will be safe there,' he said.

'Really?' Bumping into this young biker was a stroke of luck. If I had been in India, I would have been suspicious, but in Nepal everything felt completely different. Appreciating my good luck, I followed him to his father's hotel, where I was given a room with five beds for the price of a single, a luxury that allowed me to spread out for a change.

Pleased to have arrived in calm, civilized Nepal, I went to bed early, but was woken early the next morning by heavy rain pounding the corrugated iron roof above my bed. I discovered the roads had flooded overnight, but I wasn't worried about my journey as I would be climbing to higher altitudes. Hoping to make it to Kathmandu in a day, I followed eighty miles of narrow, winding, mountain roads. The roads were empty, the scenery was spectacular and there was the promise of getting to the cooler climate of the mountains. It was the most enjoyable ride I'd had since the roads of northern Thailand. After three months of heat and stickiness, I'd forgotten what it was like not to be continually covered in sweat, to wear more than a T-shirt, to feel the weight of clothes, to sleep with a blanket. But the best thing about the ride was that I was going to see my parents.

After nearly two years apart, I found the idea of meeting my parents in an unfamiliar place very odd, almost surreal. I'd changed a lot and I'd proved I was capable of achieving what I'd set out to do, so I was curious to discover their attitude to my trip now. When I last saw them, they'd been totally against it. Now I hoped that they'd be more supportive and encouraging.

That evening, I arrived in Kathmandu and booked into the Cosy Corner Lodge Hotel, a safe place to keep the bike. I spent the evening eating chocolate cake and apple pie, an extraordinary experience after four months of rice and vegetables. It melted in my mouth. Food had rarely tasted so good; I ate slowly, savouring every mouthful.

I knew I should give my bike a service, but couldn't face it, so I toured some temples the next day and slept late the following day. On my third day, I woke early, excited by the anticipation of my parents' arrival and by the prospect of staying in one place for more than one night, a five-star hotel with clean sheets, hot water and relatively good food.

After not seeing my parents for so long, for months I'd envisaged cruising up to their hotel, where they'd be standing, awaiting my arrival. I packed my bike early and prepared to leave shortly after the time my father's meticulous travel itinerary suggested they would arrive at their hotel.

Only 200 yards separated our hotels, but typically in this short distance my bike decided to break down and this time I couldn't get her started again. Maybe I should have repaired it, maybe it was divine retribution for my hubris, but it meant my triumphant entrance turned into the humiliation of me pushing my bike the last fifty yards to meet my parents. Fortunately they hadn't yet arrived, but the doorman at the hotel seemed determined not to let me escape embarrassment, throwing me out, refusing to believe I was a guest. Eventually, after much argument, I was allowed to sit in my filthy clothes in the foyer and wait for their airport bus, getting disapproving looks from all the hotel staff and guests, none of whom realized these were my best clothes, put on especially for the occasion.

Two hours later, my parents' bus finally arrived for a very tearful reunion on my mother's part. Then my mother turned to all the other members in her party.

'This is my daughter,' she announced to about twenty people, 'the one I have been telling you about.'

'Would you like to see my bike?' I asked the group around my parents.

'Oh Elspeth,' said my mother. 'I don't think anyone would want to do that.'

'Well, would you two . . .' – I gestured at my parents – '. . . like to see it?'

'I think we need to get to our room first and unpack,' said my mother.

I felt stupid for expecting them to be interested in something that had been my close companion for almost two years, something I felt was now part of me. Having achieved so much since we'd last seen one another, I'd presumed they would understand my quest a bit more and at least feign an interest in the machine that made it possible. Maybe it was too much to expect my parents' attitudes to have changed. I'd changed a lot, I felt, in the last year and a half, but they remained indifferent. From their point of view, my trip was the same as it had always been – dangerous and completely unnecessary.

13

ON TOP OF THE WORLD:
NEPAL

Kathmandu, 7 May 1984

Twenty months since we said our awkward goodbyes at Heathrow airport, I found myself standing in a luxury hotel with my parents, realizing that in spite of everything that had happened since we'd last been together, for them very little had changed. The tearful hugs now out of the way, it was back to business as usual. My mother had little interest in my trip, preferring instead to tell me at great length all about life at home. Rarely interested in family gossip before I left, I was even less bothered now. To me it all seemed tedious and unimportant, particularly when neither of my parents had asked me anything about myself or my trip, except for my mother's exclamation that I was 'painfully thin'.

I didn't understand why they still didn't take me seriously. I'd achieved something that very few people had even attempted, but I felt my mother still treated me as if nothing had changed. As for my father, he was entirely in his own little world.

'Look at this, Elspeth.' Dad lifted a layer of clothes out of his suitcase to show me rows of black plastic capsules with grey lids, neatly arranged across the bottom of his suitcase. 'Eighty rolls of film. I got them at a very good discount.' I didn't know what to say, other than to nod acknowledgement, so I left my parents and went to my room. As I unpacked my bags, I wondered if I was becoming a very different, quite insular person. Spending such long periods in my own company was bound to have an effect. The journey was setting me apart from almost everyone I met or knew.

By the standards of where I'd stayed so far, my room was extremely luxurious. It had a bed with cotton sheets and pillows and a proper bath, something I'd not seen for months, although I had to laugh when the water emerged from the tap muddy and brown. Behind the facade of Western furniture and fittings, it wasn't that different from all the other places I'd stayed.

The next day, I joined my parents in the slightly surreal confines of their air-conditioned bus for a tour of Kathmandu. Arriving at a temple with a group of wealthy middle-aged Westerners, I was unsurprised that the beggars immediately targeted us, but I was taken aback when the Nepalese tourist officials cleared the path in front of us and gave us more attention and respect than I'd ever experienced on my own. All this because they knew our group had much more money than backpackers and other budget travellers.

'What are you wearing for dinner tonight?' said my mother, as the bus returned us to the hotel.

'These . . .' – I pointed at the light trousers and shirt that I was wearing – '. . . are the best clothes I've got.'

My mother looked unimpressed. 'Really, darling?'

''Fraid so.'

In my room that evening, I tried to find something to wear. I had a pair of baggy oil-stained cotton trousers that I wore on my bike and some jeans that I kept as my smart trousers. My mother had already sniffed at my baggy cotton trousers, so it would have to be the jeans. I put them on and showed my mother.

'Elspeth!' said Mum. 'Where has your bottom gone? You've lost so much weight.'

The jeans, which had been quite tight when I bought them in Sydney, were hanging off me. I went back to my room. A few minutes later, there was a knock at my door. Dad was standing in the hotel corridor with a bundle in his hand.

'I got this in Oxfam, but it's too small for me.'

Dad thrust the bundle at me. It was a smart pair of overalls, size ten. I slipped it on. It was a perfect fit for me, even attracting compliments at dinner from an English couple who shared our table and talked only about their ballroom dancing, their obsessive chatter about quicksteps and cha-cha-chas adding to my culture shock. Clearly I didn't fit in with my parents, or with other travellers, or with the locals. Ultimately, I didn't belong anywhere; a very lonely place to be.

At breakfast the next morning, I suggested that my parents leave the bubble of organized tourist tours. By them experiencing Nepal in the way I had experienced other countries, I hoped we might connect better. 'How about going to see a village off the tourist track,' I said. 'I think it's important for you to see the real country and people.'

To my delight and surprise, my parents agreed and we took a taxi to Kirtipur, a sleepy town in a valley a few miles south of Kathmandu. Almost as soon as we arrived, a small boy latched on to my mum and insisted on taking her to meet his family, who lived in a single room, about five foot square. The boy's mother and sister were lying asleep on the mud floor with a few possessions scattered around them. Mum was visibly affected.

'I always knew that people lived like this,' she said afterwards, 'but it's totally different when you see it for yourself.'

Everywhere we looked, it was obvious that life was physically tough and demanding in Kirtipur. We passed women crouched on their haunches beside a river, washing clothes by hand, rubbing them against stones instead of using soap. Young boys and girls carried huge bundles of reeds, three or four times larger than themselves, on their backs from the river, along the side of roads and up steep flights of steps into the town. Young men hauled harvested crops across a river on a pulley system they propelled by hand. In our whole time in the village, we didn't see a single machine being used to reduce the laborious burden of anyone's tasks.

Unlike in India, the locals didn't hassle us. They seemed to sense when it was time to leave us to ourselves. We had such a good time, my father taking countless photographs and showing his camera to the kids, my mother sitting on a low wall, chatting to young girls who were interested in her clothes and glasses.

When we got back to the hotel, my parents told their travelling companions what they had seen and experienced in great detail, and I felt extremely proud that I'd shown them a glimpse of the world through which I had been travelling.

The next day, we again struck out on our own, visiting some temples and ghats around Kathmandu. At the end of our excursion, we set off to find a taxi back to the hotel, but every taxi that stopped was already booked by someone else. Eventually, one of the drivers stopped, got out of his cab and spoke to my mother and me in the street.

'I get my friend,' he said. 'He has taxi. He'll take you to your hotel.'

Excellent, I thought – until my mother, who was no closer to the driver than me, turned to me and said: 'He's got a friend who has a taxi. He's going to ask his friend to collect us.' I couldn't believe she was repeating what I'd just heard. 'I do speak English,' I snapped. As soon as I said it, I regretted it. It sounded sarcastic and chippy. In the taxi, Mum started to cry. I felt terrible, but I was also angry that she was treating me the way she did when I was a child. I didn't need English to be translated for me, as if I was stupid. Back at the hotel, I tried to explain. 'I'm sorry. It wasn't meant to sound sarcastic.' Mum still looked upset. 'You were treating me as if I was stupid,' I said, but I could see that my mother didn't understand.

Mum never understood the effect her words and attitude had on me. I'd had years of being told I was thick when I was at school. But now I'd left home and I'd proved I could survive on my own. I'd got myself a job in Sydney, then done things that few people had even attempted, yet I still felt like my achievements were not being recognized by my parents. In fairness to my mother, she didn't comprehend anything that was unconventional and her apparent disinterest was probably her way of dealing with my trip, which she simply did not understand. Like any good mother, she worried about her children, and in her view my life had taken a wrong turn that might end in disaster. I realized that nothing I achieved on my trip would change my mother's opinion of me. Her only hope was that my trip would get my restlessness out of my system and then

I'd settle down to a life that conformed to her ideas of normal. Until that happened, our relationship would remain the same as ever.

The days passed quickly, with little to worry about except getting to the dining room in time for the next meal until Mark arrived a few days later. It was good to see him, although I was worried when I saw how much weight he'd lost after travelling around India for two months. He'd been ill and, like me, found India exhausting, so was very relieved to be in Nepal now.

When Mark and I sat down to spend hours talking about our various travel adventures, I realized that I'd really missed him. Somewhere in the middle of Indonesia, while we were making our way from Bali to Singapore, I'd fallen in love with him. Having experienced many of the same frustrations and delights of travelling in Asia as me, Mark was one of the few people who understood what I had been going through.

'I want to do the Annapurna Circuit,' he said as we were walking away from breakfast one morning.

'The what?' I knew Annapurna was one of the major Himalayan peaks, but I wasn't quite sure about the Annapurna Circuit.

'It's a three-week two-hundred-mile trek around Annapurna. It involves climbing passes up to five thousand four hundred metres.'

I'd never been much of a walker. In fact, I couldn't remember ever walking more than a few miles – and certainly never with a rucksack. But I was intrigued. When I looked through trekking books and saw photos of awe-inspiring mountains and beautiful remote villages, I really wanted to see them. I just didn't know if I wanted it enough to do all the hard work involved in a three-week trek.

While I made up my mind, Mark and I spent the days with Mum and Dad relaxing, doing nothing special except eating good food. Dad found a cheap Chinese restaurant that charged about £3 each for an entire meal with drinks. It was such a good bargain that he insisted on going back every night, never once complaining about paying the bill.

On the day of their departure, we took Mum and Dad to the airport by taxi and, as expected, had a tearful farewell. Mum was very emotional, although she said that leaving me with Mark made it easier for her. My dad, as usual, was oblivious to it all.

Returning to Kathmandu with Mark, it felt good to be alone with him. Our days of five-star living were over and we were now back to living in cheap cockroach-ridden hotels, eating meals of rice and dhal. Although I would not have swapped the two weeks with my parents for anything, I was quite relieved they had gone. Staying with them in the comfort of their hotel was just what I needed to recharge my body, put on some weight and sleep well, but now I felt a great sense of freedom and independence again. The streets were no less dusty, the temperatures and humidity no cooler or drier, my daily tasks no less challenging, but after my recharge I now felt much stronger to cope with the hassles of travelling again.

Mark and I checked back into my old room at the Cosy Corner Lodge and we started to plan our trek. He'd been persistent and I'd finally agreed. I was excited at the thought of another adventure, and about spending more time together. Mark wanted to do the longest trek possible, which daunted me, but surrounded by amazing mountains in the trekking capital of the world, I accepted I ought to make the most of it. Shaped like a horseshoe, the full circuit would take us about three weeks on foot (an unpaved road built in the past decade has made the trekking route shorter) and needed quite a lot of preparation. We spent a day getting a trekking permit, which was easy enough once we handed over the fee, but we were advised that most people did only the first third or the final third of the circuit. Anyone who did the entire circuit needed a guide, which we couldn't afford, so we spent another day searching for a map, eventually locating one that was a photocopy of a very faint photocopy. It was just about legible.

With only a small daypack, some light shoes and some motorcycle boots to my name, I needed to find some boots suitable for trekking. I hired a pair from a local shop and strapped them on very early the next morning to take the bus to Dumre, which was on the road from Kathmandu to Pokhara. After stopping about halfway for two hours to wait for some more passengers, we arrived in Dumre at midday and waited for a bus that dropped us in Turture at about four o'clock, from where we started trekking straight away with the intention of walking for a couple of hours before it got dark.

Almost immediately I could tell that this trek would nearly kill me. It was agonizing. Now that we were doing it, I realized why many people avoided the first part of the trek from Turture to Manang. For all the first day and most of the first week we did nothing but climb; my daypack was so small and tightly packed that it bounced like a taut ball against my back with every step that I took. Plodding one foot in front of another, I wondered who the hell thought this could be fun.

The trail was barely visible in places and although we were both good at reading maps, we still got lost several times. Referring to the map was often pointless. Several times we arrived at junctions with no idea which of two or three paths we should take. So we would just take pot luck, often realizing our mistake a few miles later, when crossing a feature such as a river, that wasn't on the map and therefore made it obvious to us that we now had to track back to the junction to try a different path.

On the third day, we both felt very ill with the same symptoms: abdominal cramps, bloating, foul-smelling flatulence and belching. All were classic signs of having contracted giardiasis, an infection caused by tiny parasites. However, although it weakened us both, the effect of giardiasis on our stamina and strength wasn't nearly as significant as the altitude. Although I was bike fit, I wasn't prepared for the physical demands of walking uphill every day. I got very breathless and had headaches due to the altitude, the dangers of which were brought home when we were told of another trekker on the circuit at the same time as us. This trekker had started to feel ill, so he pitched his tent and went to sleep. He never woke up.

Maybe I'd have enjoyed the first week more if I'd been able to see the magnificent mountain peaks that Mark had promised me lined the route. But every morning, after a night spent sleeping in a straw barn or on the floor of a Nepalese family's hut, I'd look out into the valley in the hope of a clear view of the mountains. And every morning the valleys were shrouded in thick, low clouds that blocked any view of Himalayan peaks.

After a few days, I surprised myself. In spite of the weather, I actually started to enjoy it. Following months of riding through towns and villages, the simple act of turning up in small communities that never saw vehicles and which could only be reached on foot was a revelation.

'Guess what?' I said to Mark one day. 'I'm actually glad I'm doing this.'

A beaming smile creased Mark's face. 'Why now?'

'It's so remote. It feels as if we're completely cut off from the rest of the world.' Life in the mountains was a whole different mentality, another planet. Everyone walked everywhere. If a villager wanted to visit their sibling in the next village, they set off on foot, even if it took them two days. And as we walked, we passed dozens of porters every day, carrying loads on their backs that were often larger than themselves. One day we passed a porter balancing a load that was eight feet high and entirely made up of cartons of cigarettes.

Now that I'd settled into the rhythm, I could take in the scenery. Although we still couldn't see the mountain peaks, the views were nonetheless stunning. Walking between boulders the size of houses, we traversed green valleys on rope bridges and picked our way through villages of mud huts with thatched roofs.

The scenery was great, but it was the villages that fascinated me. The buildings were beautiful, sometimes made of mud, but more often built of stone, without mortar. Like Tuscan farmhouses, they looked as if they had risen out of the landscape, which, given that they were made from stones gathered from their surroundings, they almost had.

Every night, we found somewhere to sleep, simply by asking the inhabitants of whichever village we were passing through if they had a spare bed. We found billets for a dollar or two a night, staying in some very rustic accommodation, often on wooden platforms above cattle sheds. From the locals we bought local biscuits to eat along the trail. Brittle and dry, they tasted of very little, but kept us going until the evening, when we'd eat in our guesthouse or with whichever family had taken us in for the night. The locals were, without fail, very welcoming and kind. And I had the feeling that they hadn't yet reached the point of being tired of strangers tramping through their villages.

But the best was yet to come. Finally, on the morning of our ninth day, we woke in Manang to clear blue skies. At last I could see all the mountain peaks that we'd been walking past for the last week and a half. The view was astonishing. I'd spotted a few peaks through the clouds, but now I realized they'd been only foothills compared to the six-, seven- and eight-thousand-metre-high peaks that surrounded us.

Now fitter, I was really enjoying the walking, although the toughest day was still ahead. Over the previous week we'd walked eight to ten miles each day, distances that took us five to seven hours. Now we faced the biggest challenge of the trek, a ten-mile hike to Thorong Phedi, the last stop before crossing the Thorong La Pass, which at 5,400 metres was the highest part of the circuit. If all went well, we should arrive in Muktinath on the other side of the pass in two days.

Before leaving, we filled our water bottles from a passing stream. Another twenty minutes further up the trail, we passed a Nepalese farmer, spilling the guts of a dead cow into the same stream.

'Hmm. Lovely,' said Mark, frowning.

'Best not to think about it,' I said.

The trail was very steep, but in return offered stunning views behind us of the Annapurna massif, including the 7,937-metre Annapurna II and 7,725-metre Annapurna IV. Yaks and sheep grazed on the slopes ahead of us, which were now above the tree line and mostly made up of the loose rock and scree characteristic of moraine from the glaciers we could see above the valley. After a few hours, we reached a teahouse at 4,600 metres, at which point the path descended sharply downwards, along a narrow, steep, tortuous trail that took us down to Thorong Phedi at 4,540 metres, where we stayed at Phedi base camp, a stone building that was little more than a cattle shed bordered by two huge piles of firewood. Shortly after we arrived we were surprised when an unfamiliar voice broke my contemplative silence.

'G'day,' said a young man with a beard and long curly hair.

Credi, short for Tancredi, turned out to be the exception to my Aussies-abroad rule. He was lovely and very easy to talk to. Also travelling unguided, it was evident that Credi had similar symptoms to Mark and I and was probably suffering with giardiasis too. We all bunked down in the only room for the night and gave up on any sense of propriety. The noise and smell in the room was so unbelievable that we got a fit of the giggles in the middle of the night as we all lay there trying to sleep.

The three of us set off early the next morning, ensuring there was adequate distance between us to avoid inflicting our unfortunate symptoms on each other. The first hour was damned hard work, the altitude debilitating. With oxygen in very short supply, my head felt as if it was going to burst and I could feel blood pulsing in my skull as my heart worked overtime to supply my brain with oxygen.

As if the altitude wasn't enough of a challenge, the pass had fourteen false summits, which no one had told us about. Time after time I thought we'd reached the top, only to discover that there was another long climb ahead of us. Eventually, after five to six hours' climbing, we reached the ultimate summit of the pass, a place that looked hardly different from the previous false summits except for about half a dozen prayer flags atop a cairn and a view that now led only downhill. (Nowadays there is a big sign, thousands of flags and quite a large pile of stones, but in 1984, there was almost nothing.)

Exhilarated as much as exhausted, I lay down on the cairn, closed my eyes, enjoyed the warm sun on my face and marvelled at the fact that I, a reluctant walker at the best of times, had made it to the top of the highest tourist pass in the Himalayas. I found it hard to believe that I'd reached 5,426 metres above sea level. Then, dizzy from the high altitude, Mark, Credi and I ran down the hill as fast as we could, desperate to fill our lungs with thicker air at a lower altitude to banish headaches, nausea and dizziness.

Two hours later we were in Muktinath, and for the next four days we continued stomping down the trail, now covering significant distances each day because we were fit, the air was thicker with oxygen and it was predominantly a downward slope. On 6 June we ended our trek in Kharehawaa. For nearly three weeks, we had seen only villagers, porters and Credi on our trek, but now it all changed. Grubby-faced kids with big smiles ran alongside us, asking for 'sweetie, sweetie . . . pen, pen', a legacy of the thousands of tourists who had walked this last stretch of the Annapurna Circuit to Pokhara. Not taking a refusal for an answer, the children soon became a bit of a nuisance and I missed the solitude of the high altitudes.

The next day we caught a bus to Pokhara, where we switched buses to Kathmandu. I slept all the way and woke up in the Nepalese capital feeling fantastic. I was incredibly tired, but physically the fittest I think I've ever been. It was as if I'd had a complete physical servicing and overhaul, which was exactly what I needed to prepare me for the next stage of my journey.

PART 4

KATHMANDU TO HOME

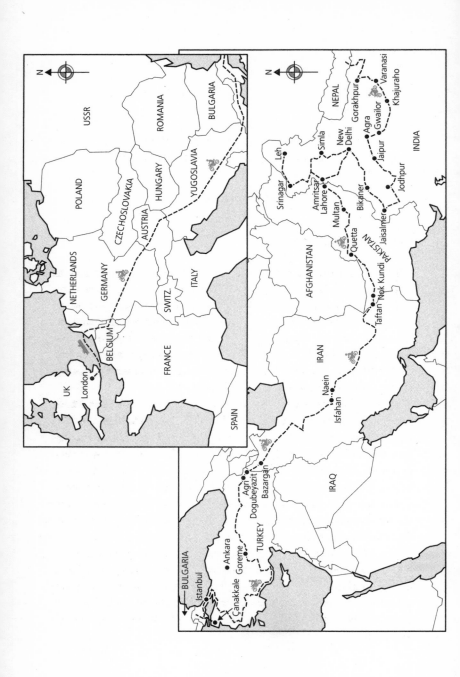

14

FROM SERENITY TO CHAOS:
KATHMANDU TO VARANASI

Kathmandu, 8 June 1984

The first thing I did on arriving back in Kathmandu was to head straight to the Cosy Corner Lodge and check my bike. Reassured that it was still intact and working, I sat down with Mark for something to eat. After nearly a month of mountain biscuits, rice and vegetables, our taste buds went into overdrive when reacquainted with the textures and flavours of chocolate cake and apple pie that the Kathmandu cafés and teashops were famous for. Food had rarely tasted so good.

Maybe the increased oxygen in the air played a role, but Mark and I felt as if we were on a high. The thrills and challenges of the trek had forced us together in heart, mind and spirit, and sharing so much had forged a deep and loving bond between us. I was very grateful and admiring of Mark for having pushed me into what became, to my great surprise, a wonderful and unique experience.

For the next three days, we did little else but eat, sleep and recover from the rigours of the previous three weeks. I was very much in love, but also extremely exhausted.

On our fourth day in Kathmandu I began to prepare my bike for my reluctant return to India. The monsoon had arrived in Kathmandu, bringing a brief but intense rain shower every afternoon that made me dread returning to the roads of India. If I didn't leave Kathmandu soon they would be knee-deep in water and mud.

Before leaving, I needed to repair several faults on my bike, including the ongoing points problem, which after a little thought I solved by replacing the condenser. However, while finishing the job, I yanked my handlebars around without remembering that I'd left my key in the steering lock. The key was badly bent and broke in half when I tried to straighten it.

I found a blacksmith's workshop down a back alley in Kathmandu and showed the remains of my key to a kid no more than ten years old who was crouching at its entrance. Using sign language, I indicated that I needed a replacement.

From a strip of metal about 1.5mm thick, the boy cut out a key shape, round at the top with a long, straight section. He filed the straight section so that it was the correct length and width, then put the round part in a vice and bent the long section over. Working entirely by eye, he used a hacksaw to cut grooves into the long section, then flipped it over and cut the grooves on the other side.

There's no way this will ever work, I thought to myself, but I wasn't going to stop him. *Anything is worth a try and it's amazing to watch him, even if the key doesn't work.*

Continuing to work entirely by eye, the boy fashioned something that looked like a very convincing facsimile of my BMW key. Although unconvinced that it would work, I paid him $2, a small price to pay for watching the boy's extraordinary craftsmanship. Back at Cosy Corner Lodge and with little expectation of my new key actually working, I put it in the ignition. It slipped in easily, a surprise in itself. Then, with no hope of it actually working, I twisted my Nepalese approximation of a BMW key.

The old girl's ignition lit up. Astonished, I grinned from ear to ear. The bloody thing worked.

The next day, I rode over to the blacksmith's workshop to show the boy how well his key had worked in my BMW ignition. Riding back to the Cosy Corner Lodge, I saw another BMW rider pass on the other side of the street. He was very tall and skinny, and because he wasn't wearing a helmet, I could see he was fair-haired and bearded, a total contrast to the small dark Nepalese locals surrounding him.

Glancing over my shoulder, I caught sight of Dutch plates on his BMW R80/7 and immediately pulled over to have a proper look. The Dutch biker had stopped in the middle of the road and was looking my way. Our eyes met, we both smiled and I felt my heart race – not because of the rider himself, but because of the unexpected thrill of meeting another person on a BMW in the middle of the third world. He was the first person I'd met in nearly two years doing a similar overland journey as myself.

Lifting my hand to wave 'hello', I watched as the Dutchman pulled his bike round, rode towards me and pulled up beside me at the side of the road.

'Hi!' He had a strong Dutch accent with a slight Aussie twang. 'Robert.'

I shook Robert's hand. 'Elspeth.'

'I don't believe it,' said Robert. 'I heard about you when I was travelling around Australia.'

'You've come from Oz?'

Robert nodded. 'From Sydney, I lived there for two years, but decided it wasn't the place for me, so I decided to ride home.'

'Back to Holland?'

'Yeah.' Robert nodded again. 'And wherever I went in Australia, I kept hearing about this woman who was on a BMW, riding around the world.'

I couldn't keep the smile from my face. 'I didn't think I'd made any impression.'

'And I kept thinking I was going to meet you,' said Robert. 'In fact, I was hoping it.'

Comparing notes, we discovered that for much of the previous six months, we'd rarely been more than a few hundred miles apart, our paths frequently crossing until Robert overtook me when I was stranded in Singapore after my money and documents were stolen. After that, Robert had been involved in a very serious accident in southern India and spent three months in hospital, so I had overtaken him. Then, if Mark and I hadn't done the three-week trek, our paths might never have crossed.

We sat on the side of some wide concrete steps in front of a trekking shop, talking non-stop for several hours about our experiences – our bikes, what we had done, where we had been, what had gone wrong, where we had broken down. We discussed the difficulties of travelling in India, the constant stares, the terrible roads, and we laughed as we compared experiences of our 'double engine, selfie start' departures, which he too had encountered.

We arranged to meet up again that evening at Cosy Corner Lodge, where, with Mark having joined us, we continued to talk about our experiences and our bikes. I'd seen Robert ride only 100 yards or so, but that short distance was enough for me to see that he was a very safe rider, so I was curious about his accident.

'I was riding up a mountain pass,' said Robert. 'It had no barrier and it was only as wide as a single vehicle.'

Just the kind of road I hated. I raised my eyebrows. Robert then went on to tell us about his horrendous accident: of the truck smashing into him, dragging him down the road and breaking his ribs, his arm, his collarbone. Of the driver putting him in the back of his truck with his bike, and how he passed in and out of consciousness with the pain.

I shook my head; it sounded like hell.

'Eventually we reached the outskirts of a town, where I was bundled into a rickshaw and taken to several hospitals. The truck driver kept arguing with the hospital staff, trying to negotiate the best price thinking he might have to pay for my treatment. We spent nearly six hours trying to find one that would treat me. And it was more than forty degrees Celsius.'

I put my head in my hands. It was one of the worst stories I'd ever heard. 'And the hospital? What was it like?'

'Terrible. Filthy and almost no doctors or nurses. I had to pay a kid to fetch me food and water every day. Without him, I would have starved.' Robert had turned pale with the memory of it all. Sensing the experience still haunted him, I touched his arm lightly. It was meant to be a sympathetic gesture, but I felt Robert's muscles tense beneath my hand. He seemed awkward. From his manner, I guessed he might be shy around women and that maybe my genuine expression of concern for his well-being made him uncomfortable.

Beside me, Mark's face was tight. He'd already voiced his fears about me riding across India on my own; Robert's experiences would do nothing to reduce those feelings. Sitting between the two men, I wondered if Robert and I might be safer continuing the journey together.

The following day, Robert and I serviced our bikes, both of us enjoying having someone with whom we could work and talk through any mechanical problems. In pouring rain, we sheltered beneath a porch as we worked on the bikes.

'I set off for a four-day trip to the Chinese border last week,' said Robert, 'but returned after a day because it was so wet and miserable. We need to get into India soon or the roads will be deep with water.'

After 20,000 miles on the road, including numerous knocks, a cartwheel down the road in Australia and an electrical fire, my BMW was carrying a lot of battle scars. Everything on it was approaching the point of giving out and I realized that I'd need to nurse my old girl carefully now if I wanted her to carry me all the way home. But before I could leave Kathmandu and escape the rain, I needed to solve the problem of my front wheel wobbling at speed. My steering head bearings were wearing out and with so much weight at the back of the bike, the front end often felt unstable, so I decided to cut down my top box to reduce the weight on the back of the bike. I also thought that redistributing the weight by moving some of my luggage further forwards might help.

Returning to the blacksmith workshop that had fashioned my Kathmandu BMW key, I sketched a design on a scrap of paper of a rack for carrying luggage above my cylinder heads. Again, a little kid twisted and welded some metal strips – without a welder's mask or any safety precautions – into exactly what I wanted and all for a few dollars in payment. I handed over the money with a heavy heart, not because of the cost, but because the kid, who looked about five years old, had already lost two of his fingers and if he continued welding without protection, he would soon lose his sight as well.

Back at Cosy Corner Lodge, I discovered my horn didn't work. Although Robert told me he managed without his horn, I considered mine an essential item, especially in India, where all the trucks had 'Blow Horn' written on the back of them. If you wanted to overtake them you had to sound your horn so they knew you were there and hopefully they would pull over, allowing you to pass. I traced the wire and found it had come out of a switch. A relatively simple repair would fix it, but we didn't have a soldering iron, so we made one by cutting a Malaysian cent coin in half, heating it in the flame of a petrol stove so that we could use this to melt some solder onto the wire and the switch. Half an hour later, the horn was repaired.

Our bikes fixed and serviced, we were ready to get back on the road and Robert left the following morning. I wanted to visit Varanasi, which he'd already seen, so we made an arrangement to try to meet near Agra in a fortnight. Sorry to see him go, I wondered if we would ever see each other again. In India, things were bound to go wrong.

Although I really liked Robert, I wasn't sure I wanted to travel with him, or with anyone else, as it meant compromise. After so long on the road alone I wasn't sure either of us could adapt to the other's idiosyncrasies and habits. But I also knew how hard I'd found India and how much a like-minded soul might help me cope with the country. If we happened to meet up, I'd soon discover if we got on and how long we'd want to travel together.

After Robert left, I went through my usual process of procrastination before leaving anywhere. Kathmandu felt very secure and, having been in Nepal for five weeks, fortified with good food and pleasant company, the road ahead felt a very hard place that I'd prefer to avoid rather than tackle. Dreading returning to India's multitudes, monsoons and miserable roads, I spent the last day in Nepal with Mark, chopping my top box down, a relatively easy but tedious job. Then, with my new racks carrying my tools on top of my cylinders, I reluctantly said goodbye to Mark, hugging him for all I was worth. We'd had a fantastic time together in Nepal, thanks largely to his efforts, and I would miss him deeply. If all went to plan, the next time we'd see each other, we'd be in

London.

As I'd feared, the roads out of Kathmandu were in a terrible state. Riding in heavy rain, I headed for Gorakhpur until I reached the Kali Gandaki River, which had burst its banks and now flowed three foot deep across the road. I stopped for a short while to watch a few locals attempt to cross the waters, then decided to turn around and head for Birgunj, adding 150 miles to my journey. By evening I was in Birgunj, staying in the same hotel I'd found when I first entered Nepal, but for half price now as I knew the owner. It felt vaguely like home and I sat at the back of the restaurant, watching *Rocky 2* being played on a communal television while I ate, but gave up after ten minutes for lack of air and being bitten to death by mosquitoes. That night, it rained heavily and by morning the area outside the hotel was like a lake and the rain was still hammering down. I took my time having breakfast and getting ready, eventually deciding I had no choice but to get going. The Nepalese border was relatively smooth apart from the problem of trying to keep all of my documents dry; of course the Indian border was a different story.

'You need to see carnet guy,' said the first official I met.

'I know,' I replied. 'Where is he?'

The official smiled.

'How long will he be?'

Another head bobble. Welcome to India.

While waiting, I was served breakfast and numerous cups of chai, all free but very frustrating. Eventually the 'carnet guy' arrived and I had the usual problems of trying to explain where he was supposed to stamp the carnet. In spite of my best efforts, he still managed to do it wrong, stamping in the space reserved for the exit from India, instead of entry to the country. I hadn't yet set foot in India, but already everything was chaotic.

I advanced from customs to the immigration post.

'You need a visa for India,' said the immigration officer.

'Yes, I have one.' I pointed at the automatic forty-nine-year visa in my passport that all British subjects were issued on arriving in India.

'No good.'

'But all Commonwealth citizens get them automatically.'

'Not any more.'

'Why?'

The immigration official looked at me with contempt. 'You don't follow the news?'

Christ, I wondered, *what's happened now?* 'I've been trekking. There were no newspapers.'

'The law has changed. Lots of problems in India – the Sikhs have been rioting.'

I'd heard rumours about Sikh uprisings, but hadn't realized they would affect me. 'What can I do?'

'You need a visa.'

'From you?'

'No,' he said with the obvious delight of being able to say it to a British subject. 'From an embassy.'

I begged and I pleaded, explaining I'd have to get a new Nepalese visa to return to Kathmandu to apply for an Indian visa. 'It could take me a month,' I said.

The Indian official looked at me, stamped my passport and wrote something in it. 'You can enter,' he said, 'but you must register at a police station and get a visa within fifteen days.'

With an unwarranted sigh of relief, I entered India. The rain had stopped, but I still had a terrible day's ride on the worst roads I had seen in the country. Thousands of buses and trucks pushed me into potholes, ditches and the mud at the side of the road. Poorly sealed roads were worse than unsealed roads, enticing me to ride faster than was safe, given the many potholes, and enabling truck drivers to drive faster and more recklessly than they did on unsealed roads.

The contrast with beautiful, serene Nepal could not have been greater. I hadn't realized that this part of India, a belt of densely populated cities stretching from Delhi to Calcutta, was so industrial, so polluted, so filthy and so teeming with people. Already, it was my least favourite part of the country.

Although the rain had stopped, it had fallen almost incessantly for two weeks, leaving the fields flooded and the roads often ankle deep in water. Arriving in Gorakhpur very wet, I was too tired to expend much effort finding somewhere to sleep and ended up in a dormitory with eight Indian women. After waiting until midnight to wheel my bike into the dormitory's restaurant for the night, I had a terrible night, bitten to pieces by mosquitoes, then got attacked by thousands of red eye flies while trying to eat my breakfast. By Indian standards, I had a good ride to Varanasi, but I got totally lost when I arrived. As soon as I stopped I was immediately surrounded by a crowd of locals and thrust straight back into the hassle of everyone touching my bike. As ever, they played with all the controls and turned the throttle dozens of times, as if I wasn't even there. I tried to stop them but within seconds their hands were all over my bike again.

Eventually, spotting a tailor's shop that appeared clean and well organized, I made my escape from the crowds and knocked on the door. Anticipating a potential sale, the owner invited me inside and thrust a very welcome cold Limca lemon and lime drink into my hands. Inevitably, he had a friend who owned a hotel, so I followed him on his bike, ending up at an excellent hotel for the price of fifteen rupees. It was full of other Westerners, including an Aussie doctor. He invited me for a Chinese meal, after which we wandered the streets back to the hotel for an early night before getting up at five o'clock to see the pilgrims take their dawn swim in the Ganges. After the usual haggling, we hired a boat and paddled along the ghats, stopping to climb the steps from the river up to the funeral pyres where we saw the burning bodies being poked and prodded with sticks, their heads smashed up so they burnt faster.

Fascinated, I took many pictures, suspecting that when processed and printed, the images would look like medieval depictions of hell. The ghats were ghoulish, the riverside was filthy, and the quantities of dead bodies, rubbish and shit thrown into the river were unbelievable. And yet there was something mystical and serene about the place. Women's bodies were covered with orange or red material and flowers, while men were simply wrapped in a white cloth. Then, with their feet pointing towards the river, they were incinerated atop funeral pyres. Depending on how much wood the relatives could afford, the whole process took about three hours. If the corpse was a child, a leper or a smallpox victim, the relatives saved the expense of wood and simply dumped it whole in the river for the vultures to eat. Meanwhile, at the water's edge, the pilgrims drank and performed their ritual ablutions in the filthy, fetid water.

I returned to the guesthouse and spent the rest of the day working on my bike. BMW bikes had a well-deserved reputation for reliability, but with more than 64,000 miles having now passed under her wheels, my old lady was showing the effects of her relatively hard life as well as several crashes. I wondered how much longer I could keep pushing her to cover hundreds of pothole-ridden miles every day. Although confident that she'd carry me all the way home, I did wonder what state she'd be in by the end of my journey.

15

NO MORE LONELY GIRL:
AGRA TO RAJASTHAN

Khajuraho, 21 June 1984

Avery long but good day's ride took me from Varanasi to Khajuraho. Riding west took me away from the monsoon and the weather was much better; dry and arid, a pleasant change from all the rain. The road was wide enough for two cars and I reached speeds of 50 mph, quite an achievement in India. Remote and situated in the middle of the Indian plains, Khajuraho had fewer people and cheaper prices than the cities I'd stopped in so far. I found a good hotel, went up to my room, lay back on my bed and stared at the ceiling. It was so hot I undressed and lay under the fan in my underwear. It felt good to rest at last.

My eyes wandered from the ceiling to the top of a wall, then across the wall towards a blemish. Thinking I saw something move, I narrowed my eyes. That mark on the wall wasn't a blemish.

It was a hole. And there was an eye behind it.

Watching me.

The eye moved as its owner craned for a better view of me. It was too much. Even in my own hotel room it seemed I was denied privacy and peace. Incensed and despairing, I reached above my head, flicked off the light in the room, lay perfectly still in the dark. When my eyes had acclimatized to the darkness, I noticed more holes in the wall. I couldn't bear to think how many men were trying to watch me. Too tired to move, I pulled the bedsheets over me and closed my eyes.

*

I rose early the next morning, keen to get dressed and out before anyone else was up, and went to see all the temples before the heat arrived. Festooned with intricate erotic carvings, the temples were beautiful and fascinating. Cordoned off to anyone who hadn't bought a ticket, they were a peaceful oasis of calm in the bedlam of India. I then headed west from Khajuraho to Gwalior, where I had intended to stay, but found the hotel scene hopeless, stomping out of the last hotel I tried as it couldn't even tell me the price of a room. I found my way to Gwalior's fort, perched on a high hill with the town all around. Climbing up to a nice relaxing spot with few people, I wandered around alone, basking in the architecture. In spite of all my struggles in India, I loved many aspects, especially its buildings. The beauty of some of India's palaces and forts almost outweighed the hardships and irritations of getting to them. Many were deserted, so I could lose myself in their magnificence, unencumbered by hassling crowds, left to wonder how a single culture could produce such structured beauty as well as such chaos.

Having decided Gwalior's accommodation was a dead loss, I continued west towards Agra. The town of Agra was nothing special, a messy collection of factories, warehouses and rundown houses, but the Taj Mahal was something else. My first glimpse of the ethereal palace – like most tourists and travellers, seen through an arch that led into the gardens in front of it – simply took my breath away. I was bowled over and returned to the building and its grounds four times, including at sunrise and sunset, but unfortunately failed to see it with a full moon or any water in the ponds. Nevertheless it left me speechless. The Taj's proportions, its beautiful pale cream stone and its position in its environment were perfect.

As agreed with Robert in Kathmandu, I left a message in the post office for him in case he arrived after me. He'd left no message for me, so I assumed I was ahead of him or that he'd passed through without stopping and that we might meet in Jaipur, the next city at which we'd agreed to leave messages for each other.

At the end of my third day in Agra, I returned to the walled compound where I and a few other Westerners were staying. To my surprise, I found Robert sitting there, beside his bike. Robert introduced me to John, a long-haired, bearded man in his mid-twenties who smiled nicely and nodded at me.

I guessed John was the owner of a Honda XL500 with a British number plate I'd noticed parked next to Robert's BMW.

'And I'm Sarah, John's mother,' said a hippyish woman in her mid-fifties.

'Hello.' I shook hands with John and offered my hand to Sarah, who hesitated before shaking it.

'Did you travel here together?' I asked Robert and John.

'Well, I didn't have much choice,' said Sarah. 'I was on John's pillion.'

Surprised by Sarah's spikiness, I tried to clarify my question: 'I meant did all three of you travel here together or did you meet here?'

Robert explained that they'd met on the road a few days ago and joked that John was pioneering the ultimate low-tech approach to long-distance motorcycle touring.

Glancing over at John's bike, I could see what Robert meant. John had bungee-strapped a blue milk crate to carry all his kit onto the back of his single-cylinder XL500. As a dual-purpose trail bike with a short seat, it was not designed to carry a passenger any distance, nor much kit.

'Did you ride like that all the way from London?' I asked John and his mother.

'He did . . .' – Sarah pointed at her son, a scowl on her face – '. . . and then he picked me up at Delhi airport.'

'That must have been nice for you.'

'It's meant to be a holiday,' she replied, her eyes cold, her expression unsmiling. 'We've just come down from Kashmir.'

'I see.' I was feeling more and more awkward. 'Are you enjoying yourself?'

'It's not about enjoyment. It's a challenge.'

I was completely thrown by John's mother, but determined not to show it. 'So how's it been?'

'Amazing.' Her voice was flat, as if she couldn't be bothered with me.

Sensing the awkwardness, Robert chipped in. 'Elspeth is riding around the world. She started in London and we met in Kathmandu.'

'That must be nice for you.'

I didn't know what to say, so I simply smiled. As the evening went on, I watched John and Sarah. Although John was very quiet, the two of them appeared to get along well, but there was a lot of tension, which reassured me that I wasn't the only person who put her nose out of joint.

At breakfast the next day, Robert suggested that we ride together to Jaipur.

'With her?' said Sarah, nodding her head towards me with a look of disdain.

'Of course,' said John and Robert in unison.

We had a good day's ride, but the best of it came when we stopped in a village to buy some vegetables. Leaving John to look after our bikes, Robert and I glanced back as we walked away. John was lying back on his bike, surrounded by hundreds of Indians. It was as if none of the locals had ever seen motorbikes before. They were hanging out of windows and even standing on rooftops all along the street, craning for a view. John just lay back and stared up at the sky, his expression one of total despair and helplessness. Robert and I laughed at the absurdity of it all. I was relieved to be travelling with Robert and John, their company a huge comfort in these crowd situations that seemed an inevitable part of riding a motorbike in India. Not having to deal with it all on my own made a hell of a difference.

Later in the day, with darkness approaching fast, we stopped near the edge of a small town to discuss where to camp.

'We can't camp here,' said Robert. 'Far too many people.'

'Maybe if we ride another five miles, we'll find something,' said John. 'But it's nearly dark. We need to get on with it.'

'I'll lead,' I volunteered, 'You follow me.'

Within a minute of setting off, I regretted my offer. In the short time we'd stopped, it had become fully dark and chickens, dogs, goats, people, cyclists, cars and trucks coursed everywhere, appearing randomly around me as I led our three bikes deeper into the darkness. The fact that none of the vehicles had lights didn't stop them moving just as fast as in daylight.

'How can these people see?' said Robert when we stopped in a field. 'You can't see them; how can they see us?'

I wondered if the Hindu philosophy of death and reincarnation might have something to do with it. I explained to Robert their belief that everyone enters the world with their life's journey determined, meaning that the time of their death is pre-ordained. Robert gave me a puzzled look. He found it a difficult concept to grasp.

We pitched our camp, cooked and ate a meal, then crawled into our tents. I'd sent my tent home from Perth, so I shared with Robert, pressed against each other like brother and sister. The next morning, I sensed that Robert and I were not alone when we woke. It was quiet outside, but I thought I heard occasional murmurs and could see shadows on the side of the tent. Leaning close to Robert, I mouthed, 'I think there's someone out there?' Robert sat up, leant forwards, pushed the bottom of the zip up a few inches and peered through the gap. He almost jumped back with surprise and beckoned to me to look through the gap.

A row of little dark toes stretched in front of the tent from left to right as far as I could see. 'Oh my God . . .' I whispered. 'How long have they been waiting there?'

'I know . . .' whispered Robert. 'They're fucking mad.'

Taking deep breaths, we lifted the zip all the way and crawled out of the tent.

'Aaaaah!' A collective gasp of astonishment greeted us.

Smiling, we bowed to our audience, then stepped forward in the hope that the crowd of about twenty would step backwards to give us some space, but no one shifted.

'What now?' said Robert.

'Pack up and go, I suppose,' I said.

Fifteen minutes later, we were ready to leave with John and his mother. I swung my leg up and eased myself onto my bike, gripped the throttle and pressed the magic button.

'Oooh, selfie start . . . selfie start,' rippled through the crowd. It was going to be another long day.

A few hours later, we arrived in Jaipur, a beautiful city famous for its red and pink sandstone buildings, among them the Palace of the Winds and the enormously impressive City Palace, which we visited in the afternoon. This first stop in Rajasthan immediately felt different from Uttar Pradesh and the industrial belt that we'd left behind. The air seemed sweeter, the climate milder and less humid, the streets less frenetic and more colourful, the people calmer and less intrusive. The locals even looked different from those in the industrial belt, the men wearing amazing turbans in startlingly bright colours. This was closer to the India of my imagination, a place of exoticism, colour and mystery.

At breakfast after our first night in Jaipur, John announced that he was going to ride up to Delhi and put his mother on a plane back to England.

'She's been moaning for days about the discomforts of riding pillion,' he said. 'I think we've both had enough of each other.'

I was ready to leave Jaipur too, but first I needed to get the visa that the border official specified when I entered India. Robert and I rode to the police station, where we were directed to the office at which I could obtain the required documents. Predictably, the official demanded 150 rupees *baksheesh* to process my visa within the regulation forty-eight hours. Two other travellers waiting in the queue, a New Zealander and an American taxi driver recuperating from hepatitis, also refused to pay the bribe, so we spent five days together, drinking tea and moaning about the difficulties of dealing with Indian bureaucrats. On the final day, we all returned to the office and obtained our visas in five minutes flat.

A short day's ride took Robert and me to Pushkar, a pilgrim destination beside a small lake in the middle of a rocky desert that had become a magnet for hippies. Although the journey was short, the road was littered with crashes. Most days we'd see eight or ten accidents, but on this short stretch of road, we saw two or three times as many. Some of them were totally bizarre – a lorry lay overturned in the middle of a field; a truck that had collided with the only telegraph pole, ending up perpendicular to the road, blocking it completely.

When vehicles were damaged or broke down, the drivers never moved them to the side of the road. Instead, they repaired them in the middle of the carriageway, jacked up and supported on rocks they'd collected from the surrounding area. Then, when they'd finished their repairs, they drove off, leaving the huge rocks in the middle of the road, ready to cause another accident.

About halfway between Jaipur and Pushkar, I was riding behind Robert as a truck approached on the opposite side of the road. Even from a quarter of a mile away, we could see that it was alarmingly overloaded. The goods strapped to the sides and top of the truck more than doubled its width and height. As the truck approached, the payload started to wobble, so the driver steered from side to side in an attempt to counteract this. But the more the driver tried to correct it, the further his payload leant over, until he lost control of the truck and it started to swerve from one side of the road to the other.

Robert and I pulled to an abrupt stop in the middle of the road, our eyes fixed on the truck. Waiting for the moment when it was almost upon us, our hands gripped our throttles, ready to gun our engines and ride whichever way would dodge the errant vehicle's path.

Fifty feet in front of us, the truck skidded and toppled over, smashing onto its side in the middle of the road. For a few moments, the road was silent and nothing moved. Then the driver and several passengers appeared, scrambling out of the cab. Assured that no one was hurt, Robert and I looked at each other, shook our heads in disbelief and rode on. Everything here seemed to end in complete chaos.

At Pushkar, we found a spot on a lawn in the Tourist Bungalows compound, pitched Robert's tent, then walked around the town and had a relaxed day. In spite of the crazy traffic, I was enjoying Rajasthan. Being with Robert helped, but Rajasthan itself was definitely less hassle. From Pushkar, we rode for four hours to a beautiful valley, where we hired a camel to take us up from the small town of Ranakpur to a spectacular Jain temple with 1,444 marble pillars, each of which was uniquely carved. We spent most of the day wandering around the temple, transfixed by its scale and beauty, then spent a night in Ranakpur before heading for Jodhpur along a wet and muddy road. We'd stopped in a village to buy some vegetables when I pointed out to Robert that his bike's rear tyre was soft.

'Fuck!' Robert kicked the ground. 'A fuckin' puncture.'

Although generally mild-mannered, Robert was reacting increasingly angrily to any stress or obstacles he encountered. I wondered if it was a delayed reaction to his accident and his horrific experiences in the Indian hospital.

Robert crouched down by the side of his bike and started to deal with the puncture. I bent down to give him a hand. On a good day, we could both repair a puncture in less than half an hour. On this occasion, we were surrounded by onlookers within a couple of minutes, their toes pushing closer to us as new voyeurs joined the crowd and craned forwards for a look. Within ten minutes, we were surrounded by a huge crowd of men, most of whom had no idea that we were at the centre of the melee, their curiosity piqued only by the crowd.

At the centre of it all, crouched over the punctured tyre, Robert and I sweated; superheated by the throbbing mass of people as well as the usual heat of India, we nearly expired. Surrounded by dozens of heads, some peering from behind us over our shoulders, others standing in front of us, staring into our faces, all of them breathing heavily, Robert and I started to suffocate.

'There's no oxygen!' shouted Robert. 'I can't breathe here.'

Looking at Robert, he was pale and clammy. I grabbed my tank bag, thrust it out in front of me repeatedly and shouted 'Get back!' Pushing into the crowd, I swung my bag ahead of me to make them back off. 'Back!' I yelled.

Robert stood up, tipped his head, swaying as he sucked in oxygen, then returned to crouching beside his wheel while I now concentrated all my efforts on securing enough space around Robert for him to be able to breathe. Rajasthan was turning out to be just as demanding and exhausting as any other part of India.

After repairing Robert's tyre, we spent two days and nights in Jodhpur, before heading to Jaisalmer, the supposed pearl of Rajasthan in the heart of the Thar Desert, close to the Pakistan border.

About forty miles out of Jodhpur, riding along an empty road, Robert was roughly fifty yards ahead of me when I spotted a man in a white knee-length tunic. He was walking along the side of the road, holding the hand of a girl I assumed to be his daughter. As Robert passed him, the man looked at Robert on his bike, then turned around and looked straight at me. For a brief moment, everything stopped moving. A shiver ran down my spine. I was sure he'd spotted me. And something about it really didn't feel right.

Drawing level with the man, my mouth felt dry, my knees weak.

And then it happened. A sudden movement and a blur of brown limbs. The man's bright white tunic flashed near me. A head with long dark hair smacked against my headlight.

Don't stop. Don't ever stop.

The words I'd heard so many times in India rang through my head: *If you hit anyone, do not stop. Just keep going.*

But I looked in my mirror and saw a body lying at the side of the road.

It was the little girl, the one who'd been holding the man's hand. And she wasn't moving.

Like many travellers, I'd heard stories of scams that desperate parents apparently pulled in India. I'd questioned the truth of tales in which children were deliberately blinded or crippled to elicit sympathy when begging. I'd thought that stories of parents throwing their children in front of vehicles to extort compensation were just lazy Western racism. But now something very similar seemed to be happening to me.

But the girl – an innocent, no more than nine or ten years old – was lying motionless on the road. I had to stop.

I turned my bike around and rode back towards the girl in the dirt as her father came running up the road, away from her, directly towards me. Swerving around him, I rode to the girl's side, got off my bike, dropped to my knees beside her. I touched the girl's face. Her eyes were closed.

Behind me, I heard Robert's engine. Suddenly the man in the white tunic was in front of me, pressing a finger against my chest. 'Rupee! Rupee!' His face close to mine, he rubbed his fingers together. 'Rupee!'

For a second I was speechless, then I came to my senses. 'You haven't even looked at your daughter. She's lying there and you don't even know if she's alive.'

Now that he was close to me, I could see the father was filthy and bedraggled. Unkempt, greasy grey hair poked out from beneath a stained and dirty turban. 'Rupee!' The father rubbed his fingers in my face again. 'You give me rupee.'

I was so angry that I pushed him aside and crouched down beside the girl again. 'Are you okay?' The girl smiled weakly. She had a few splinters of glass in her forehead, but she was not bleeding heavily.

Robert and I helped the girl sit up, then I ran over to my bike, the girl's father permanently by my side, hectoring me for rupees. Rummaging through my panniers, I located my first aid kit.

'Rupee . . .' – the father was still rubbing his fingers in my face – '. . . you give me rupee!'

'Fuck off!'

Turning away from me, the father grabbed Robert by the throat. 'Rupee! Give me now!'

Fearing that Robert would hit the man, I jumped up and pulled the man's hand away from Robert's throat.

'Leave us alone!' I yelled. ' Look at your daughter – she's injured.'

While I attended to his daughter's injuries, picking glass out of her forehead and hair, checking she was otherwise not harmed, her father breathed down my neck, repeating his demand for rupees.

Delving deep into my panniers, I found the *cura* given to me by the farmer's wife when I hit the dog in rural Thailand and used it to disinfect the girl's wounds. I put cream on her burns, then dressed and bandaged her arms and head. While I was nursing the girl, a bus pulled up beside us. Dozens of Indian heads poked out of windows all along the side of the bus, most of them shouting to the father, working him up into an even greater state of agitation. Inside the bus, arms were waving and mouths were yapping. It appeared everyone had a very strong opinion about the poor girl's accident. And I suspected none of those opinions favoured me.

Twenty minutes later, a second bus arrived and parked behind the first bus. Another sea of Indian faces appeared, protruding through the bus's open windows. As if prompted, the occupants of the first bus all sat down as their driver started up the engine and drove off. The second bus advanced a few metres to give its occupants a turn at shouting and gesticulating at the father, who now stood silent, too overwhelmed to maintain his faked outrage and trumped-up demands for compensation.

A third bus turned up, disgorged its occupants onto the highway for a closer look of me tending to the girl. Robert tried to hold them back, but like Canute, he was powerless against the tide.

'Can't you do anything?' I asked Robert.

'There's too many of them,' he said.

Finally, a military Jeep pulled up with an official dressed in a smart khaki uniform.

'What's going on here?' The official's imperious tone silenced the crowd.

I explained what had happened.

The official sighed. 'Just give them some money. Twenty rupees or they'll never let you leave.'

'And if we don't pay?' I said.

'They're very tribal around here. The whole village will come after you.'

I finished bandaging up the girl and gave her father as much as the official had suggested, a sum equivalent then to two US dollars. His eyes lit up and a beaming smile revealed several missing teeth. From that I took it he was extremely pleased with the result.

Riding away, I consoled myself that I hadn't seriously injured the girl and that the accident was not my fault. But I was shocked at the desperation of the father and the lengths he was apparently willing to go to secure a few rupees. I was also surprised at how little I thought of the girl in the coming days. After only a month in India, the country had hardened me.

16

THROUGH THE STORM:
DELHI TO SRINAGAR

Rajasthan, 6 July 1984

We didn't make it to our intended destination of Jaisalmer by nightfall, and were forced to camp in the desert in a sandstorm. By the time we'd unpacked, everything we owned was encrusted with fine white granules. The weather had changed, becoming very hot and sticky, which made the sand stick to everything even more.

As usual, Robert and I spent every moment chatting about ourselves, our surroundings, our thoughts, our dreams and our ambitions. It felt as if there were never enough hours in the day to squeeze in all the things we had to say. Even as the wind whipped sand around us, we jabbered to each other for the entire time we were pitching Robert's tent.

Eventually dropping off to sleep, I awoke the next morning to silence. The storm had passed, but when we clambered out of the tent, we saw that the damage was extensive. Both bikes had been blown over and the engines were clogged with sand that had to be cleaned away before we could ride.

By afternoon we were in Jaisalmer, once again chatting away as I repaired an electrical fault on my bike and Robert cleaned his air filter. By trade a mechanic, Robert had ridden nearly 200,000 kilometres on his BMW R80/7, so there was very little he didn't know about our bikes. His assistance, particularly after months of never being sure if my repairs were the right thing, was enormously helpful and reassuring.

Robert and I spent the next day exploring Jaisalmer, the most beautiful city I visited in India, the highlight of which was a stunning fort that, unlike most in India, was still inhabited and working. Then, for three days, we did very little except wander the streets, rest, eat and drink. With anyone else, I would have found spending every hour of every day with just them for company quite intense and stressful, but I found being with Robert effortless. We always seemed to have something to say to each other and the time passed in a blur.

'We could just ride through the desert into Pakistan,' suggested Robert over breakfast one morning. 'Save ourselves the hassle at the border.'

The idea of exiting India immediately was beguiling, but I'd always wanted to see Kashmir. So we continued our journey the next day by riding parallel to the Pakistan border to Bikaner, an uneventful ride apart from seeing the same workmen shovelling the same sand dunes as when we'd approached Jaisalmer from Jodhpur five days earlier. Like the painting of the Forth Road Bridge, clearing sand dunes appeared to be an unending task. The workmen cleared sand from one stretch of road, moved along a few hundred metres to clear another stretch, by which time blown sand was re-forming a dune at the location they had just cleared. It was like Sisyphus trying to roll his boulder to the top of a hill. What a life.

From Bikaner, we headed east to Delhi, a long ride on a very busy road. By late afternoon, I needed fuel and we pulled up at a shack beside a petrol pump. No attendant appeared, so I got off my bike and stuck my head inside the shack, then reported back to Robert.

'Empty.'

I looked around.

'Nobody,' I said. Robert sucked in a deep breath, held it, then exhaled with a long sigh. 'Let's try somewhere else?' I swung my leg over my bike and was about to leave when a man in a tunic appeared from behind a bush. He held up his hand as if to say, 'Don't move', then crossed the road and entered a house. A few minutes later, a boy came out of the house, followed by the man, and ran off across a field.

'Do you know what's going on?' I said to Robert.

He shook his head. 'No idea.'

The man returned, ignoring us as he walked past Robert and entered the shack.

'What now?' I said.

'Fucking idiots,' murmured Robert. 'I don't know.'

I got back off my bike, looked in the shack and found the man sitting on an oil can. He smiled weakly, then looked away. We were about to leave when the boy ran up, carrying a handle.

'Ah! For the pump,' said Robert.

The man reappeared, fitted the handle to the manual petrol pump and gestured for me to fill up my tank. I looked at my watch. Nearly twenty minutes had passed since we stopped for some petrol.

'Elspeth. Look at this.' Robert was pointing at the pump. 'The gauge isn't turning.'

'Again?' It wasn't the first time we'd encountered a pump with a rigged, faulty or broken gauge.

By now, my tank was full. The attendant held up six fingers and asked for enough rupees to pay for six gallons of fuel.

'But my tank takes only five gallons.'

'Six.' He showed me his palm.

'No.' My patience was wearing thin.

The argument went on for a few minutes until I'd had enough. I put the correct amount of money to pay for five gallons on the attendant's upturned palm and we rode off immediately, with the man shouting and waving his arms as he chased us down the road. The simplest task always turned into a major performance, taking hours and invariably ending up with an argument. Why did everything have to be so difficult?

Dealing with the hassles of riding in India – sometimes a dozen or more of them in a day – pulled Robert and me closer together. We became a team, helping each other get through it all. But I worried all the time that eventually it would be too much for Robert – he seemed to be becoming increasingly frustrated with it all. I started to worry that, when I least expected, he would completely lose it.

*

We didn't quite make it to Delhi that night, so we stopped and camped out in the scrub. No sooner had we got the tent up than a very heavy monsoonal rainstorm broke. To a soundtrack of screams, yelps and giggles, we shot into the tent, pulled off our soaking clothes and lay back on the groundsheet.

'What about our sleeping bags, our things?' I said. Most of our belongings were still packed on our bikes.

'When the rain stops, we'll get them,' said Robert. 'Right now, we can't even see our bikes through the rain.'

But within ten minutes, the water outside the tent was several inches deep and coming in through the zip. If we hadn't been inside the tent, it would have floated away. Wearing only pants and a vest, I joined Robert outside to dig a trench in the downpour.

'This is hopeless,' I said. 'Everything's soaked.'

We decided to pack up in the dark and move on. About three miles further on, the road and all our surroundings were bone dry. We stopped at a small stall that sold chai during the day. Open on all sides to the elements, it was no more than six posts that supported a grass roof. The owner was lying on the floor, so we asked him if we could join him and sleep under the cover of his stall.

'Why not?' he said.

I looked at Robert, who laughed and said, 'Well, there's no answer to that, is there?'

We rode our bikes under the roof, unrolled our sleeping bags and tried to fall asleep, but within a few minutes the storm caught up with us and drips started to fall from the ceiling.

'Fuck,' said Robert. I knew how he felt.

We packed up our sleeping bags, put on our waterproofs, rolled out a tarpaulin and tried to go to sleep on it. The rain became heavier.

'Fuck,' said Robert again. He fetched two green plastic bags from his bike, gave me one. 'Put it over your head to keep it dry.'

By six o'clock we abandoned any hope of sleeping that night, boiled water in the billycan and had a cup of tea before leaving for

Delhi. Approaching the city on a dual carriageway, we came to a complete stop because a truck and trailer had attempted an overtake and ended up perched on the central reservation. The central barrier was higher than the truck's axles, raising the driving wheels of the truck above the road, dangling impotently. Of course every vehicle had to stop and have a look, and the inevitable crowd of a few dozen Indian men were standing in the road, waving hands and shouting, all barking instructions at the driver, who sat forlornly in his cab. We weaved through the hold-up and continued into Delhi, finding a place to stay in the Tourist Camp, a totally chaotic place. This stretch of green parkland was surrounded by buildings made of concrete breezeblocks that could be rented. Although the buildings were like prison cells and the parkland was filthy and overrun by rats, the Tourist Camp was a guarded compound and therefore the only place we knew in Delhi where it was safe to leave our bikes.

Like many of the occupants of the concrete cells, I'd come to Delhi primarily to obtain visas and permits for my onward journey. I needed an Iranian transit visa and a permit from the Ministry of Home Affairs to enter Punjab, a new requirement for foreigners following Sikh unrest and rioting in the state.

The Iranian visa was relatively straightforward, as the number of Westerners making applications had dwindled to a trickle since the Iranian revolution and the outbreak of the Iran–Iraq war. The Punjab permit, administered by Indian bureaucracy, was far more complicated. Robert and I spent two days at the ministry, trying to find out which official and which department could issue us with the necessary paperwork. Eventually we tracked down Mr T. O. Khakha, a short, clean-shaven man in his forties who seemed to revel in his position of power. After a succession of refusals, we were told we could return in a week to collect our documents. I killed time riding around with Robert, visiting Edwin Lutyens's many beautiful buildings in New Delhi. One evening, we met a very well-dressed Indian in Connaught Place who took delight in telling us about what he regarded as the 'idiocy of tourists'.

'They spend heaps of money,' he said. 'I have seen them paying one hundred rupees just to have their ears cleaned. And a Canadian tourist who I met paid twenty rupees for a pair of shoelaces.' Our newly acquired Indian friend shook his head. 'I took him back to the shop to get his money back. He should only pay one or two rupees.'

'And what did the shopkeeper say?' I asked.

'He was not too keen about all this.'

'So what did you do?'

'I told him his fortune.' The Indian smiled and we knew exactly what he meant. From then on, 'tell him his fortune' became shorthand between Robert and me for any situation in which we felt someone needed to be made aware that their behaviour was unacceptable.

Back at the camp, Robert and I sat outside our concrete cell while a bunch of Nigerians, South Americans and Iranians played football and, like us, waited for their travel documents to be processed. With spare time on our hands, at last I had a chance to meet some other travellers, including a very nice English girl called Monique, who had bought two 1940 Indian motorcycles with sidecars and was hoping to take them home to sell for a profit but was struggling with the mountain of paperwork needed to export her bikes. I also met Michel, a French taxi driver who had driven a Renault 4 van from Paris to Bali and was now on his way home. His journey had started with two cars and four people, but all his fellow travellers had abandoned the trip when it became too much for them. Michel was very nice, but travel-weary. Desperate to fly home, he had to drive back to France because, in common with us, his carnet didn't allow him to exit India without his vehicle. He also had a contract with his sponsors that he had to fulfil.

One evening I found Robert running his finger over a logo that I'd drawn on my top box in Sydney. 'Is that meant to be you?' he said, pointing at the simple graphic, which showed a figure leaning a motorbike into a bend. 'Yes,' I said. 'I designed it ages ago, in London, then put it there after I built my luggage boxes.'

'I noticed it some time ago,' said Robert. 'I like it.' He asked if I could draw it in his diary so he could keep it as a memento. I handed the diary back when I'd finished and as he looked at the motorcyclist logo, he traced the outline of my sketch with his finger and smiled.

A few days later, I returned with Robert to the Ministry of Home Affairs. Having been told to wait a week for our documents, we were again made to jump through numerous needless bureaucratic hoops until, towards the end of the working day, we were finally allowed into Mr Khakha's office.

'You want your travel permits?' Mr Khakha said as we entered.

'Yes.'

'And you've been waiting how long?'

'Eight days.' I tried to keep the frustration and impatience out of my voice.

'Come back tomorrow.'

Two days later, travel permits in hand, we finally left Delhi. The documents permitted us to travel through Punjab for twenty-eight days, which we hoped would be just enough to pass through the state on our way up to Srinagar in Kashmir, then return through Punjab on our way to the Pakistan border.

After an overnight stay in Jagadhri, at the foot of the Himalayas, we started the slow ascent up to the mountains, stopping for a night in Solan that turned into an unintended longer stay. Having felt weak for a few days, by the time we arrived in Solan, I felt quite ill. As soon as we entered our guesthouse room, I ran to the toilet, not quite sure which end of myself to point at the bowl first. Vomit and diarrhoea gushed from either end of me, although there was little to tell them apart. Eventually I worked out how to expel from both orifices simultaneously by sitting on the toilet with my head bowed between my knees.

Faced with the symptoms and consequences of dysentery, I was hugely relieved to have Robert at my side. For months I'd been worried about falling ill somewhere on my own, becoming gradually weaker and possibly even dying because I had no one to get water or food. Lying on my bed in the guesthouse room, staring at its bare white walls, I felt as if I was going to die. The stomach cramps, weakness, sweats and my complete inability to keep anything in myself were the worst I'd ever experienced. Even a tiny sip of water would make me immediately throw up. Fortunately Robert had found us a room with an en suite bathroom and a proper toilet, not a hole in the ground. Even so, the three steps from my bed to the toilet often felt like an insurmountable hurdle.

After not eating or drinking anything for several days, I felt totally drained and helpless, but knew we needed to get moving. Weak and aching, I climbed on my bike and set off for Shimla. A few hours later, we stopped by a river so that I could go to the toilet and wash off the road dust. Pulling up my trousers, I realized I'd taken them down without undoing them, an indication of how much weight I'd lost. I looked at Robert. He was even thinner than me, just skin and bone, largely from the months he'd spent in hospital after his accident, barely eating while waiting for his broken bones to mend.

We rode on, my illness dominating the day, making me overlook the routine tasks of travelling, such as removing the bottom part of my tank bag from my bike at the end of that day's ride. As we left our hotel in Shimla the next morning, I discovered someone had stolen the base of my tank bag from my bike, even though it was totally useless to them. Infuriated that I now couldn't attach my tank bag to my bike, I stomped up to the manager, who had guaranteed us the safety of our bikes.

'I'm not paying our bill,' I said.

'But you have to pay.'

'Not if you don't keep to your side of the bargain.'

'What did we do wrong?'

'You let someone steal part of my tank bag from my bike.'

'That's your problem.'

'Whoever stole it, stole it only because you didn't secure our bikes properly,' I said.

The manager bobbed his head. 'It's not my problem.'

We argued for half an hour, eventually ending up at the police station, where I submitted a complaint against the manager, although I held little hope of a result. Three hours later, to my great surprise, the police had intervened and we were absolved of having to pay our hotel bill. Nevertheless, we still had to find some way of securing my tank bag to my bike. Robert had an old belt, which he cut in two lengthways. Using some of my pop rivets, he fixed it to a scrap of leather that we found. We fastened it to the top of my tank and used the belt buckle and a bungee to secure my bag. It worked, although now, while riding, my tank bag would slowly slip off the tank, down to one side until it rested on my right knee. I had to haul the bag back up onto the top of the tank a few times every hour, an irritation and a constant reminder of India that I would now have to endure all the way home.

As we put on our helmets and prepared to leave the town, Robert turned to me and said with a smile, 'Maybe we'll see the person who stole your tank bag base walking down the street, wearing it as a hat.' We both laughed at the thought of it. Nothing would have surprised me any more.

We didn't leave until early afternoon because of the theft, and consequently only reached Shimla that night, where we were offered a cheap hotel room in return for taking a message to Srinagar. Continuing to climb up into the mountains, we rode for the next few days along cool tree-lined roads through dense forests. It was stunningly beautiful, but also very demanding. Some of the roads were terrible, washed away or obscured by landslides brought down by the monsoon. Riding often in the rain, it was hard work. Random potholes dotted the roads (when there was a hard road surface) and many of the other vehicles behaved as if they were the only road users in India. The basic rule of the road was that size mattered; most of the time we seemed invisible to other road users, only cyclists and pedestrians acknowledging us.

Approaching Palampur, a hill station town surrounded by tea plantations, I was riding along a single-track road when a cow appeared as if from nowhere. I swerved, but clipped the back of it and was thrown off my bike, which careered on its own into a river.

Brushing mud off myself, I clambered down the riverbank and with Robert's help pulled my bike out of the river. I'd almost got it out of the water when a group of Sikh bikers turned up on Royal Enfields. In their blue waterproof ponchos and matching plastic bags over their turbans, they looked really cool. They were friendly and spoke very good English.

'Where are you going?' one of them said.

'Srinagar,' said Robert, 'then maybe Ladakh.'

They warned us to take care. 'The roads are worse there than here. Are you going back through the Punjab?'

We explained that we needed to pass through Punjab to get to the border.

'Be careful there, too. There's a lot of trouble. Don't exceed the time allowed by your permit.'

It was enlightening to hear about the troubles in Punjab from the Sikh perspective. Travelling constantly, it was difficult to keep abreast of current events. Although English-language newspapers were rarely available, I'd heard about the Sikh demands for an independent homeland, called Khalistan, in Punjab. And I'd also picked up on reports of Indian troops storming the Golden Temple in Amritsar, which had been occupied for several years by Sikh militants, some of whom had supposedly been armed with machine guns and rifles.

However, until we met the Sikh bikers, I hadn't realized that the Indian army's bombardment, shelling and storming of the temple had led to the deaths of so many civilians. According to the Sikhs, who said the government's official figure of 493 civilian casualties was a cover-up, more than 20,000 civilians had died in the five-day military operation.

At the bikers' recommendation, we found accommodation in Palampur at the Agricultural University, where we got an entire house and VIP treatment for a bargain eight rupees. By the end of the next day we were in Dharamsala, home to the Dalai Lama and the Tibetan government in exile. Although very pleasant, it was crawling with tourists and drugs, both of which I avoided by taking residence in the television lounge of our hostel, getting a rare fix of the box by watching three hours of the Los Angeles Olympics over a huge banana pancake, much to the disappointment of Robert, who hated television.

Two more days' riding, including an overnight stop at Mansar Lake, brought us at last to Srinagar. At the end of a beautiful

day with scenery to match, we arrived   shortly before dusk and
went straight to the American Express office, where I picked up
letters from Mark and my family. After rejecting dozens of offers of
houseboat rentals, Robert and I wound up in a small hotel, where
I lay on my bed and turned first to the letter from Mark, feeling
slightly guilty that I had barely thought of him since we said our
farewells in Kathmandu.

'I've been thinking about you a lot lately,' Mark wrote from
Jaisalmer.

> I find it hard to believe that in ten days I will be on the plane home
> and you will still be fighting it out in India. Every time we say
> goodbye I try to be light-hearted, but last time was particularly
> hard as I knew you were starting on the most difficult part of
> your trip and I wouldn't be there to see it through.
>
> Looking back, I think it was absolutely right for me to go to
> New Zealand when I did. I did it for love, and I'm glad.
>
> I've got to get used to the idea that the last one and a half years
> has been a thing for me, you, my pack and your bike, and that
> people at home will not begin to understand because it's so far
> outside their frame of reference.

The events that drew Mark to New Zealand now felt to me like
something that someone else had told me had happened to them.
Two months had elapsed since Mark and I had last seen each other
and I'd spent all of them battling India, fortunately with someone
who made the hardships a little easier. But as I read Mark's letter, I
realized that although he had slipped from my thoughts, I was very
much still at the forefront of his mind. At the end of his letter, Mark
warned me about the restrictions he'd experienced as a result of
what he called the 'farcical performance as a result of the change in
visa rules'.

'Bit tricky getting used to the change of status from forty-nine
years to a police report on arrival in every town,' Mark wrote.
'When I arrived in Bombay, I read in the paper that they were
actually stopping people getting on their planes if they didn't have

the correct documents. Typical lack of initiative by those petty officials too scared to make a common-sense decision on their own. Some things in India I won't be sad to leave behind.'

My father wrote to me on his new typewriter, which he proudly informed me had '3KB of memory and would function as a printer if connected to a Word Processor etc.'.

Mostly, the letter relayed news about family weddings, exam results and my father's attempts to lay a new carpet in his consulting room and buy a car at an auction, his latest penny-pinching discovery, all of which seemed very remote from Kashmir, but towards the end he wrote something that reminded me strongly of home.

One thing I did while Mummy was away (a good time because it makes a temporary mess of the kitchen) was to brew a lot of wine. When Woolworths had a sale, I bought a lot of tins of grape concentrate, reduced from £2.50 to 99p. I have had these for a long time and one of the tins blew, which made an awful mess, so I thought I would use them up and I used up eighteen tins today. One tin makes one gallon. The wine isn't awfully good, but it's drinkable.

Reading about my father's industrial-scale winemaking brought a lump to my throat, which grew in size when I read the final sentence in Dad's letter.

'I hope that trekking around Annapurna went well (Justin was amazed at the idea of you trekking), that Delhi, Agra and Varanasi were enjoyable and not too incredibly hot, and that you and Mark are both well and happy.'

I read the final line again and thought about my father's association of Mark travelling with me and his concern about our mutual well-being. Then I looked across at Robert, dozing on the bed next to mine and wondered what was really going on between us.

Travelling had become so much easier with Robert. Thanks to his friendship and support, I felt like I was on holiday for the first time in the entire trip. Everything felt right; we were travelling, getting along great, making the journey easier for each other by laughing about the eccentricities of India and its mindless bureaucracy. I was relaxed and we never argued, even in the most demanding circumstances.

Of course I realized that Robert and I were two young, fit and relatively healthy people, and I was very aware that many couples in similar circumstances ended up sleeping together. In some cases, they even fell in love. I didn't find Robert unattractive, but I was certain I didn't want any kind of romantic relationship with him. I was enjoying every moment of every day with Robert and didn't want anything to risk ruining a fantastic friendship. After throwing everything I had into my relationship with Alex, who I'd thought of as a soulmate, and being rewarded with heartbreak and confusion, I was wary of making the same mistake again. Maybe that's why I'd recently become more comfortable about thinking of Mark as a partner. In all sorts of ways, Mark and I were very different, but events and common experiences had pulled us together. Maybe it was better that way.

I didn't want to allow anything to make my life in India any more complicated than it already was, particularly as I had no idea how Robert felt about me. In my mind, I was still with Mark and I vowed to do everything I could to avoid thinking about Robert as anything more than just a very good friend.

17

FALLING AGAIN:
KASHMIR

Srinagar, 3 August 1984

The summer capital of Kashmir lived up to its reputation of being idyllic, cool and beautiful. After the heat of the Indian plains, it felt like we had entered an oasis in which the temperature was always pleasant. Built around a lake and very tranquil, Srinagar's only shortcomings were the huge crowds of tourists and the number of hippies it attracted, so on the second day we looked for a houseboat located outside the town. Eventually we found a suitable boat about four miles from Srinagar in a restful, peaceful location that was safe enough for us to leave our bikes parked on the shore, next to the boat.

After a very pleasant evening eating off china plates in the luxurious dining room of the boat, we were abruptly woken early the next morning by the boat's owner. 'Out . . . out . . . out . . .' he shouted as we forced open our eyes. The owner had been offered a better rate by a tourist group and now wanted us off his boat as soon as possible. We managed to find another houseboat nearby and spent the day servicing our bikes. I discovered my rear bevel seal was leaking, which explained why I had no rear brake, but without the parts and the specialised BMW tool there was no way we could fix this. My entire bike was now becoming a bit of a challenge, in particular the electrics, which took all the following day to repair as we attempted to fix my ignition yet again and solder the horn wire back into the switch.

That evening, after we had eaten, Robert and I were lying on the deck, reading books and writing in our diaries. I'd noticed that Robert had been much quieter than usual that day. For once, we hadn't spent every available minute chatting.

'Are you all right?' I asked.

Robert nodded. 'Yeah.'

'You sure?'

He nodded again, a bit too vigorously. 'I'm fine.'

I sensed he wasn't as fine as he claimed. He didn't seem himself and I knew something was bothering him.

Later that night, lying in the bedroom of our houseboat, Robert seemed restless, tossing and turning in the bed next to mine. 'Are you okay?' I said again.

'Yeah – it's nothing.'

'Nothing?'

Robert didn't reply, just groaned before sitting up in his bed and swinging his legs onto the floor. Switching on a small light, he sat on the edge of his bed, his head in his hands.

'What's the matter?'

A long sigh, then silence.

'Come on,' I said. 'What's the matter?'

Another sigh. 'I can't do this any more. I just can't.'

'What?' I was worried that Robert wanted to ride on without me.

'I just can't . . . I really can't . . .'

'Can't what, Robert?' I sat up in bed, laid my hand on his arm and spoke softly. 'What can't you do?'

Robert held his breath, then exhaled suddenly through his nostrils. He was clearly troubled.

I moved over to Robert's bed, sat beside him and held his hand. He seemed really agitated. 'Come on,' I said, 'you can tell me.'

'I can't . . . I can't . . .' he said, shaking his head.

It all felt very weird. I had no idea what was going on in his head, but started to worry that maybe he was as confused about our friendship as I was. We had become so close, and yet I guessed that, like me, Robert didn't want to risk anything that might change our wonderful friendship.

After a long silence, Robert squeezed my hand, unable to meet my eyes as he spoke. 'I've never felt this way before, about anyone. Being with you, day after day . . .' – he paused as he stared at the floor – '. . . lying next to you, night after night; it's driving me mad.'

Not knowing what to say, I remained silent. I realized I'd been kidding myself. Being with Robert felt right. It was effortless. From the moment we met, it was as if we'd known each other for years.

I thought of Mark. How could I do this to him after everything I had put him through? But Mark and home seemed like a million miles away. Day-to-day survival in India meant I no longer thought about the future at all. It had become about just surviving the day, living for the moment and who knew what would happen tomorrow?

I kissed Robert gently on the cheek to comfort him. 'No,' he said, 'you don't understand.' Another long pause. He looked at me. 'I've never had a girlfriend before.' I tried to make sense of what he'd just said. Did I understand him correctly? I couldn't believe it. Surely it wasn't possible.

'Right . . . okay . . .' I said, realizing that my friend was at a complete loss and that it was up to me to make the first move.

We slept together that night. Robert was nervous and painfully shy, even more so than me. He was like an awkward adolescent teenager, which I found very endearing. But it didn't take him long to overcome his inhibitions and we stayed in bed all the following day and did little else for the next week.

It was both uncomplicated and intense, everything I had always wanted in a romantic relationship. The fact that I was Robert's first lover made me feel as if he was all mine. There was something very pure about a man who was so true to his feelings that he had remained a virgin until he was twenty-five years old. I found it wildly romantic, beautiful, beguiling, exciting and genuine. He offered me a blank piece of paper, clean and brimming with beautiful potential. He brought no baggage, no complications to the relationship. It was just about the two of us in our own little world.

*

After a week on the houseboat, Robert and I knew we needed to get back on the road, which was when we discovered that someone had stolen my penknife and my BMW lighter. I was furious. My lighter was of sentimental value, but my penknife was absolutely essential to me, on a par with the three plastic bags that I'd carried and carefully looked after all the way from Australia to wrap up belongings that needed to be kept dry in my tank bag. Like decent plastic bags that wouldn't rip or tear, a proper penknife with sharp blades was a rarity in India.

At the police station, I braced myself for the same old routine of official indifference to any crime reported by a Westerner. To my astonishment, the Srinagar police were amazingly efficient and actually threatened to put the owner of the houseboat in prison if he didn't find the thief, but then Robert noticed one of the officers shouting down the wrong end of a telephone earpiece and my hopes were shattered.

'It's all an illusion,' said Robert. 'Nothing will happen.'

He was correct.

In the wake of the theft, we rethought our plans for our trip up to Leh and Ladakh. We'd intended to halve our costs by leaving my bike behind and both riding on Robert's bike, but now we decided to take both bikes. Ensuring their security was more of a priority than saving money on fuel. As we left, we asked the houseboat owner if the road to Ladakh was open.

'Yes, yes. Good road. Good road,' he replied. 'Yes, yes. Open, open.'

By the time we'd ridden sixty miles out of Srinagar, Robert and I wanted to throttle the houseboat owner. The road was terrible. Large sections of it were dirt track. The occasional sections of hard-surfaced road were strewn with gravel, boulders and other detritus, as well as riddled with potholes. And then came the final blow: shortly after the sixty-mile mark, a sign said the road was closed.

I stopped and looked at Robert. 'What now?'

'I don't know.'

We got off our bikes, and looked at my very basic Bartholomew map, which resembled something from an atlas rather than a proper road map. There wasn't an alternative route. About ten minutes later, we spotted a pony train in the distance, carrying goods and approaching from where we wanted to go. Sitting on the front pony was a young man with a very old, weather-beaten face. As he arrived, Robert flagged him down and asked him if the road was open. He shook his head.

'Does that mean the road is closed?' I said. 'Or does it mean he doesn't understand?'

Before we could find out, the pony train moved off. Robert put his helmet back on. 'If he got through with those ponies, we can do it on our bikes,' he said.

Unconvinced, I followed Robert past the sign and up the narrow, twisty road as it climbed towards a pass. A few miles later, we caught up with a convoy of Indian army trucks. So much for the road being closed.

The convoy – the first of several – was a nightmare. Negotiating hundreds of trucks throwing up dust along a windy, single-track road with no protective barriers and steep drops of several hundred metres was exhausting and frightening, but gradually we made our way past them all. Like dozens of other Indian operations we'd encountered, the convoys were a masterclass in chaos. Instead of moving in a single continuous column, each convoy had broken up into dozens of small sections, some of which would arbitrarily stop at the most inconvenient places to wait for the section behind them. The convoys became so disjointed that some sections decided to overtake other sections, resulting in gridlocks, standstills and, occasionally, trucks teetering with several wheels off the edge of the road.

When we weren't negotiating the anarchy of army convoys, the ride wasn't that difficult, although it became more challenging when we had to ride over the mudslides that we encountered two or three times a day. I rode with a permanently tight stomach, anxious about what I'd find around the next bend – a river, a missing section of road, a mudslide, a convoy, a fast-moving truck coming towards me with no regard for anyone else on the road. Having never encountered dirt roads before Australia, I was less confident than Robert when off the tarmac and I took things slowly.

Robert was a bit more gung-ho than me, so when he was riding in front, I usually followed in his tracks.

At the end of the first day, we overnighted in Dras, then spent most of the next day riding through rain to Kargil. Robert really suffered, the cold making the knee damaged in his accident six months earlier ache painfully.

The toughest part came when we had to cross the Zojila Pass. Several sections were cobbled and as we reached the summit at 3,528 metres, the second-highest point on the road from Srinagar to Leh, both our bikes spluttered in the oxygen-deprived air. Stopping to take pictures beside a stone marker at the highest point, I felt as if we were on the top of the world. The views over a barren, rocky valley were astonishing. Everything was perfect – the scenery, the journey – and in Robert I had found the perfect companion. In the first flushes of love, I felt like I had infinite amounts of energy. I was as high as the mountains that surrounded me.

Maybe I should have spotted the approaching rain clouds that were about to shatter my blissful state of mind. They struck shortly after I got back onto my bike to start the descent from the Zojila Pass. With the rain pelting down and no back brake on my bike, riding down a steep, narrow pass built for mule trains was terrifying. Controlling my descent entirely with my gears, I didn't dare touch my front brake. The track was so steep that I would have been straight off my bike. I rarely left first gear. Eventually we arrived in Dras extremely wet, cold and tired. Even my feet were soaked after I'd dropped my bike in a river crossing.

The next day we rode about forty miles to Kargil, where again a sign declared the road ahead closed. This time, instead of ignoring it, we booked into a hotel, collapsed and slept from early afternoon through to the next morning, when we continued our journey. Ending in Khalsi, we had an excellent day's ride, the scenery changing as we climbed from lush green forests to completely barren mountains in a rocky desert. Unable to store our bikes at our guesthouse, we parked them outside a nearby shop. The next morning, Robert returned to the guesthouse after checking the bikes were still in place before we had breakfast.

'Still there,' he said with a nod. 'But the owner of the shop wants fifty rupees from each of us for the privilege of parking our bikes in the street outside his shop.'

Another scam, I thought. 'What did you do?'

'I told him his fortune.'

Later that day we arrived in Leh, the capital of Ladakh, formerly a Himalayan kingdom, now the largest region in the Indian state of Kashmir. Leh was a fair-sized city dominated by a vast ruined palace that was once the home to the royal family and then the Dalai Lama. The city was largely populated by Tibetans, beautiful people with aquiline features and leathery skin from the altitude.

Overwhelmed by the vast number of tourists, almost all of whom had flown to Leh, we were searching for a hotel to escape the crowds, when an unexpected voice came to our rescue.

'Mister . . . Mister . . . you want hotel?'

I looked around, saw nobody, then looked down and found a scruffy Tibetan boy with a fantastic smile beaming up at me. 'Yeah, I am looking for a hotel,' I said. 'Do you know one?'

'I know lots of hotels,' said the boy. With a twinkle in his eye and a cheeky manner, he made me think of a Tibetan version of The Artful Dodger. 'I help you find.'

Our new friend climbed up and sat on top of Robert's green bag on the back of his bike, then perched there as he directed us through Leh, having the time of his life. Riding with us through town, he made sure all his mates could see him, waving and shouting out to them as if he was the King of Leh. I guessed that few of them had ever seen such large motorbikes and none of them would have managed to hitch a ride on one. Ten minutes later, trailing a string of Tibetan kids as if we were pied pipers, we'd found a good hotel, thanks to our friend.

We spent three days in Leh, eating Chinese food, which was a welcome change after months of Indian cuisine, and riding around the area visiting the old Buddhist monasteries, or gompas. Many of them had a strange atmosphere, almost as if they were witchcraft venues. The centrepiece was always a shrine with photos of the Dalai Lama and other artefacts covered in dust. There was lots of incense and lamps fuelled with yak butter and on the floor the kneeling cushions were so filthy and full of wax that the fabric had become as stiff as a board. It was very interesting at first, but most of the gompas were overrun by hordes of tourists, had high entrance fees and were overflowing with tacky souvenirs which spoil the mystical experience.

The return journey to Srinagar was largely uneventful. Now used to the demands of the passes, we descended quickly. At midday on the first day, we parked our two bikes outside a food shack. We were about to leave when I noticed that Robert's tyre looked a bit soft. He had another puncture, which took us an hour to mend. Then, as he tried to start his bike, he discovered that the throttle was broken. 'Fucking children!' His face contorted with anger as he stomped around his bike. 'Every time we stop, their little hands twist my throttle. My bike does twice as many miles parked than it does when I'm riding it. So, now it's *kaput.*'

It took us until beyond midday to take Robert's throttle apart, then bodge a makeshift repair. After a terrifying crossing of the Zojila Pass, this time with no rear brake and a front brake that was either full on or full off, so I didn't dare use it, we arrived back in Srinagar in the early evening.

Now that we were back in Srinagar, it was obvious to me what we should do next. I'd seen the best of India so there was no reason to stay in the country any longer.

'Let's get out and go home,' I said to Robert as we finished repairing our bikes. 'Straight down to the border and into Pakistan.'

The first leg took us to Mansar Lake, riding for about forty miles through thick cloud over one of the passes, where visibility dropped to less than five yards. Without Robert taking turns to ride at the front I would have found it exhausting, but he took the lead whenever he sensed that I was nervous. That night, we camped rough near Mansar Lake, down a really bumpy track on which I almost dropped the bastard, as I was now calling my bike. Bit by bit, my BMW was becoming more of a liability and less of a friend, not through any fault of its own, but simply through the wear and tear of more than 20,000 miles on extreme roads and tracks since leaving London. The next day, I noticed the clutch was becoming difficult to engage, all because of a little spring that cost £2 at home, but was unobtainable in India.

From Mansar Lake, we headed for Amritsar, close to the Pakistan border, near Lahore. Having spent longer than intended in Srinagar, our Punjab transit permits had lapsed, but having never been asked to show our paperwork on the way up to Srinagar, we assumed it was of little importance. We'd heard rumours that foreigners were being detained at roadblocks in Punjab, but consoled ourselves that this was India, and with the usual disorganized chaos anything could happen. Surely, we thought, it's worth a try.

A few miles into Punjab, we came to our first roadblock, a string of empty oil barrels across the road, staggered to prevent traffic from passing. But on a bike we could ride straight through without stopping, so we kept going. Anywhere else but India, we might have taken the roadblocks more seriously, worried the guards might have pursued us, but we guessed they wouldn't bother. Our hunch was right; the guards slouched in their chairs, barely looking up as we passed through at speed.

Every ten to fifteen miles, another roadblock spanned the road. When we were waved down, we just waved back and carried on until we found ourselves in the centre of Amritsar. In a narrow street, 100 metres from the Golden Temple, our quest to get to see the holiest Sikh place of worship was brought to an abrupt stop by a rifle-toting soldier standing in front of a van that blocked the street. My explanation that we only wanted to see the magnificent golden shrine from afar was met with a simple shake of the head and two words: 'Go back.'

Conceding that there was definitely no arguing with someone holding a rifle, we turned around and decided to make our way to the Pakistan border at Wagah. We arrived a couple of hours later, after the crossing had shut, but ready to pass into Pakistan the next day.

That night, in Robert's tent, we assessed our chances of getting out of India.

'I think we'll be fine,' I said. 'I know our Punjab permit's not valid any more, but now that we're leaving the Punjab and India, surely it won't matter.'

'I hope you're right,' said Robert. 'Because if you're wrong, we're in a lot of trouble.'

With the Punjab effectively closed, no one could reach the border, and there was no queue there the next morning. The place was deserted, so we pushed our bikes forwards to the barrier that marked the end of Punjab and the beginning of no-man's land between India and Pakistan. A guard checked our documents, then lifted up the barrier. Trying not to smile with excitement, we entered a stretch of road, about 100 metres long, with barriers at each end. Technically we were now out of India. 'We've bloody done it,' I whispered to Robert.

At the side of the road there was a row of officials, sitting behind a trestle table with nothing to do. In the full glare of the early morning sun, we parked the bikes and walked slowly towards the table until we were in front of a man in the uniform of an Indian border official.

'Papers?'

We handed the official our documents – passports with visas and permits, and our carnets. The official passed back our carnets and started to flick through our passports.

'Dollar?' The official raised his eyebrows.

Prepped for the expected bribe, I had a ten-dollar bill in my right hand, folded and held so that the customs official could clearly see the '10' in its top-right corner.

The official's gaze darted from the banknote in my fist to me, then to Robert, before he nodded almost imperceptibly, but enough to acknowledge that $10 would do the trick.

'*Playboy*?' Again the raised eyebrows from the official.

I caught Robert's eye. The request wasn't entirely unexpected, but we hadn't prepared for it.

'We don't have *Playboy*,' I said.

The official paused for a couple of seconds, as if considering our response, then said, 'Where are your Punjab permits?'

'We don't have one,' I said, my heart starting to race.

The official straightened his back. 'So how did you ride through the Punjab?'

'We just rode,' I said.

'But that's not possible. You need a permit.'

'No one told us that,' I said.

'That's impossible.' The official narrowed his eyes. 'You would have been stopped.'

'No one stopped us.'

'Everyone is checked.'

'Not us.'

The border official pushed our passports across the trestle table towards us. 'You need to go back into the Punjab to get a permit.'

Robert and I looked at each other not fully believing what we were being told to do. This didn't make sense. 'How can we go back into the Punjab to get a permit if we don't already have a permit?' I said.

'You must go to Amritsar and get a permit that allows you into Punjab.'

'How do we do that without a permit?'

The official gave us a dismissive wave; as far as he was concerned, the conversation was now over. Robert tried again.

'But what you're asking us to do,' said Robert, 'is impossible.'

Sighing, the official spoke very slowly to us, as if we were children. 'Go away and get a permit now.'

'But we're not in the Punjab any more,' I said. 'You're sending us back into the Punjab to get a permit to enter the Punjab. Surely that doesn't make sense.'

'You need a permit.'

Maybe we did need to have a copy of *Playboy* in our luggage.

18

NO EXIT:
NEW DELHI

Amritsar, 28 August 1984

An hour later we were in Amritsar. After the usual hassles of being sent in dozens of different directions, all of which were wrong, eventually we found the office of the Senior Superintendent of Police.

'We need a permit to pass through the Punjab,' I told the Senior Superintendent of Police.

'But you are already in Punjab.'

Smiling in a way that I hoped would convey my understanding of the ridiculousness of our situation, I explained. 'I know. We were sent here from the border.'

'If you came from Pakistan, the border officials should give you your permit for the Punjab, not me.'

'But we didn't come from Pakistan.'

The SSP looked confused. 'So where is your permit?'

'We don't have one.'

'I can't issue you with a permit; you'll have to go to Delhi.'

'Delhi?' The rising tone in Robert's voice was a forewarning that he was about to lose his temper. 'Delhi?'

The SSP nodded.

'But that's five hundred kilometres,' I said.

The SSP nodded.

Fifteen minutes later, after a lot of swearing by Robert, we were back outside the SSP's office, resigned to riding to Delhi, a place I'd hoped I would never see again. To save petrol, we decided to ride to Delhi on one bike; we both rode back to the border, packed some bare essentials on Robert's bike and locked up my bike, which was useless at night since my headlight had been smashed when I hit the child.

Wanting to get the permit as soon as possible, we set off immediately, riding all day and through most of the night on the worst and busiest road we'd experienced in India. In daylight, the road would have been chaos. By night, with everyone driving without lights at ridiculous speeds, it was like being trapped in a nightmarish video game. Eventually, when the first rosy glow of dawn appeared on the horizon, we stopped in Sonipat, about thirty miles before Delhi, and found a place to pitch Robert's tent in a government-run campus. For once, we had nothing to say to each other at the end of a very long day simply because we were too exhausted to speak. I clambered into the tent, pulled down the zip, flopped back on my sleeping bag, sighed and just lay there, staring at the canvas ceiling of the tent, thinking of nothing, saying nothing, just letting the experiences of the day and long night wash over me. At times, travelling through India felt like nothing more than simple survival.

After a short sleep, we arrived in Delhi at midday, just in time to pay a visit to our old friend, T. O. Khakha at the Ministry of Home Affairs. Of course nothing had changed for the better since our last visit to the ministry. I had hoped that our previous experience of its bureaucracy might have taught us a few lessons about how to work our way through a system that seemed to be designed to obstruct, not aid, anyone who set foot in the ministry's halls. I was wrong.

Our initial enquiry at the reception desk was met with a response that was typical of all dealings with the ministry's bureaucrats: 'No permits. Fly the bikes to Lahore.'

Having left my bike at the border, flying wasn't an option for us, although our circumstances were less complicated than those of other travellers we met in the ministry's long, lime-green-painted corridors, such as a Dutch guy who had a huge Jeep and trailer laden with heavy equipment.

For three days, the bureaucrats led us on a succession of wild goose chases. We were sent to buildings that hadn't been built to obtain documents that had never been printed from people that didn't exist. Eventually we realized we were being fobbed off. We spent long, frustrating periods in empty concrete corridors, waiting to get pieces of paper stamped so that we could get a lift up to the next floor, where we waited on another bench in another corridor to obtain yet another piece of paper that allowed us access to an official who issued chits that allowed access to another building, in which there was someone who might be able to help us obtain a permit to allow us to see T. O. Khakha.

To make matters worse, T. O. Khakha's office in the Ministry of Home Affairs was open to foreigners only from ten o'clock until two o'clock. When we were finally permitted entry to Mr Khakha's office, he smiled and said: 'It's two o'clock. You're here too late. We're closed.'

'Can we come back first thing tomorrow morning?' I asked.

One of Mr Khakha's assistants answered, 'Yes, but you'll need a new permit to see Mr Khakha.'

Fearing that the prospect of never getting out of Delhi, let alone India, would cause Robert's temper to blow, I pushed Robert out of Khakha's office before he let his feelings show. I knew that Robert was at the end of his tether. I needed to get him out of India as quickly as I could.

Back at the tourist camp, seven other groups of people with vehicles were marooned in India because of the troubles in Punjab. They included a Dutch family in a Land Rover who I'd met at the camp six weeks earlier. In the time that Robert and I had travelled up to Kashmir and back, their many attempts to obtain a permit to drive through Punjab to exit India had got them nowhere, but in that time one of their children had fallen very ill. Still the Indian bureaucrats wouldn't let them go home.

'We've got "Land Rover imported" written on all our passports,' said the softly spoken Dutch father, 'so we cannot leave the country without it.'

'Same as us,' I said. 'We have our bikes written in our passports. Why don't you drive to Bombay and ship it home?'

'It's not allowed. The customs officials won't let us export it by air or sea. We have to drive it across a land border and the only land border heading west is into Pakistan, through the Punjab, where foreigners are banned.'

'Have you spoken to Khakha?' I asked.

'Pffft . . .' The Dutchman made a sour face. 'I told him I was running out of money and would have to start stealing if he wouldn't allow us home soon.'

'And what did he say to that?'

'He said, "You go steal. You go steal."' The Dutchman shook his head. 'You can't talk sense to people like that.'

After three days at the ministry, we finally got to see T. O. Khakha. Having collected all the documents we needed, we presented them to him and explained our situation. 'We're completely stuck,' I said. 'Please give us a permit, if only for twenty-four hours to get to the border.' Leaning back in his chair with his hands clasped against his chest, Khakha listened impassively. When I'd finished, he leant forwards and said one word. 'No.' Khaka leant back and crossed his arms.

Beside me, Robert was clenching his fists by his side. Then, he leant forwards over the desk until his face was inches from Khakha. 'What the fuck do you expect us to do?' he said.

Khakha shrugged. 'Your problem.'

'My problem?'

Khakha nodded. 'Now get out.'

Robert grabbed Khakha around the throat and hit him several times. Guards appeared. We were thrown out of the building.

Standing in the street outside the ministry, our hopes of getting to the border now in tatters, I realized that Robert had long passed the point of being able to control his reactions in India. He'd had more than enough of the country and would lose his temper at the slightest provocation. If I didn't get Robert out of India very soon, he'd do something that might result in him not leaving for a very long time.

'Are you okay?' I said.

'No,' said Robert. 'It's like being in a war, on the front line, when you're shot at all day but you can't shoot back.' I knew exactly how he felt.

Back at the camp, we considered our options. I suggested riding down to Bombay to ship our bikes out of the country to somewhere in east Africa, but the monsoon had started and it was a long way in heavy rain and we had neither visas nor carnets for African countries.

'We need to go back to the border,' I said eventually. I was becoming increasing worried about my bike getting stuck there permanently.

Robert looked surprised. 'Without a permit?'

'We've got no choice and we made it there before. The situation in the Punjab's getting worse by the day. They're never going to give us a permit now.'

Robert nodded. 'You're right.'

We left the next morning.

We left Delhi at 4.30 a.m. to avoid all the traffic in the old city. 'If we see a roadblock, just don't stop,' I said to Robert as I climbed onto the pillion seat behind him. 'Once I've got my bike back, we can deal with whatever they throw at us, but I've got to get my bike back first.'

Despite being pillion, it was the longest and mentally toughest day's ride I've ever done. The security on roads entering Punjab had been tightened since we rode down to Delhi because of a special conference between the government and Sikh representatives in Amritsar.

Riding at great speed, we passed without stopping through five roadblocks manned by army and police, all of whom frantically waved us down and shouted at us. I simply waved back, pretending not to understand what they wanted. Shortly after midday, the monsoon rain started, which played into our hands as the soldiers retreated into their huts, allowing us to pass through their roadblocks faster than they could react.

In places, the road was flooded up to a foot deep, but we kept pushing on towards the border, soaked to the skin, shivering with the cold of the wind. Darkness fell and we entered a curfew area that felt very edgy and unsafe.

Shortly before midnight, extremely wet but very relieved, we finally arrived at the border at Wagah. To my relief, my bike was still there. I vowed then that I would never leave my bike anywhere like that again; I couldn't believe I'd been so stupid. Robert and I wheeled both our bikes into an empty warehouse building near the border, collapsed onto the floor beside them and almost immediately fell asleep.

Exhausted, we slept late, then considered our options while eating for the first time in more than twenty-four hours. From where I was sitting, eating my breakfast just outside the gatehouse, I could see the border post. Pakistan was tantalizingly close.

That afternoon we turned up at the border, hoping we'd encounter a different group of officials who might be more inclined to overlook gaps and anomalies in our immigration documents. But just our luck, the same line of officials who had sent us back to Amritsar a week earlier were sitting at the trestle table. As before, the border was deserted. The officials immediately recognized us, probably because they'd had few other customers in the meantime.

'Passport please,' said the official who'd previously demanded dollars and a *Playboy* as a bribe.

As I handed over my passport, the personal registration document that I'd been issued with when I re-entered India from Nepal slipped out and fell onto the desk. The official picked it up, looked at it.

'Ah! Your Punjab permit,' said the official.

'Er . . .' I was confused, but decided to go with it. '. . . yes.'

The official turned my personal registration document over, looked at the back of it, then turned to Robert.

'Passport please.'

Robert gave the border official his Dutch passport.

'Punjab permit?' said the official.

Robert looked at me, confusion and a mild panic in his eyes. Unlike me, he didn't have a personal registration document because Dutch passport-holders required a different type of visa from Britons and Commonwealth members.

'But I am Dutch,' said Robert.

The official ignored Robert and passed my registration document to his colleagues. *Shit*, I thought, *they'll tell him it isn't a permit.* But my document was passed from official to official, each of them examining it closely. *Any moment now,* I thought, *one of them will realize it's the wrong document.* 'Ahhh . . . permit, permit,' each official exclaimed with mild excitement as my document was passed down the line from one to another. I realized none of them had a clue what a Punjab entry permit looked like.

The official handed me my passport and registration document, looked at his watch and smiled. 'It's late.' He pointed at me. 'Come back tomorrow and you can go through.' He moved his index finger towards Robert. 'But you can't.'

We pitched our tent near the border gatehouse. Lying inside it, we had an agonizing discussion trying to decide what to do. Should I go across the border and leave Robert behind? Or should we wait until we could both pass across the border together, even if it required another battle with bureaucracy in Delhi? For hours we stayed up discussing it.

'You should go,' said Robert eventually. 'Just get out of India while you can.'

But I couldn't leave him. He was like a coiled spring about to pop and I could see his short temper getting him into some serious trouble if I wasn't there. 'Maybe he knows it's not a permit,' I said, 'but he's just being nice because he knows we tried once before.'

'Maybe.'

'So maybe he'll let you through too.'

'Maybe.' Robert sounded sceptical. 'But probably not.'

By the morning I'd decided anything was worth a punt. 'Come on,' I said to Robert. 'Let's just give it one last go. It's India – anything could happen.' Returning to the border, I worried that a different official would be on duty.

When we got to the trestle table, our friendly official wasn't on duty. My heart pounding, my palms damp, I offered my passport and personal registration document to his replacement. The official examined it, nodded, then turned to Robert. 'Passport.'

As cool as anything, Robert handed him his Dutch passport. The official flicked through its pages, stopping on some of them to examine immigration and visa stamps. Then, without saying anything, he picked up his rubber stamp, pressed it into an inkpad and pushed the exit stamp on a page in my passport. He lifted the stamp off my passport and looked at the page.

It was bare. No stamp.

I nearly screamed. I slowed my breathing while praying the official wouldn't change his mind before we got the stamps in our passports. Pulse racing, I watched as the official tried to squeeze enough ink out of the pad to wet his rubber stamp.

Bang. I got the stamp in my passport.

Bang. Robert got the stamp.

We were out of India.

For weeks afterwards I looked at that stamp. *Exit Amritsar*, it said on what felt like the most valuable page in my passport.

Leaving the immigration trestle table behind us, we walked to the hut where we had to collect another stamp, this time on our carnets, to export our bikes. 'Don't run,' I whispered to Robert. 'Just walk. Keep calm.'

We ambled to the hut, trying to look like we didn't have a care in the world. For once, the carnet guy was at his desk and with no preamble, no questions, no delay at all, we both got the necessary stamp smacked on our carnets.

I glanced over at the immigration table. With nothing else to do, the officials behind the table were passing my personal registration document between themselves, discussing something. I tried not to stare at them; surely they couldn't change their minds now?

Slowly and carefully, we got on our bikes, put on our helmets and gloves, casually started the engines and rode steadily to the barrier that took us out of no-man's land and into Pakistan.

With a smile, Pakistani border officials raised the barrier as we approached, but I couldn't wait. Crouching down, gunning our engines, I ducked under the barricade as it lifted, Robert by my side.

Twenty metres into Pakistan, we stopped. I jumped off my bike, took a couple of steps towards Robert and hugged him before he'd even switched off his ignition.

'We did it!' I could see the relief on Robert's face. Months of tension had lifted. 'We bloody did it!'

19

ROAD TO REVOLUTION:
PAKISTAN TO IRAN

Lahore, 5 September 1984

Arriving in Pakistan from India felt like riding out of the Dark Ages into the light. It was calmer, it had fewer people on the streets, and they seemed busier and more driven. After India, Pakistan had energy and a sense of urgency. We rode a short distance into Lahore and found a room in a Salvation Army hostel that was in a quiet backstreet, away from the bustle. When darkness fell and the town came to life, we left our room to explore the markets and street traders.

'Look! It's amazing.' Robert held up a reel of tape he'd found on a stall. 'Insulating tape that actually sticks.' Thrilled to find basic items we desperately needed that actually worked, we bought spark plugs, tape, wire, screws and some tools. Now I could properly bodge all the little things that needed attention if my BMW was going to survive the long ride back home.

My most pressing problem was my Iranian entry visa. After wasting so much time trying to get out of India, it was due to expire in two weeks. Without it, I wouldn't be allowed to pass through the country, but the only place I could renew it was Delhi and there was no way I was ever going back there. I also had another problem. When I was organizing my carnet in Sydney I was told that to have Iran included on the list of valid countries, the deposit would increase from £1,500 to £4,500. This was beyond my budget so my carnet wasn't valid for Iran, meaning there was a good chance that I wouldn't be allowed to take my bike into the country. With no other choice, I would have to try and bluff my way into Iran without one.

Iran really worried me. Since the Islamic Revolution in 1979, it had cut all ties with the West and much of the rest of the world. Now at war with Iraq, it was the great unknown gap on my travel itinerary. I'd heard so many conflicting stories about travelling through Iran, but when I looked at my maps, I had no other option. To our north lay Afghanistan: out of bounds to Westerners since the Soviet invasion in 1979. To our south lay the Arabian Sea, but I had no information about boats from Karachi to anywhere on the Arabian Peninsula. And the prospect of sailing as far as Africa, then trawling my way up the continent, across the Sahara, seemed daunting. Iran seemed the only viable option and after my experiences at the India–Pakistan border, I persuaded myself that I could somehow wangle my bike into Iran, even if it wasn't the official way.

Relieved to be out of India, I was now feeling desperate to get home, particularly with worries about Iran playing constantly on my mind. I also had to readjust to Muslim culture as well as contend with Robert, who was becoming angry and quite upset by the constant unwanted attention I was receiving. 'If it wasn't for you, I would never have known what it's like to travel as a woman,' he said.

After two days in Lahore, servicing our bikes and visiting the Badshahi Mosque, we set off shortly after six in the morning for Multan. It was a very difficult ride, made harder by the complete unavailability of food to be bought because it was a Muslim religious holiday. Towards the end of the day, Robert spotted a stall that he thought was selling oranges. He pulled over, asked to buy some, but the stallholder didn't understand him. Exhausted from the ride and weak with hunger, Robert returned to his bike, dug through his bags for something to eat.

'I can't find any fucking food.' The contents of Robert's bags came flying over his shoulder. Within seconds, his belongings were strewn all around us. I tried to calm him, but he was almost uncontrollable in his rage. I'd hoped things would be better once we were away from the frustrations of India, but Robert seemed just as uptight.

'I've fucking had enough,' he yelled, leaping onto his bike and slamming it into gear. Robert's gearbox crunched ominously to a halt. 'Fuck!' screamed Robert as I stood well back. The scale of his rage at the world and the way in which the smallest of hurdles could trigger a completely disproportionate response was starting to frighten me. I felt his frustration, but worried that it would get us into trouble. If he punched someone, we'd be arrested. My sightseeing itinerary did not include the inside of a Pakistani jail.

Eventually I managed to calm Robert and get him back on his bike. Riding very carefully and struggling to change gears, he moved off, but I could feel his anger still bubbling beneath the surface. By the end of the day, he'd cracked his goggles and ripped the strap off his tank bag. He had just had enough.

We found a decent hotel in Multan that was very generous with free cups of tea and snacks. Woken by heavy rainfall at six the next morning, we found those endless free cups of tea very difficult to refuse and left Multan much later than intended, for which we paid dearly later in the day.

The traditional route west from Multan led via Islamabad into Afghanistan, where it passed through Kabul and Herat, then left the country and skimmed through a short stretch of northern Iran on its way to Turkey. However, with Afghanistan now out of bounds, the traffic followed a more southerly route via Quetta that was often no more than a series of tracks across a desert. Sometimes the tracks disappeared altogether, leaving us to orientate ourselves only by the dust plumes of trucks in the distance, which worked well until rain turned dust to mud, which it did shortly after we left Multan, the road and weather slowing our progress even more.

Riding towards Quetta, I sensed the approaching border with Afghanistan. Every time we crossed a mountain pass, the faces of the people changed as we encountered more and more Afghani refugees. Hanging around in the desert with rifles slung over their shoulders, most of the refugees, like the locals, were members of rival tribes, either Pashtun or Baloch. As outsiders, we were regarded with great suspicion. It felt threatening and unsafe, so we pushed on as best we could towards Loralai.

By five o'clock the sun was nearing the horizon but we still had more than 100 miles to ride to the nearest town. I still hadn't been able to fix my headlight so we rode as fast as we dared while daylight remained. When darkness fell, we rode side by side so that I could see the road ahead by the beam of Robert's headlight. The road, where it existed, was in a terrible state and I dropped my bike doing an emergency stop ahead of a deep trench across the road that I only saw at the very last moment.

After having crossed two fairly small rivers in the half-light of dusk, we followed the dirt road into a wide riverbed in darkness. At the centre of the bed, we came to a stop at the shore of a fast-flowing river. Knee deep and strewn with huge boulders, it was about twenty-five metres wide. The beam of Robert's headlight picked out a collection of trucks and fifteen to twenty truckers hanging around, waiting for the river to subside before attempting a crossing. Already, a few trucks were stuck halfway across the water.

'We could camp,' said Robert, 'and cross it in the morning, but . . .'

I knew exactly what he was thinking. Even in the beam of Robert's light, I had spotted too many daggers and guns on the truckers' belts for either of us to be able to sleep there that night. The atmosphere was very edgy. Pitching a tent didn't appeal.

'No,' I said. 'Let's keep going. I don't think this is a good place to camp.'

We hung around for a while and watched a Jeep attempt the crossing. It got across, so we decided to have a go.

While Robert rode my bike through the water, I stood on the shore, watching until water got into the points at the front of the engine and it cut out halfway. Wading into the water, I helped Robert and some of the truckers push it to the far bank. Then Robert rode his bike through the water, almost making it all the way before his engine cut out.

Safely across the river, we removed the front engine covers on each bike and dried off the points by the light of a torch while a large group of truckers looked on.

'Why don't you take off your helmet?' said Robert.

'I can't,' I whispered. 'They all think I'm a bloke and I think it's best left that way.'

The truckers were friendly and helpful, standing back and not engaging, watching us rather than imposing themselves. A few of them smiled or gave us curious looks, which reassured me that they didn't regard us as threats. But I didn't want to find out if their attitudes changed when they realized I was a woman. They all carried rifles openly and I had no doubt that most of them also had several other weapons tucked under their belts. Not knowing if they were innocent truckers, refugees, bandits or mujahideen, I thought it safest not to take any chances.

'We've got to get out of here quickly,' I whispered to Robert, 'before they realize I'm a woman.' We focused on drying our points and half an hour later we were on the move again, only to be confronted by yet another river, this time with a bed of sloppy mud instead of rocks. After crossing the river and dropping one bike in the process, we still had another twenty-five miles to the nearest town. At the speed we were travelling in the dark, it would take us at least two hours if we encountered another river.

'Follow me,' said Robert. 'And don't use your brakes. We don't want anyone seeing our taillights.'

Robert switched off his headlight and turned off the dirt road into the desert. Keeping as close as I could to Robert, I rode by feel, hoping there were no ditches or holes in front of me. Gradually my eyes acclimatized to the dark and we pulled up beside a sand dune, pitched our tent behind it and crawled inside for a much-needed sleep.

When the sun rose the next morning, I discovered we were in the middle of a pancake-flat landscape in which our sand dune was the only bump. There were no other features – no hills, no rocky outcrops, no grasses or bushes. It was totally flat.

Convinced that there were people walking through the desert past our tent all night, I'd hardly slept. We decided to ride immediately to Loralai, where we breakfasted, found a hotel and slept for a few hours, then spent the day working on the bikes. Now in the city, we looked at ourselves and realized we must have looked quite alarming to the locals. After riding for days through dust, we were filthy. My light cotton trousers that I'd bought in Sydney were stiff with dirt and flecked with my attempts to repair rips with patches I'd cut from my towel. Robert wore a pair of dungarees that hadn't been properly washed for months. My dysentery hadn't completely cleared up and I was now so thin that I looked quite haunted. Food continued to be a problem for us.

Early the next morning, we left for Quetta. Now focused entirely on getting home, I'd decided the way to deal with the stresses of the road was to think no further ahead than reaching the end of each day. Days might start well, but they often degenerated in ways we couldn't control. Smooth city roads in the morning would become rough desert tracks in the afternoon and by nightfall we might find ourselves trying to cross knee-deep rivers. With no way of knowing what lay ahead, it made no sense to plan any further ahead than a few hours. As it turned out, the ride to Quetta was long but reasonably uneventful and we arrived early that evening, then treated ourselves to a good meal of chicken, a bit of a rarity for us.

Knowing that the ride from Quetta through Balochistan to the Iranian border was going to be long and hard, we spent the next day resting and prepping our bikes. The main task on my bike was replacing the bevel seal in my final drive, a job that usually required an expensive special tool from BMW, but which Robert and I needed to bodge in best Heath-Robinson fashion. At the critical point in the operation, where the seal had to pass over a groove before it was secured in place, we filled the groove with some string, covered it with a plastic bag and some oil, then slid the seal over the groove perfectly. We were so pleased with ourselves.

That night I totted up my assets. I had 210 rupees in cash, $1,733 in American Express travellers' cheques and a twenty-pound note that I kept permanently in my wallet because it reminded me of home. As long as nothing unexpected happened it ought to be enough to get me home.

Balochistan filled me with trepidation. Roughly one and a half times the size of Britain, it was Pakistan's largest, poorest, most inhospitable province. For decades various Baloch tribes had been fighting for independence from Pakistan and the area had a reputation for bandits, but that didn't worry me as much as the fact that the thin red line marked on my map would be no more than an approximation of a road at best.

A few miles outside Quetta, riding through one of the last villages before we met the empty desert plains, a sign by the side of the road caught my eye.

London 9,476 km.

I had to stop and take a picture. Just seeing *London* painted on a sign for the first time in two years was a very significant moment in my journey. For the first time I felt completion was within my grasp. Now I really wanted to get home quickly. I was tired. I was ill. I was weak. My bike was just hanging on, bandaged together by too many makeshift repairs.

Continuing to ride west we passed through a vast empty landscape of scrub and rock. Except for occasional clusters of nomad tents, the only sign of human life we saw that day was a rackety old train comprising half a dozen passenger carriages and a few goods wagons, propelled by two large steam engines, one at each end, spewing thick black smoke. That evening we stopped at a rest house in Nushki, but the owner told us his rooms were full so we asked if we could camp. As soon as the owner saw us put up Robert's tent, he came outside and offered us a room inside his rest house for free. We were mystified.

Then, to our further surprise, the owner phoned a friend in Dalbandin, the next town on our itinerary, to arrange a free room at his rest house for the following night. Completely baffled, we thanked him and felt very grateful for his help . . . until we arrived in Dalbandin the next night. Standing in the doorway of his rest house, the owner looked at me in a way that immediately made me feel uneasy. 'You stay in rest house,' he said, pointing first at Robert, then at me. 'And you stay in my house.'

Robert stepped forward. 'No, we stay together.'

The rest house owner spun a story about there not being enough room in the rest house for both of us. 'Maybe we'll camp,' said Robert.

'Yes, you can camp,' said the owner. 'And she stays in my house.'

'Look, we need to be together,' I said. 'Either we both camp together, or we both stay in the rest house together, or we both leave together and find somewhere else to stay together.'

The owner abruptly conceded. 'Okay . . . okay, you both stay here for free. Is good.'

In the end, we stayed for two nights without paying, then rode to Nok Kundi, along a road that was so badly potholed it was easier to ride through the sand along the side of it. But that was nothing compared to what was to come. After a night spent in a dormitory, we set off, unaware that Nok Kundi marked the end of the supposed sealed road and the official start of ninety miles of terrible dirt road. With each passing kilometre under our tyres, the road became less distinct. In place of tarmac was a dirt track marked only by small heaps of boulders along each side.

Eventually even the rocks and stones petered out into nothingness. Now we were riding across sand dunes and dust plains. In some places there was a narrow path of slightly firmer, compressed sand upon which we pinned our hopes that it was the route to the border. When the trail of compressed sand disappeared, we orientated ourselves relative to a line of telegraph poles, reasoning that they had to lead somewhere. Weaving our way through the sand dunes, we occasionally spotted a dust plume from another vehicle running parallel to us, travelling in vaguely the same direction, any concept of a road completely gone now. And then the wind picked up.

Grinding along in first and second gear through a sandstorm was sheer hell. Deep corrugations, in places covered by sand or gravel, slowed me down to no more than 20 mph, although Robert wanted to ride much faster. Anything to get to the border sooner. 'I just can't ride that slowly,' he said.

'And I just can't ride that fast,' I replied.

Robert's theory was that if he rode fast enough, his tyres would skim over the top of the corrugations, but I found the thought of losing control frightening. 'I've tried it and I can't do it,' I said. 'I know the theory, but I don't have the strength to control my bike if things go wrong. I'll do it my way.'

'Then I'll ride ahead,' he said. 'And wait for you.'

Taking off at 50 mph, Robert was completely out of sight before long. Behind him, I felt terribly lonely; just me in a vast, empty expanse. To make matters worse, I had to stop every twenty to twenty-five miles to clean the sand out of my points. It only took a few minutes each time, but crouching beside my bike, focusing on my points, I felt extremely vulnerable and wished Robert was with me to watch my back.

About an hour later, I caught up with Robert. Bent double, sitting astride his bike with his head rested on his tank bag, he was having a snooze. As I approached, I noticed Robert's rear tyre was flat.

'You know you've got a puncture?'

'Aaagh!' A succession of swearwords followed.

We unpacked Robert's panniers to get at his tools. Sitting on the floor of the desert, we then repaired his puncture.

'I'll get my pump,' said Robert.

Both our bikes came with a small pump as part of their tool kits, fixed to the main frame under the seat. Robert connected his pump to his repaired tyre, started to blow up his tyre, but the tyre wouldn't inflate.

'Fuck! The connector's perished.' Robert held up the rubber tube that connected the pump to the valve. 'Fuck, fuck, fuck.' Robert threw his pump on the desert floor and stomped away from his bike. 'You carry these fucking things for thousands of miles and the one time you want to use it, it doesn't fuckin' work!'

'Calm down,' I pleaded.

Robert stopped abruptly, picked up his pump, bent it over his knee and hurled it as far as he could into the desert as if it was a boomerang.

'Don't worry,' I said, before Robert could take out his rage on other items of his equipment, 'I've got my pump. We can use that.'

I passed my pump to Robert and he attached the connector to his valve, started to blow up the tyre.

'I don't fucking believe it!' Robert looked like he was about to burst a blood vessel. 'This one is also fucking *kaput*.'

When Robert had calmed down, I suggested that I ride to Taftan, which was less than two hours away. 'I could come back with someone with a truck and pick you up,' I said.

'If you can find someone with a truck . . .'

'You know what it's like. Money talks. I'll get someone.'

But Robert was not easily convinced. For ten or fifteen minutes we discussed the best course of action until we saw a plume of dust approaching. It was a truck, like us heading for Taftan.

We waved down the truck. After a lot of negotiation over payment, the driver agreed to load Robert's bike onto the back of his truck. Leaving Robert to ride in the cab beside the driver, I rode the last forty miles on my own to Taftan along the roughest part of the road. The relief I felt at the sight of Taftan in a valley below me as I came over a hill is something I'll never forget.

Like many border towns in third-world countries, the place was a dump, but Taftan even pushed the deprivations of shitty border towns to a new low. Five years earlier it had been a handful of huts, but since the Soviet invasion of Afghanistan drove the east–west route further south, Taftan had grown fast and furiously. Now a shantytown of hastily constructed corrugated iron shacks arranged arbitrarily along some dirt tracks, it was unbelievably grim. We found a cell-like room in the worst hotel I had ever seen. The floor was our bed. There was no water. When I asked to go to the toilet, I was handed a key and pointed towards a door. Opening the door, I found myself in a walled backyard scattered with piles of excrement, picked over by goats wandering freely. While Robert guarded the door in a forlorn attempt at protecting my privacy, I picked my way through the turd heaps, found an empty space, pulled down my trousers and crouched down, flies swarming around me in the heat.

Iran couldn't come too soon.

In the morning, we repaired Robert's tyre and, after a short ride, we were at the Iranian border by 10 a.m. After passing out of Pakistan relatively easily, I approached Iranian immigration with more trepidation than on any other crossing on the trip. Iran had a fearsome reputation as the most foreboding country for any Westerner to attempt to enter.

The immigration office wasn't a problem. Robert and I both had transit visas and were waved through courteously. Then we presented ourselves in a very dark room in the customs building, where an official examined Robert's carnet, stamped it and handed it back to Robert without a word passing his lips. Robert was free to go.

Knowing that Iran was not included in the list of countries which were typed on the front cover for which my carnet was valid, I handed it to the official, fully prepared to do whatever was needed – a bribe, a vaguely plausible explanatory story – to get my bike into the country. But the official didn't even look at me as he shook his head and tapped the list of countries for which it was valid. Every country along my route was on the list – except Iran.

Hoping to appeal to his good nature, I beamed my widest, friendliest smile, but the expression on the official's face didn't soften. Instead, he tapped the list of countries again, this time a bit harder, raised his eyebrows and handed the carnet back to me, leaving me trying to fathom meaning from his silence.

I thanked the official with a nod of my head, stepped away and huddled with Robert. 'I think he's suggesting that I add Iran to the list of countries on my carnet.'

'You sure?' said Robert.

'No – but I've got nothing to lose if I do it.'

'Except being thrown in jail for forging documents.'

It was a good point, but I was convinced I could talk myself out of trouble if necessary. 'I'm going to give it a go.'

Turning around, I smiled at the official and pointed at a biro lying on his desk, thinking that if he lent it to me, I could suggest that he had condoned my alteration of my carnet. The official nodded and handed me his pen as he looked away. With 'Iran' carefully added and my heart in my mouth, I handed my carnet back to the official. The official didn't even glance at the list of countries, which now included Iran neatly added in my own handwriting. He opened my carnet, found an empty space and stamped it, then spent ten minutes filling out a large, blue customs document that he handed to me with my carnet and a wide smile. I felt like hugging him. At last, an official who was understanding and helpful. And in Iran, of all places.

I climbed onto my bike, barely able to believe I'd got into Iran so easily, then moved off, crossing lanes as I entered the first country in which vehicles drove on the right-hand side of the road since leaving England two years earlier.

Another step closer to home.

20

BELL HELMET FOR A BURKA:

IRAN TO ISTANBUL

Zahedan, 18 September 1984

Five miles into Iran, I ran out of petrol and realized that since filling up in Quetta, I'd ridden more than 350 miles on a single tank. For the first time during my entire trip my tank was completely empty, ironically in the country where petrol cost a few pence for a gallon. I wheeled my bike about a quarter of a mile to a petrol station, filled up then rode along to Zahedan, the first town inside Iran. These last twenty-odd miles on sand would, I hoped, be the last stretch of sand or dirt I'd have to ride through for the rest of the trip.

Needing Iranian currency, Robert exchanged $100, his smallest US dollar banknote, on the black market. Instead of the official rate of 100 rials, he received 550 rials to the dollar. Suddenly we had so much money we didn't know what to do with it. Stuffing Iranian banknotes into any space we could find in our bags, we went in search of somewhere to stay. Money being no object, we hired an entire igloo-shaped house, then both took long, luxurious showers, the first chance we'd had to wash in four days.

Iran was a revelation. To my surprise, it turned out to be the first country since Australia that felt Western. Of course 55,000 rials burning a hole in Robert's pocket helped, but oddly it was the little things that made me feel closer to home, such as sugar lumps, tea in a pot, butter served with bread, and the locals going about their own business and taking very little interest in me when we stopped to eat, drink or refuel our bikes. I soon realized, though, that keeping my helmet on for most of the day minimized any unwanted attention, as the locals automatically assumed I was male. Our British and Dutch number plates attracted little more than cursory glances, possibly because most Iranians had more pressing and weighty concerns than two young, Western travellers passing speedily through their country.

Nevertheless, I was very nervous about passing through a country that had a hard-line Islamic government that had recently seized power through revolution and that was at war with its neighbour. Although there was little overt sign of the war with Iraq, there were soldiers everywhere, standing on city streets, sitting in trucks on the roads between the towns, loitering at crossroads in villages.

As well as dealing with the effects of the war, Iran gave me the impression of being a nation trying to come to terms with massive changes within its own borders. A populace that was brainwashed with pro-Western propaganda for decades and told to embrace everything associated with American and European values had had a complete mindset change forced upon it almost overnight. The Islamic Revolution had forced them to reject their common past and embrace an entirely new way of life that involved going back almost to the Dark Ages. The mood on the streets was quite tense and we often had the impression that many of the locals wanted to welcome us, but were frightened to do so in case they were seen talking or laughing with a Westerner. It was as if the people didn't know how to behave towards us. We were thrown out of restaurants several times, then five minutes later slipped free Pepsis, as if they felt guilty about it.

After a night in Zahedan, we wasted no time in heading for Kerman, our next stop. With our visas allowing us seven days to ride the length of Iran, a distance of more than 1,500 miles, Iran was about one thing only: getting miles under our wheels. Both of our bikes were only just hanging on. Anything could go wrong at any time and a puncture or a repair requiring a spare part would leave us stuffed, so it was a great relief to discover that the roads were fantastic. Perfect, black tarmac as smooth as a billiard table and even without chippings. There were some aspects of Iran that I was growing to like very much, although our progress was slowed by the endless number of roadblocks. Set up every fifty miles, they were no more than shacks, erected and guarded by armed soldiers who looked about eighteen years old. A barrier across the road forced us to stop and every time I would go through the same performance of having to show my passport, which caused great excitement. Then I'd have to remove my helmet so they could check I really was a woman riding the bike. They'd stand around, laughing and joking, and although I didn't feel threatened, the roadblocks became a real irritation that took up several precious hours every day.

Arriving in Kerman, we decided to blow some of our vast stack of rials on an expensive room at a luxury hotel. We pulled up at a hotel that looked like it had been a part of one of those large American chains, such as Sheraton. Walking up to the door, we could see dozens of staff, but not a single guest. It was completely deserted.

'Do you think we should go inside?' I said. 'No guests usually implies it's not very good.'

Robert was upbeat. 'The only reason it's empty is because there are no tourists in Iran.'

He opened the door and I stepped forward. About to enter the hotel, I was stopped by a manager standing in front of us, his hands shooing us away.

'Out! Out! Out!'

I could see fear in his eyes. He was scared of us crossing the threshold. Even though his hotel was empty, he clearly didn't want two scruffy Westerners for guests.

We stepped back. As we walked away, I glanced over my shoulder. The manager was standing outside his hotel, nervously scanning the street, watching us anxiously until we reached the corner. He appeared to be very frightened of anyone having seen us approach his hotel.

'It's like being given a million pounds,' I said, 'and having only a week to spend it in a country where everything costs only a few pence. This is mad.'

Scratching around for places to stay, eventually we resorted to renting a flat for a week, although we needed to stay only one night. In Naein the next night, we found it even harder to find somewhere that would accommodate us and ended up in a dirty room above a shop that had a prayer cubicle in one corner and sand all over the floor and furniture.

Midway through our crossing of Iran, we arrived in Isfahan, where I'd wanted to stop to see its two famous mosques, both of which were considered to be among the world's most striking buildings. Again we were turned away from several hotels, so we stopped to eat in a café, where we bought a tasty meal of grilled meat and rice. At the end of the meal, when the manager brought our bill, I held two hands against the side of my face to indicate that we were looking for somewhere to sleep. Nervous glances shot between the manager and his staff before we were ushered into the back, then upstairs to a room, where it was made very clear in sign language that we were not to show our faces downstairs that night. The next morning, after a good night's sleep, we were escorted to the back door. The manager opened the door a few inches, glanced through the crack, opened it enough to stick his head out. Having assured himself that no one would see us leave his café, the manager bustled us out into a dirty alley and slammed the door shut behind us.

Touched and impressed by this local's kind attempt at hospitality in the face of an unforgiving regime, Robert and I set off for the Shah Mosque, renamed the Imam Mosque following the revolution. Vast and reminiscent of the Taj Mahal, it was beautiful and very impressive. Apparently constructed of 18 million bricks and 475,000 tiles, many of them in various shades of blue, it was overwhelming in its scale and beauty, but as I walked around, I started to feel very ill. I'd been feeling tired and completely drained of energy, so I put it down to another gut episode, but this time I also ached all over, as if I had flu. I just felt crap and every step was an effort.

Returning to the café, we were quickly ushered up to our room, where I ran for the bathroom to pass a lot of very watery diarrhoea. A dodgy gut was nothing new, but now it seemed much worse.

Lying on the bed, I groaned to Robert. 'God, I feel dreadful,' I said. 'I don't know if I'll be able to get on the bike. I'm not right.' I felt so weak I wouldn't even have managed to get up to go to the toilet, if Robert hadn't been there to help me.

According to our itinerary, we needed to leave Isfahan by mid-afternoon and ride for a couple of hours before darkness. A second night in Isfahan would put us behind schedule, making it unlikely that we'd leave Iran within the strictly prescribed seven days. Even so, I couldn't face riding that evening, so I asked Robert to go downstairs and ask the café owners if we could stay a second night.

Robert returned with some food, water and the news that we could stay one more night. Then he nursed me through the night. The next morning, I still felt dreadful. 'Elspeth.' Robert was sitting on the side of my bed, dabbing my forehead with a cool, damp cloth. 'We've got to get out of the country before our visas expire.'

'I don't know if I can do it,' I said. 'I'm so weak.' When I compared my symptoms to those I'd seen Mark suffer in Indonesia, I was convinced I had hepatitis. I looked at myself in the mirror, and noticed that the whites of my eyes were yellow. But I knew we had to move on.

Robert lifted me out of my bed, carried me down the stairs and helped me onto my bike. We rode off. Every twist of the throttle or squeeze of the clutch or brakes was a superhuman effort for me. I dreaded having to stop because I'd have to put my feet down to support the weight of the bike.

Even before I fell ill, riding my bike had become a considerable challenge. With no front or rear lights, no back brake and a lethal front brake, it was falling apart. To avoid using my constantly slipping clutch, I had mastered the art of clutchless gear changes, only using the clutch when I first set off. As long as I kept moving, I could ride all day without using it at all, a skill for which I was thankful in my weakened state. I rode head down, my eyes squinting ahead, praying that traffic lights would change from red to green before I got to them. When we stopped at a petrol station, I toppled over because I didn't have the strength in my legs to hold up the bike. Robert came over, helped me lift the bike back up, put me on it. Without his help, I don't know what I would have done.

Fortunately the roads were excellent, so I could just hang on to the bike and hope to get out of the country as soon as possible, then look for a hospital in Turkey.

We stayed one night in Saveh, in a room behind a shop. The next morning, hungry for the first time in days, I bought a slice of melon from a stall at the side of a road. But I took one bite and knew I wasn't ready for it. My liver felt sore within minutes of eating it, another sign that I was fighting hepatitis. I passed the slice of melon to Robert. Ever hungry, he finished it quickly.

We rode on, through desert scenery and past women working in irrigated fields near villages who didn't take the slightest notice of us when we stopped to repair a few things on Robert's bike. It seemed that for them, we were just there, a temporary feature in the landscape. It was a complete contrast to India, where we would have been surrounded in seconds. While Robert worked on his bike, I lay on the ground nearby, trying to regain some energy for the next leg of our journey.

That evening we reached Zanjan in the north-west of the country, about midway between Tehran and the Turkish border and found a room to stay. Early the next morning, feeling a bit stronger than the previous day, I left the room to get something from my bike. Running out into the street in a T-shirt and jeans, my head uncovered, my gaze on the ground to avoid stumbling when I still felt weak, I was initially oblivious to the commotion I was causing. It was only when I reached my bike that I noticed the Iranians in the street stopping dead in their tracks. My uncovered hair, my T-shirt and jeans, did not conform to the dress standards expected of a woman in public. Although few Iranian women completely covered themselves in 'black tent' *burkas*, nearly every woman wore a *chador* full-body cloak that left only their faces uncovered. Western women were expected to cover their hair and shoulders. Realizing I'd committed an offence against their concept of propriety, I ran back inside, slipped on a top and covered my hair before going back outside to my bike.

Riding slower than planned because I was still ill, we eventually made it to Marand that night, before continuing to the border town of Bazargan the next day. I'd previously thought that Taftan, the border crossing from Pakistan to Iran, was the nadir of awful border towns, but I was wrong. Bazargan was worse. Close also to the Iraq border, it had a particularly edgy atmosphere, even by the standards of border towns. As usual, lots of unsavoury characters roamed around, but Bazargan was also bristling with soldiers and official-looking characters, who we suspected were secret police and who watched us very closely. And as if we didn't already feel on edge, the border post had a huge painting of Ayatollah Khomeini on the wall beneath a sign stating 'Welcome to Islamic Republic of Iran' and beside it, painted inside a flower-shaped logo, the words: 'NO WESTERN'.

The border office was a mess. No one knew where we should go or what the carnet was about or who could stamp our passports to let us out of the country. It was utter chaos and I didn't have the energy for it. While I sat in the shade, Robert ran from office to office, trying to sort out our exit procedure from Iran.

'You need to come into the office,' said Robert, after he'd spent a couple of hours queuing in various buildings.

'Why?'

'Because we overstayed our visa by two days. You need to explain that it was because of your illness. They won't take it from me.'

We went into a shabby room with a counter, behind which several uniformed border officials were creating a fuss with every single person they encountered. However, it was nothing compared to the hassle that erupted when we presented ourselves and tried to explain the reason why we'd taken ten days instead of seven to cross Iran.

'Penalty . . . penalty . . .' said one of the officials. In a stream of invective, it was the only word we managed to understand.

'Do you know what's going on?' I asked Robert in a break from the tirade when the official took our passports into another room.

'I think they're threatening to put us in prison,' he said.

Suffering with hepatitis, I was so weak and exhausted that I could barely stand, my bike was falling apart and now they were threatening me with prison, I didn't think things could get any worse.

Lots more shouting followed, accompanied by people going in and out of rooms, carrying our passports. Robert didn't have a clue what was going on and I was too weak to care. I just stared at the floor, prayed it would all be over soon, so that I could crawl into a bed somewhere to rest and recover.

After a while we realized that very few people passed through the border post other than locals, so the officials had very little idea of how to process our paperwork. We were the first Western overlanders they'd seen in months – and then we'd overstayed our visa, which completely flummoxed them.

'We call police,' said one of the officials at one point.

'Okay,' I said. I didn't have the energy to care any more. Even a prison cell appeared attractive, as long as I could lie down until I felt better. Eventually the guards and officials realized that involving the police would create more work and upheaval for themselves. Opting instead for a quiet life, they stamped our carnets and passports, then waved us into Turkey.

If I'd had more energy I would have been triumphant, or at least slightly excited, but instead I wobbled into Turkey, desperate to rest and recuperate from my illness. Before I could do that, though, I spotted a bunch of bedraggled exhausted-looking people, who I thought might be refugees, on the Turkish side of the border, heading into Iran.

'Give them our rials,' I said to Robert.

'What?' Robert looked very surprised. 'But we might need them.'

'They're worthless out of the country.'

'But we might be able to use them or exchange them later.'

'We won't,' I said. 'And they take up loads of space in our bags.'

That convinced Robert. He immediately walked over to the bedraggled bunch and gave them our vast hoard of unspent Iranian currency. They were overjoyed.

As I watched him, I thought: I've done it. I'm in Turkey and almost home now. If anything goes wrong, I can get it sorted. The rest will be easy.

*

At first, Turkey still felt very Eastern. Fresh vegetables and bread were readily available, but in the area between the border and the first mountain range, everyone dressed and looked exactly the same as the people in Iran.

We stopped for the first night in Doğubayazit about forty kilometres inside Turkey, with the intention of staying for a few days to allow me to recuperate. We found a shabby hotel with green-painted corridors and dingy rooms, but I didn't care what it looked like as long as it enabled me to lie horizontal and still for a few days. Shortly after we got to our shoddy room, I went down the corridor to have a shower. I heard a noise outside the door.

I remembered having left the light on outside the bathroom, but now I noticed the keyhole on the door looked dark. Standing naked, I lowered my head to the keyhole.

An eye stared back at me through the keyhole.

'Fuck off!' I yelled, suppressing my immediate reaction to scream.

I kicked the door, then hit it several times.

Footsteps receded down the corridor.

Opening the door, I glimpsed the waiter disappearing around a distant corner.

I staggered back into the bedroom, dressed myself, then fell on the bed and slipped into a deep sleep, I was completely exhausted. When I woke later that evening, I felt uneasy.

'I'm sure we're being watched,' I whispered to Robert.

'Don't worry about it,' he said. 'You're just paranoid after what happened earlier.'

I didn't think Robert was right, so I got up from the bed. Keeping to the edge of the room, I crept across the room to the wall where I would be out of sight of anyone looking through the keyhole. Tiptoeing along the wall, I made my way silently to the door, then flung it open.

'Fuck off!' I yelled again.

A crowd was standing in the corridor, gathered around one man, who was on his knees, his eye at the exact position of our keyhole.

'I don't care how ill I am,' I said to Robert. 'I'm not staying here another night. Let's get out of here first thing.'

When we climbed on our bikes the next day, the clouds over Doğubayazit had cleared, affording excellent views of Mount Ararat, centre point of the Armenian Highlands and the supposed resting place of Noah's Ark. Still not feeling well, we rode past it, but only as far as Ağri. If it hadn't been for the peeping toms in Doğubayazit, we wouldn't have made the journey at all, which deposited us in another crap hotel room with green painted walls. Cruddy, concrete and Spartan, it had a bed in each of its four corners and a small desk upon which we dumped our belongings.

There was a knock on the door. I reached for the door handle, started to open it.

Crash!

The door slammed open and I was pushed aside. Four uniformed policemen burst into our room. One of them went straight for my tank bag. Another officer targeted Robert's pannier, while a third policeman picked up my diary from the desk, flicked through it. In seconds, they were everywhere.

'For fuck's sake!' I looked at Robert. 'Watch them . . . watch them! Or they might plant something on us.'

Maybe my paranoia was unwarranted, but ever since *Midnight Express*, a 1970s book and film about an American student caught smuggling hashish out of Turkey, the Turkish authorities had gained a disproportionate reputation for corruption and ruthlessness regarding drug trafficking. We had nothing to hide and should not have had anything to worry about, but I knew that didn't guarantee the police wouldn't emerge with some form of contraband that they would triumphantly claim they'd found in our possession.

'Stop!' I shouted. 'What are you doing?'

The policemen pushed Robert and me out of the way.

'Stop . . . please stop,' I said. 'We have nothing.'

'Police.' It appeared to be the only English word they knew.

One of the officers stopped rifling through our belongings to look Robert and me up and down. When I saw the look of suspicious contempt on his face, I realized how Robert's and my bedraggled, exhausted appearances must have looked to him. Yellow-skinned from jaundice, pasty-faced with illness, weak with exhaustion, severely underweight, my clothes hanging off my bones and filthy with dust from three weeks riding through the deserts of Pakistan and Iran, I looked little different from the clichéd image of a junky. And outside the hotel stood our bikes, mud-spattered, beaten wrecks that could easily lead impartial onlookers to think we were penniless and desperate enough to consider trafficking drugs for some quick cash.

'Keep watching them!' I shouted at Robert as the police ripped through our belongings and tore our possessions apart. Half an hour later, they'd finished and one of the policemen was holding the only contentious object they'd found: Robert's Bowie knife that he'd shipped from Holland to Sydney and had now carried all the way back to Turkey. With a long blade, the knife was so precious to Robert that it rarely left his side. He slept with it under his pillow, but now the police were making clear that they were confiscating it.

'You cannot do that!' Robert was jumping up and down. 'That's my property. I have done nothing wrong. You have no right to take it.'

But the police ignored him. Amid all our property strewn across the floor of the room, they responded with only one word: 'Bikes?'

We followed the police downstairs to watch as they stripped our bikes apart, removing the panniers, seat and tank. They searched inside the frames and prodded all parts of the bike, looking for contraband we didn't have. It took hours. They were convinced we had to be carrying drugs. Why else would we have made the journey?

Eventually they pulled a small package, wrapped in plastic, out of the frame of my bike. 'Look! Look!' said one of the policemen, brandishing the package like an excited schoolboy.

The other policemen gathered around him, several of them exclaiming and gesturing wildly, competing to be louder and more animated than their colleagues. I didn't need to be able to speak Turkish to understand what they were saying: at last they'd found exactly what they were looking for.

A silence fell as they pulled the inner contents of the package out of its plastic wrapper: about $100 in cash. Eyes narrowed as they questioned why I had hidden the money, before realizing that it was a matter of common sense to stash some emergency savings somewhere that few people would find it. With a disappointed look, they returned the cash to me and looked around the hotel foyer at the mess they'd created. Then, without a word, they turned away and walked out of the hotel into the street.

'That's mine! You can't take it,' Robert shouted after them. 'The knife is mine.'

'Maybe,' said the chief policeman. 'Come to the police station tomorrow.'

We reassembled our bikes and repacked our bags and panniers. That night, Robert hardly slept for worry about his treasured knife. The next day we turned up at the police station.

'Yes?' said the chief policeman who had taken Robert's knife.

'I've come for my knife.'

'Your knife?'

'You took my knife yesterday. I want it back.'

The policeman gave Robert a long, cold stare, dropped his hand under the counter and pulled out Robert's knife. Holding it by its tip, he passed it to Robert with an icy look that made it plain that he resented having to return it.

Without a word of undeserved thanks, Robert turned and left the police station. We spent the rest of the day replacing the steering head bearings on my bike, a frustrating and difficult job that took many hours, then I went straight back to bed for more recuperation.

From Ağri we rode as fast as we could out of Eastern Turkey, which had a very strange atmosphere. There were police everywhere and we felt as if we were being watched all the time. As we rode through towns and villages, we spotted kids standing at the side of the road in a line of four or five boys and girls, aged about ten, their hands behind their backs. As soon as we were within range, they chucked their missiles at us. Their aim was good and we were hit several times by stones and large rocks, never knowing whether it was for fun and sport, or if it was a more sinister reaction to strangers in their midst. Eventually we got wise to them and rode on the other side of the road from them as fast as we could. It was surreal and left us in no doubt that we were unwelcome here.

After a night spent sleeping in the back of a trailer in Erzurum, I noticed that I was starting to regain strength and began to feel marginally better. The gamma globulin doses I'd got whenever possible over the past year had reduced the intensity and duration of the symptoms when the hepatitis struck.

We rode on, camped for one night in Sivas, then made our way south-west into the Cappadocia region in the centre of Turkey. We stopped at Göreme, a volcanic valley with houses carved out of the soft tufa rock. Inhabited by troglodytes, the buildings looked like they had risen out of the ground. For the first time in two weeks, I felt stronger as I hauled myself around the ruins, although it was still an effort.

From Göreme we headed south and spent almost a week travelling along the Turkish coast, visiting castles and ruins, and indulging ourselves with swimming and good food. At last I felt safe eating meat regularly, which after more than a year on a largely vegetarian diet, tasted amazing, especially as the Turks cooked it so well with lots of herbs. We also ate lots of fish and delicious bread, crusty and white like French bread, with lots of good, salted butter.

Civilized and pleasant, this part of the trip felt like a small holiday. In the 1980s, this part of Turkey was largely untouched by tourists and the people were lovely. Our stay was marred only by the theft of my Walkman from Robert's tent. But now that I felt so close to home, I didn't really care.

After nearly four weeks making our way slowly across Turkey, a country that was far larger than I'd realized, we arrived in Istanbul. I loved it. The city was frenetic and intoxicating. Cars, taxis and buses buzzed everywhere. The manic traffic was alarming and exciting. We toured the sights, including the Blue Mosque, and we got talking to a local who took an interest in our bikes. On his advice and following his directions, we located a warehouse down a backstreet that made knock-off copies of BMW exhausts for a few dollars and dozens of other parts that we didn't really need, but which were so cheap we couldn't resist them. Laden down with our spare parts, we rode back down the coast from Istanbul to Çanakkale, a fishing port that is the nearest modern city to the site of ancient Troy.

Shortly after arriving in Çanakkale, Robert complained of feeling weak and tired. 'I've got a pain right here,' he said, pointing at his liver. I immediately thought of that slice of melon I offered him in Iran, immediately after I'd eaten a chunk of it. My greatest fear was that I had passed on the hepatitis to Robert who, unlike me, had not vaccinated himself with gamma globulin and was therefore likely to suffer a far worse infection.

Within a couple of hours, Robert was feeling so weak he was in bed. For the next three days, I nursed him, but could do little to improve the way he felt. His symptoms – fever, aching limbs, vomiting, weakness, liver pain, dark urine – all suggested hepatitis. Four days after taking refuge in Çanakkale, he was so yellow that I insisted he went to a doctor. The doctor took one look at Robert's symptoms and sent him immediately to hospital.

The hospital was a bit rough and ready, but okay. The doctors put Robert on a drip of sugars and salts to overcome dehydration and his lack of appetite, then left him to rest. I visited him every day. Robert couldn't move and was too weak to speak. When I wasn't seeing him, I found I had very little to do. To while away the time, I bought huge sacks of pistachio nuts for very little money and then sat all day eating them beside Robert's bed, joking that I'd bought 'pistachios for peanuts' and hoping he'd soon recover.

21

HOME ALONE:

TURKEY TO LONDON

Çanakkale, 28 October 1984

After five days in hospital, Robert was allowed to leave and moved back into the hotel, where he did very little except lie in bed all day. With November approaching, I was becoming concerned that we were running out of time. Europe would be getting cold and the only clothing we had was designed for riding in the tropics. My jeans and Robert's dungarees would not keep us warm across the Alps or into northern Europe. We needed to get moving if we wanted to get home for Christmas.

Thoughts of being at home were starting to enter my mind and with them the conundrum of what to do about my relationship with Mark. Until we reached Turkey, I wasn't certain I'd even get home, but now that the end was in clear sight – and in the near future – I wondered how I should resolve the complications of my love life. I had not picked up any letters since India as my plans had been so uncertain, so it had been several months since I had heard from Mark. I knew I had to be absolutely straight with him, but fretted over how to break the news without hurting him any more than was absolutely necessary. I still had fond feelings for him, but I also knew that Robert was the only man I wanted to be with now. Having written only once to Mark since leaving Kathmandu four months earlier, I wondered if maybe Mark already suspected that I had met someone else. My one consoling thought was that I had always warned Mark not to count on a relationship with me because I wasn't ready for it.

After eleven days recuperating at the hotel, Robert thought he was strong enough to continue the ride home. Neither of us felt particularly healthy, but we were okay. I was down to six and a half stone, technically dangerously underweight for a woman of my height. Robert was already skinny, but now he looked like he had been on a starvation diet. I could see every bone in his chest.

Setting off from Çanakkale, we rode until dusk, then pitched a tent in an olive grove. We spent the next three days riding up through Greece and Yugoslavia, staying in a hotel near a lake, then camping among poplar trees near Thessaloniki. Now in Europe, border crossings were relatively straightforward.

Our first stop in Yugoslavia was at Kumanovo, now in Macedonia, where we spent a very cold night camping in a field. The days were cold, too, and I had to put on everything I had to wear and stuff newspaper inside my jacket as insulation. It helped a bit, but I was still freezing, the coldest I have ever been. Worst of all were my hands, as my gloves had worn tissue-thin. Somewhere in the middle of Yugoslavia, we passed a building site where the workers were throwing out large thick plastic bags used to carry concrete. Robert and I nicked the bags out of the skip, then spent half a day fashioning some handlebar muffs from wire and the plastic wrapping, then fitting them to our bikes as windbreaks. They helped a lot.

Our route through Yugoslavia took us up the so-called 'Road of Death', a treacherous 250-mile two-lane highway between Zagreb and Belgrade that carried the bulk of the traffic heading from Europe to Asia. Renowned for its death toll, it was littered with crosses, shrines and memorials to thousands of deceased drivers and their unfortunate passengers. One truck driver we met told us he saw 'dozens of vehicles turned into tin salad every time I drive through'. Turkish workers returning from Germany in their summer holidays used the road as a rat run on their way home. Faced with 1,500-mile journeys, they were renowned for putting bricks on their accelerators to rest their feet, then dozing off at the wheel, often killing all the occupants of their vehicle and several other vehicles too.

The further we ventured along the 'Road of Death', the more we realized why it had gained its reputation. Coming over the brow of a hill or around a blind bend, we'd often be confronted by an approaching truck being overtaken by another truck on our side of the road, which was in turn being overtaken by a third vehicle, bouncing along the edge of the highway, one wheel on the road and one wheel on the dusty verge. Again and again we faced these moving walls of trucks, stretching from dirt verge to dirt verge, occupying the entire road and more, approaching fast. It was terrifying.

Had we been driving a car, there would have been no escape, but on bikes we could ride onto the banks at the side of the road and wait for the lunacy to pass us by. I thought I'd left chaotic roads behind in India, but this was worse than anything I'd experienced in the subcontinent because everything moved so much faster. No wonder the death toll was so high.

With every mile we rode further north, the temperature dropped, until we crossed the border from Yugoslavia to Austria and found ourselves riding along roads lined with snow. Since we were still dressed in clothes suited to the tropics, the cold was now becoming dangerous to us and we were stopping every thirty miles to force blood and warmth back into our extremities.

In our current state, the thought of crossing the Alps was incredibly daunting. Struggling to keep warm now, when we were surrounded by a mere few inches of snow, I was starting to wonder quite seriously if we could survive the deep snow and ice we'd encounter in the mountains in the gear we were wearing and on bikes held together by string, tape, bits of wire and rubber bands. My brakes were still not working properly and we'd have to cross several passes where the snow would be several feet deep and the temperatures even more brutal than where we were now standing. I didn't know how much longer I could take it.

At one rest stop, Robert went off to look for somewhere to buy hot food and returned with a very small Turkish man with a huge smile.

'This is Suleyman,' he said. 'He's got an empty van. He can give us a lift across the Alps and into Germany.'

I didn't need to hear it twice. Twenty minutes later, we were sitting in the cab of Suleyman's van with the heater on full blast, trying to warm up while Suleyman, still with a beaming smile, sweated in his jumper and jacket. Our bikes safely stowed behind us in the van, Robert and I knew we'd just made one of the best decisions of our journey together. A few hours later, passing over the Alps, we saw the depth of the snow and realized that we would never have made it across the mountain range.

At a rest stop on the autobahn between Salzburg and Munich, we waved goodbye to Suleyman and rode northwards through Germany. After two years of travelling slowly through the developing world, sometimes at walking pace, it was a massive shock to find myself on German autobahns. Whenever I ventured into the overtaking lane, hugely powerful BMW and Mercedes cars would bear down on me at frightening speeds, their headlights flashing. Suddenly I was back in the manic thrust of Western Europe.

'Have you noticed how everyone looks so miserable?' I said to Robert at one of our stops for petrol. 'All these people driving big cars seem so stressed, angry and unhappy.'

Robert smiled and nodded. 'Strange, isn't it?'

It was quite an eye-opener and a considerable shock to be thrown back into the melee of Western Europe, but the biggest surprise was how much my journey had changed my outlook in the time I was away. It struck me that people in poorer countries appeared happier, even though they had very little. Life was much simpler in the less developed countries we'd travelled through, and it seemed the more people had the more they wanted. It was clear to me now how easy it is to take things for granted and forget to be grateful for the basics in life: family, food, and shelter.

Staying in roadside motels, we headed further north through Germany. At another autobahn service area, we met several BMW riders, all riding immaculate bikes and wearing matching gear. When they saw our BMWs, they looked horrified, as if they couldn't quite understand what we'd done to them.

'Have you come a long way?' said one of the German bikers.

'From Sydney,' said Robert.

I didn't have the inclination to explain that I'd come from London via Sydney, so I simply said: 'Australia.'

The bikers stared at us, as if they didn't know how to react or what to say next. It wasn't the first time we'd encountered people, intrigued by our beaten and battered bikes, then rendered speechless by our answers to their questions about our journey.

We continued our journey through Germany to the Dutch border, which we crossed near the city of Gronau. A couple of hours later, I was standing with Robert in a detached house at the edge of a flat Dutch plain, trying to come to terms with the fact that my journey was almost done and I'd returned in love with a new man, whose mother was welcoming me into her home.

Over the next few days, Robert and I decompressed in the comfort of his mother's modest home. Rested and fortified by his mother's simple, delicious home cooking, Robert and I slowly regained strength. Days were spent being shown the local sights – a visit to Gouda, a look over a windmill, a canal and a couple of churches – by Robert. In the evenings, I'd listen to Robert explain our journey to his mother in Dutch while we feasted on her healthy, hearty stews.

Staying at Robert's mother's house was a strange way to end my journey. It felt unreal, like a dream, mainly because of the culture shock at suddenly finding myself back in the familiar surroundings of a family home in Western Europe after two years of living a nomadic lifestyle, largely in the developing and undeveloped world.

At the back of my mind was the nagging thought that Robert and I really needed to talk about our future – together or apart – but neither of us appeared to have the mental or physical energy to begin the conversation. I'd had such an amazing, life-changing experience with Robert that I didn't want our adventure to stop. Already I was considering a plan to service and repair my bike back in London, then take off with Robert to ride around Africa, South America or some other remote part of the world. I didn't want my life on the road with Robert to end.

After three days at Robert's mother's house, I realized that these deliberations about my future were delaying my return to London.

Although sad to leave Robert I was longing to see my family and get home. Robert sensed my restlessness; we were both mentally and physically exhausted and we spoke little about the future. I felt a sense of loss after such an adventure, missing the intensity of life on the open road. We had lived every minute of every day and suddenly it had all come to an end. 'We can work out our future later,' I said. 'Right now, I need to get home and see my family.'

The next morning, I hugged Robert, thanked him and his mother for their hospitality, then set off for home. I rode south to Calais with no problem, but it felt strange not having Robert at my side. I could feel a storm building, becoming stronger the closer I got to the port. By the time, I joined the line of vehicles waiting to board the 2 p.m. ferry, the wind had become a gale and rain had started to fall. The ferry was scheduled to dock at Dover at 4 p.m., which I calculated would mean I could easily get home by seven, just in time for dinner.

Struggling to believe I would be on English soil again within a couple of hours, I found it hard to contain my excitement. Only seventy-five miles from Dover to London remained to be completed. Against all the odds, I had achieved exactly what I'd set out to do.

I'd strapped my bike down securely in the hold. With a force nine gale now blowing, I knew it was going to be a rough crossing, but I didn't appreciate quite how rough until we pulled out through the port wall into open sea. The ferry was tossed around like a rag doll in a washing machine. The passengers staggered around the decks, looking green as they headed for the toilets or fresh air outside.

A couple of hours later, we reached Dover and sailed into the Western Docks, only to be told that the vehicle ramp at our quay wasn't working so we couldn't disembark. For several hours, we waited on the ferry without any further information from the crew about how we were going to dock. With the seasick passengers getting more tired and disgruntled, an announcement was eventually made. The captain told us he had considered re-routing to the Eastern Docks, but decided against it because the docks didn't have a train station for foot passengers, and now we couldn't dock at either dock because the tide was too low.

A collective groan went up from the passengers. Over the next hour, things turned nasty as a series of irate complaints directed against the captain and his crew twisted into a dispute between the foot passengers and vehicle passengers, each side blaming the other for the ferry's predicament. As tempers flared, a new announcement was made over the tannoy. 'Ladies and gentlemen,' said the captain. 'I regret to inform you that the crew has gone on strike.'

Bedlam reigned as passengers, officers and crewmembers shouted at one another in English and French. Meanwhile, the captain, stuck beside a dock at which he couldn't berth his ship, his crew having gone out on strike, decided to make a new announcement over the tannoy.

'Ladies and gentlemen, this is the captain,' he said. 'We were going to sail over to the Eastern Docks to allow you to disembark, but unfortunately one of the engines has broken down.' The moans, complaints and arguments between passengers and crew were immediately silenced. 'A diver has been dispatched,' continued the captain, 'to investigate possible damage to the propeller. I apologize for any inconvenience.'

Darkness had fallen, hopes of docking had disappeared and I had abandoned any hope of arriving home in time for dinner. Checking my watch, I realized that my parents would soon be going to bed. It seemed ridiculous; I could see the lights of Dover through portholes. They looked so close I felt like I could touch them and yet they were far beyond the reach of anyone on the ship.

Hours ticked slowly past until we heard the captain's voice come over the public address system again. He explained that they had been unable to repair the damaged propeller, then added: 'So I'm going to give it a go. I'm going to try to dock.' It was a farce of Indian proportions.

Shortly before midnight, the captain reversed the ship out of the Western Docks. Passing through a gap between two long breakwaters into open sea, the waves were so high that the two lighthouses on either end of the breakwaters intermittently disappeared from view. 'After all I've been through,' I thought, 'my bike and I are going to bloody sink and end up at the bottom of the English Channel just outside Dover.'

Eventually we arrived in the Eastern Docks and I disembarked at 2 a.m. on a freezing November night. The journey to London felt like the longest, most painful ride I had on my entire trip. Having become acclimatized to seeing distances in kilometres, each of the seventy-five miles felt like it went on for ever. The road was empty, nowhere was open, and although I'd repaired my headlight in Holland, I hadn't managed to find a proper halogen bulb, so it was very dim, forcing me to ride slowly through the starless night.

Shortly after 5 a.m. I finally arrived in London. It felt very strange. The streets were deserted and lifeless. After the bustle of India, Pakistan, Iran and Turkey, my still and silent home city felt entirely alien. Everything felt simultaneously very familiar and very different as I looked at London through an entirely changed perspective of more than two years on the road, existing entirely by my wits.

Passing the Gus Kuhn shop in Clapham Road, I thought of Lester and Daniel, who put me up in Auckland after I met them in the shop three years earlier.

I rode on, crossing the Thames on Vauxhall Bridge, beneath which flowed the river on which my BMW had begun its voyage to New York 799 days earlier.

Riding up Marylebone High Street, I passed my bank and found myself surrounded by the shops and pubs that had been the cornerstones of my earlier life. Somehow they seemed to have shrunk.

I turned a corner into New Cavendish Street, then another into Wimpole Street. Riding smack down the middle of Wimpole Street, I slowed the bike, savouring the last few tens of yards, relishing the moment until I rolled to a stop outside the house, one up from the corner. I parked my beloved BMW perpendicular to the kerb, its headlight pointing directly at the very familiar door of my childhood home.

I looked at the door and the glass fanlight above it, painted with 15 Upper Wimpole Street. *My God*, I thought as the BMW's engine ticked over between my legs. *I've bloody done it.*

Lowering my head until it rested on my tank bag, I felt my leather jacket squeak against the cold metal. Reaching forwards, I touched the key in the BMW's ignition, turned the key one click to the right to turn my headlight off, clicked it again to turn off my dipped light, and paused for a moment before the third and final turn to shut down the engine.

We were done. It felt wonderful.

PART 5

THE AFTERMATH

22

ALL THINGS MUST PASS

London, 22 November 1984

Standing outside my parents' house, three hours before dawn and two years after leaving home, I had a problem: no front door key. I rang the doorbell for Justin's flat at the back of the house. He opened the front door, bleary-eyed and dishevelled.

'Elspeth?'

'Justy?' I still didn't quite believe I was home at last. 'Yeah – it's me.'

Justin gave me a huge hug and, although desperate to return to bed, he made me tea and covered me in a blanket while I shivered and huddled in front of a gas fire in his flat. For about an hour, Justin listened to me unload my thoughts and experiences from the road in a babbling stream of consciousness before leaving me on my own after insisting he needed more sleep. Although I felt tired, too, I couldn't sleep. I was too excited and still could not believe I was home.

At about eight o'clock, my mother came downstairs to collect the papers. 'Elspeth! You're here!' We hugged and after a few comments about my appearance, I felt her interest wane. Life had returned to normal for my mother.

'Why hasn't the Sunday paper been delivered?' she asked.

'I don't know.'

'Hmm.' Mum looked annoyed.

While she disappeared to solve her newspaper crisis, I went upstairs and found something to eat in the kitchen. Emerging from the kitchen, I bumped into my father on the landing. 'Oh hello,' he said, showing no surprise or excitement at my arrival. It was almost as if I'd never left home. I hadn't expected bunting, streamers and banners to herald my return, but some kind of minor celebration wouldn't have gone amiss. Upset and confused, I tried to rationalize my family's indifference, telling myself that this was because my parents had always expected me to do what I'd set out to do. Their apparent disinterest, I told myself, was a tacit vote of confidence in my abilities.

Later that day, I caught a glimpse through a window of my bike standing in front of the house, its headlight peering towards me expectantly, like a dog hoping to go for a walk. Already my BMW seemed like an old friend from my past with whom I'd shared exceptional, special experiences, but with whom I was now losing touch. I went outside, ran my hands over the BMW badge and along the tank, then wheeled the old girl around to the mews, where I parked her in the back of the garage and took a note of the mileage. The odometer said 74,574 miles. When I left New York on 4 October 1982, it displayed 45,447 miles. My speedo cable then broke in Sydney, leaving around 5,000 miles unrecorded by the odometer. I did the mental arithmetic: a few miles short of 35,000 – that's what it had taken me to ride around the world.

Over the next few days, I slept a lot, ate a lot and tried to tell my parents about my experiences, but I found it hard to hold their interest. I was in the middle of describing my journey through Iran, when my mother perked up.

'Mark has been on the phone,' she said, her expression expectant.

'Oh . . . there's something I need to tell you,' I said.

After I'd told Mum about Robert, Mum said very little and we didn't speak about him again for some time.

The next day, I contacted Mark and we arranged to meet. Although pleased to see each other, it wasn't an easy meeting. I was honest, telling Mark immediately about Robert, who he had of course met in Kathmandu. I described how awful India had been and how it had been such hard work, a battle to survive every day. And I tried to explain how fighting those outside forces pushed Robert and me closer together.

'We were travelling and it just happened,' I said, knowing that my words were probably no consolation to Mark, but hoping they might reduce his disappointment and hurt. I tried to explain that it was nothing to do with him, but the result of being in a hostile, foreign environment with someone who was undergoing exactly the same things and who therefore saw the world the same way. Mark was quiet, but I felt he understood. 'I don't know what I want,' I said. 'I don't know what I want to do. I am still trying to get my head around being back at home. I'm really sorry.'

Mark was very good about it. He told me he was still in love with me and it was hard to see him upset, but I think he knew it was pointless making any demands on me and he left me alone, giving me the time and space to work out my feelings.

A few days later, I met up with all my biking friends. Johnny, Mike, Rick and Nick all sat with me over a pint in the pub, and I shared with them some of the highs and lows of my epic trip. But after a while I could tell that they were losing interest, so I shut up. I felt nobody understood what I'd been through. My life over the last two years had been so far from the norm, so extreme and different, that people found it hard to relate to. 'So what's been going on with all of you?' I said, changing the subject.

But nothing at all had changed for my friends since I'd been away. They were still doing exactly what they'd been doing when I left London in October 1982, just over two years earlier. Meanwhile, *everything* had changed for me and I felt a deep need to reconnect with my pals after so many life-changing experiences for me. Just as they had found it hard to engage with my stories, I struggled to take an interest in their very normal London lives now.

I longed to see Robert and, shortly before Christmas, he visited and I introduced him to my parents. Although my mother was always very polite to visitors, she treated Robert in a way that made it clear to me that she didn't think he was the right person for me. 'Mark is an engineer, darling,' said Mum after Robert had left.

I knew exactly what she meant: engineers were professional, respectable, safe and secure, everything that my mother thought mechanics, such as Robert, were not. To make matters worse, Robert was an adventure biker and might drag me away from her again.

The indifference and disinterest I encountered from my family and friends soon made me retreat into myself. I moved into the front basement flat, where I hunkered down, sticking photographs, mementoes and carefully annotated hand-drawn maps of my route into a series of albums that I constructed from card and gaffer tape. I researched the names of every monument, temple, fort and mosque I'd visited. It was painstaking, obsessive behaviour, but it was my way of not letting go of my trip. At times I longed to be back in the middle of a desert or on the side of a mountain, often solitary but never as isolated as I now felt in London.

Over the next few weeks, I wrote letters to bike magazines, newspapers and book publishers, asking if they'd be interested in my story. A few replied, but only to brush me off with similarly worded explanations each time: 'Your story not quite right for us.' It seemed nobody wanted to know.

In early January, I received a letter from Robert, written after we'd spoken on Christmas Day. 'When I phoned, you sounded pretty down,' he wrote. His bike, now repaired, *runs like a new one*, he informed me before extending an invitation to ride with him from Holland to Cape Town. 'It wouldn't surprise me that I have to go alone. I don't know what you want, but you've got more things to sort out than I. For the moment this doesn't matter much travel-wise, although it does matter feeling-wise.'

Unsure of my intentions, Robert signed off his letter with 'Good luck and maybe goodbye', so I immediately wrote back to explain my dilemma to him. Although I was unhappy in London and very tempted to depart on a new trip, especially with him, I knew that the time for responsibility had arrived, which included returning to college to finish my architecture training. A few days later, a letter arrived from Robert. 'I understand the situation, therefore no hard feelings,' he wrote. 'But the harder I try to forget you, the more you're on my mind.'

Robert was having just as hard a time as me readjusting to life at home.

I manage all right but only because I know that I will leave again, otherwise I'd go mad. I would like to come over to see you and try to settle what we have for good or bad. It's not so much that I'm in a hurry; it's more that I want to know where I stand. It would be nice to go to South Africa together, but if there is no future for us then I don't really want to attempt it together, as such a trip would bring us together even closer. And to do such a thing with no future in mind is crazy feeling-wise for both of us.

I don't know how you feel, but if you've got half a mind to stick it out with me, there will be a few things to take into consideration. I'll never be a high-flyer. All I want is a small cottage with a big shed and a couple of bikes.

Like Robert, I felt restless at home, but I wasn't sure that running away was the answer, which was one of the reasons why my BMW was gathering dust in the back of the garage. Another reason was that the journey had changed my feelings about riding my bike. The trip had been very hard work and with many days spent anxiously hoping she wouldn't break down, my BMW no longer represented freedom and escape so much as survival. By the end, my bike had become no more than a tool for getting me to my destination. And now that we were both home, I didn't dare look at her in the garage because she represented the journey that no one I loved and cared about seemed to want to acknowledge.

In early spring I finally wheeled my bike out of the garage and sat on it for the first time since my return. I looked down at the dusty petrol tank, filthy frame and dirty engine. A part of me felt guilty for neglecting her, but then I realized why I'd been so reluctant to clean her up. For as long as my bike was still covered in the dust of the road and her frame was still bent and twisted, her brakes hardly worked, oil leaked from every gasket, then my memories of my journey were still intact. I looked at the numerous bodged repairs I'd done, remembering exactly where I was when I had done them. If I took her apart, washed off the dust, the squashed insects and all the other relics of Iran, Pakistan, Nepal, India, Thailand, Malaysia, Australia and America, then I'd also be washing away the memories of my journey with Robert. And with no one but Robert to share and relive those memories, I was worried that everything about my trip would soon be gone.

A few days later, I contacted a journalist from *Motorcycle News* to see if they would be interested in writing a feature about my trip. Thinking that at last I might get recognition for my achievement, I relayed my story in detail, but when the feature appeared at the end of March, I was very disappointed. The article implied that I'd succeeded mainly because I came from a privileged, wealthy family, ignoring the fact that my parents had almost no involvement in my trip. I'd told the journalist that returning to Europe had been a culture shock after travelling through many countries that were less materialistic but where the people seemed happier. But my observation was twisted to make me sound naive and spoilt. A week later, *MCN* published a letter entitled 'Biting the hand that feeds you', which accused me of criticizing comfortable materialistic existences while coming from a privileged, wealthy background myself. It managed to miss the point altogether.

There was no good reason why I'd succeeded in riding around the world when few other people had done it, other than it had never seemed to me to be something I couldn't do. Possibly the energy, optimism and naivety of youth got me through it and stopped me giving up. But a major impetus was that I simply wanted to prove to my family, my friends and most importantly to myself that I could succeed.

In early April I received a letter from Robert:

I hope my love for you dies soon. I am missing you terribly, but what we have does not make sense. There are too many things I can't get even with, therefore it's best left to die a slow death. Wish we had had an argument. It would make it easier to forget you. I've tried everything to hate you.

More than anything, I had wanted a relationship with Robert. I'd arrived back in London convinced that I'd met the love of my life, but returning home had changed the nature of our relationship.

Robert and I still saw each other whenever possible. I travelled to Holland and he came to London, but each visit seemed only to highlight our differences. Most of all, the excitement of not knowing what was going to happen each day was gone and for the first time we were running out of things to say. Thinking that we'd rediscover what it was that we'd found so exciting and attractive about each other if we rode off on another trip together, I suggested we took our bikes around Iceland for a few weeks.

Robert wrinkled his nose. 'I don't know . . .' he said. 'I'm not sure.'

I was surprised. 'What do you mean, you're not sure?'

'I just want a quiet life,' he said. 'I just want to stay at home.'

Looking at Robert, I was confused; his last letter had talked about going off to South Africa together so our life of excitement could continue. But for Robert, I think it had to be all or nothing. I suspected he had also felt things falling apart between us, and a two-week holiday in Iceland would just be a short interlude postponing the inevitable. I began to realize he was a different person from the one I'd thought he was on our travels. Since our return, he had developed an obsessive interest in military binoculars, whereas I was reawakening my interest in architecture. Things that hadn't mattered to him when we were on the road, such as our different backgrounds and ambitions, suddenly bothered him. 'You want to do things that I can't imagine,' he said to me at one of our meetings. 'You want to be an architect and you want to travel the world. I'm not like that. I'm just a simple fellow.'

It was very painful. Something that I thought was resilient and fantastic was slipping through my fingers and I found myself drifting away from Robert, towards Mark. As there were few people I could really talk to, Mark and I had remained good friends, often meeting up for a drink, much to my mother's delight.

A short time later, I started working as an architectural assistant. It got me out of the basement flat for the first time in three months and I enjoyed the work, but I found it difficult to engage with my new colleagues. Over the next few months, I smiled and did all the right things, even being a bridesmaid at my sister Poppy's wedding, but I never felt right or happy, a situation that wasn't made easier by the next letter from Robert, which revealed he was struggling as much as me with the crumbling of our relationship. 'The cooling-down bit and taking a distance doesn't come easy for me,' he wrote. 'But it's the only solution to the present and future. The love will always be there, but it makes no sense.' I felt desperately sad but at the same time I knew he was right.

By early summer in 1985, I was feeling that the time had come to move on with my life. I went out to the garage, looked at my BMW sitting there, untouched and unloved. Accepting that my trip now belonged to my past, I started to strip down my bike, believing that if I renovated it, my bike would no longer remind me of my journey. I completely stripped down the engine, replacing all the bearings, seals and piston rings. Every part was removed and either cleaned or replaced. I felt that after all she had done for me, all the miles she'd carried me, she deserved a face and body lift. While I was working on the bike, I received another letter from Robert, this time asking if he could come over to London to collect some tools and manuals that he'd lent me. 'Don't worry,' he wrote. 'I promise you nothing heavy on my visit.'

It was good to see Robert, although he told me he had now abandoned all plans to travel again on his bike. After all we'd planned while still on the road, I was very disappointed to see my friend, lover and companion abandon his ambitions. However, I soon understood Robert's change of heart when he revealed the real reason for his visit. 'I've met someone,' he told me. 'And she doesn't want me to be in contact with you. I have to respect that wish.'

It was a great shock, but I vowed to adhere to his request and never to contact him again, although I hoped he would eventually get in touch with me and that we might one day be friends. It was so painful and I found it almost impossible to accept that we might never see each other again after all we had been through. It tore me apart

Unlike Robert, I was determined not to let moss grow under my bike's tyres. A few weeks later, I set off with Justin on a trip through Europe heading for Syria and Jordan, but when I got to Turkey, I stopped. Somehow riding my bike wasn't the same now. I couldn't see the point of riding hundreds of miles every day, only to turn around and come back, Justy was his usual easy-going self and didn't object, so we turned around and rode back home.

I started back at the Polytechnic of Central London to do my architecture diploma and Mark and I started seeing each other again. It was good. He'd grown up a lot and we soon slipped back into our routines.

Over the next two years, I struggled to get through my diploma. After such an exciting period away, I was bored at college. To make the diploma more challenging and interesting, I decided to do no drawing at all. Instead, I only built models of all my designs. I found it therapeutic, losing myself completely in my models. The Head of Architecture was not impressed and threatened to fail me because I had no drawings in my portfolio.

Incensed by the narrow-mindedness of his box-ticking attitude and rejection of anything or anyone that stepped or thought outside the norm, I stubbornly refused to present my designs as drawings. For my viva, the final exam for an architecture diploma, I was put forward as a fail but the external examiner overturned this decision and gave me a pass, saying that my 'models are a breath of fresh air'.

In the autumn of 1987, I returned to work to complete my Part III, a further year's work experience required before taking the Royal Institute of British Architects Professional Practice exam so I could finally call myself an architect. In early 1988, my phone rang in the office. It was Alex. We'd not spoken for years, and now, out of nowhere, he'd got in touch. He told me about an amazing water tower he'd seen near Guildford that was for sale. 'Maybe you could buy it.'

I dismissed Alex's crazy idea, until a few weeks later, when Mark and I were driving through the Surrey hills and I mentioned the water tower to Mark. 'We could have a look for it,' I said. 'If Alex thinks it's amazing, maybe it's worth seeing.'

Stopping in Godalming, we asked a passer-by if they knew of a water tower anywhere in the vicinity. Fifteen minutes later, driving on a back road we suddenly saw a magnificent 130-foot redbrick tower rising above the trees with a 'For sale' sign. Quite different from what I expected, it was like a giant turret for a missing castle. The minute I saw it I knew I had to have it. The tower was derelict, full of pigeons and had been disused for twenty years. To add further complication, it was a listed building with no planning permission, but I decided to go for it. In October 1988 Thames Water auctioned the tower. Sitting in the auction room with Mark and my father, we managed to secure it for £121,000, a few thousand pounds below my absolute limit.

Buying the tower was a huge risk. It was the first water tower conversion the local council had ever dealt with so there were many obstacles to overcome. But that didn't matter: now on a mission, I wasn't going to take no for an answer. Slowly but surely, I found ways of dealing with each of the council's objections. Over a year later we had successfully dealt with all the council's concerns and overcome all my neighbours' objections, a process that ultimately went to appeal.

My mother was overjoyed. She had persuaded my dad to lend me the money to buy the tower. Knowing I still had a restlessness, she thought the tower would anchor me to Mark in the conventional and conformist way that she understood. And although I sometimes still thought about Robert, I was very happy with Mark.

By early 1990, I finally had planning and listed building consent and could start work on the building. On a joint mission, Mark and I were getting on really well, even managing to find fun in shovelling several tons of pigeon droppings out of the tower, sometimes until late into the night.

Then, in the spring of 1990, just as the renovation of the tower had begun, I discovered I was pregnant. I had mixed feelings, but Mark and I had been together for nearly five years and we were happily working on building our home together, so in many ways it felt like good timing. But I did have fears about becoming a mother and losing my independence.

'You've got to understand that I'm never going to be a stay-at-home mum, cooking, cleaning and looking after kids. It's just not me,' I said to Mark one evening. 'So if we go ahead with this, you need to promise me that you'll do your share of the childcare, fifty-fifty.'

'Absolutely,' said Mark. 'I promise: fifty-fifty. I'll do my bit.'

Although unintended, falling pregnant felt like a good thing. I'd always wanted children, but suspected it might never happen because

I was always too busy doing other things. Having motherhood thrust upon me was possibly the only way I was ever going to have a child, even if right now wasn't the best time for it.

At that time, however, being pregnant had to take a backseat to the tower renovation. After working all week in London, Mark and I would drive the thirty miles down to the water tower, where we'd camp and spend the weekends working on our home. For the entire nine months of my pregnancy, I worked on the outside of the building, inspecting and cleaning all the brickwork with a pressure washer that I hauled up and down the scaffolding, squeezing my bulging stomach through spaces between the scaffold 'lifts' until I could no longer fit through the gaps. Finally I had to ask the scaffolders to adjust the boards to allow me easier access.

It was knackering work, but I was in a rush to get as much done as possible before our baby was due. On a self-employment contract, I couldn't afford to take much time off, so I worked right up until the baby was born in December 1990.

Mark and I returned home to Wimpole Street with our son, Tom, and stayed there, as my mum was keen to help me during my first few weeks of motherhood. Mark took two weeks' paternity leave and was very helpful until the end of the fortnight, when he returned to work.

I found being at home all day with Tom very hard and knew I needed to get back into some sort of routine for my own sanity. Since Tom's birth I'd struggled to adjust to my new life as a mother.

While I nursed Tom and got used to being a mother, my mum helped me by cooking meals and giving me much-needed breaks from looking after him while Mark was at work. Mum also helped me find a childminder, as after only six weeks I had arranged to return to work.

On the evening of 9 February 1991 I was just drifting off to sleep when I heard a loud thud on the floor downstairs. I'd been vaguely aware of my dad down in the kitchen, indulging in his habit of a midnight snack before bed. As I sat up in bed, I heard my mother's footsteps running to the kitchen, and then a long scream. I ran downstairs and found my father lying on the kitchen floor, a small pool of blood seeping from the back of his head. Mum frantically tried to resuscitate him while I called an ambulance.

We followed the ambulance to the hospital where the accident and emergency staff managed to restart Dad's heart and moved him into intensive care, but we were told that he was officially classified as brain-dead. He never woke up and after two weeks his life support was switched off. It was devastating for all of us. My mother was completely distraught, so I put my return to work on hold to help her deal with her grief. Justin and Poppy took time off work and we made sure one of us stayed with her at all times. Mark did his best to be supportive but he didn't understand at all, never really knowing what to do or say.

Within four months of Dad's death, Mum had sold our family home where I had lived for thirty years. I found leaving my childhood home very traumatic, my mother clearing out the contents of the house in a manic frenzy of grief. It was an understandable reaction to my father's death as she adjusted to her new life without him, but it made losing him much harder for me.

In June, when the family home was finally sold, Tom, Mark and I had no choice but to move into the water tower, which was still a building site. Tom was six months old. It had no floors, no bathroom, no kitchen, no running water, no heating and no sanitation.

I found it difficult to move out of the only home I had ever known. Packing up my belongings I found my aluminium panniers and top box in the attic. Ten years had passed since I'd left on my journey, which now seemed like a distant memory. I'd hung on to the boxes for purely sentimental reasons, but now, thinking I'd never use them again and that no one gave a damn about my journey anyway, I found a skip outside the garage and sat them on top of a pile of builder's rubble. I stood there looking at the stickers of all the countries I'd ridden through. There were signatures, little notes and drawings that friends I had met along the way had scribbled onto them, cherished mementoes of our time together. I took one last look, turned around and walked away.

*

As well as supporting my mother in her grief and house move, and building the tower, I had gone back to work full time while looking after Tom. Mark had been promoted and was working all hours, which meant he wasn't able to give me the help and support I so desperately needed.

My days consisted of getting up at 5 a.m., driving for an hour and a half into London in my unheated twenty-year-old VW Beetle and then dropping Tom off at a childminder. I worked all day, then drove home with Tom to the tower, where I sorted out the builders before I fed Tom and put him to sleep. Mark wouldn't usually get back from London until about 10.30 p.m.

This relentless routine continued for nearly six months until, in October 1991, I found myself standing at the parapet on the roof of the tower. I looked over the edge and was thinking about jumping, but something stopped me – call it survival or bloody-mindedness or maybe even defiance – I took a step back from the edge, breathed deeply and asked myself if ending my life was what I really wanted. *I've done this before*, I thought. *I've found myself in situations like this.* Even when problems seemed insurmountable, I'd learnt there was always a way to deal with them. *Do what you've always done when faced with more problems than you can handle*, I told myself. *Break it down. A big problem is no more than lots of small problems.* I stepped back from the parapet, went downstairs and checked on Tom. I didn't realize at the time, but I was suffering with postnatal depression. I think the combination of the stresses of a new baby, grieving for the loss of my father and my childhood home, living on a building site and supporting my mum had really taken its toll.

A few hours later, Mark returned from work and I explained how close I'd come to ending my life that evening and that I desperately needed his help. He was very quiet. I'd thought Mark had grown up when we were travelling together through Indonesia and Nepal, but I now realized he was at heart still the same little boy who'd pursued me a decade ago. After all I'd had to cope with, as well as becoming a mother, it was disappointing to discover that none of this seemed to resonate with Mark.

Mark moved out and I spent the next four years on my own,

nailing floorboards, tiling bathrooms, fitting cupboards and doing all the work needed to convert the water tower into a home for Tom and me. It was hell and I hated every moment of it. It was the toughest period of my life, harder than anything on my global bike trip, in part because I had always known my trip would be a solo venture, whereas I had taken on the tower and Tom on the understanding that they were shared endeavours. Sadly, I was wrong and I had to readjust mentally to dealing with everything on my own.

Four years after Mark left, and with the tower almost complete, my hard work began to reap rewards when the tower received several prestigious architectural awards. On the strength of my awards I decided to set up my own architecture practice in 1998.

Over the next few years things settled down and I began getting my life back together again. Although being a single mother in those early months had been the toughest part of my life so far, I'd survived it and created a beautiful home for us at the same time. I semi-retired my faithful old girl, the R60, to the back of the garage, and bought another BMW, the last of the 'airheads', an R80GS Basic.

Occasionally, I heard from Alex. I found it curious how he would pop back into my life at intervals, then disappear for years on end. Without his impetus, two of the three biggest achievements of my life would not have happened. Without Alex, I would not have bought my BMW and might never have left on my journey. And without Alex, I wouldn't have found the water tower.

On 27 February 2009, an envelope arrived at my office. It was from Holland. I didn't recognize the handwriting and my address was incorrect so it had taken over two weeks to arrive.

I opened the letter and took out a small leaflet with a picture of a man on a motorbike, seen from behind riding down a winding track that led to a distant horizon. For a second I was confused. Above the motorcyclist was printed a name that started Wijnand Joris . . .

The third Christian name was Robert and the surname was Albregts. Beneath it was Robert's date of birth and beside it, written in Dutch, 19 februari 2009.

Unable to understand what was written in Dutch, I could only assume the second date was the date of Robert's death and the leaflet announced his memorial service.

Having heard nothing from Robert for twenty-four years, it was a huge shock. The leaflet trembling in my hands, I sat down and used Google Translate to decipher the words printed on it. I discovered it was not a memorial programme, but a notice sent out to all his friends, informing them that Robert was dying and inviting them to visit him one last time, before he ended his life on 19 February. I checked the date on my watch. It was now 27 February.

A few days later, I wrote to the address on the funeral card and received a reply from Robert's brother, Herbert, in mid-March. Writing in broken English, Herbert explained the circumstances of Robert's death.

After a year of acute back pain that culminated in an extreme loss of weight, Robert was diagnosed with terminal bone cancer in early January, Herbert told me. By then, the pain was so extreme that Robert was crawling around on all fours and on a morphine pump. Voluntary euthanasia, an option in Holland, was his way of ending the excruciating pain he was experiencing.

Herbert had attached a copy of an obituary written after Robert's death and its English translation. In a picture accompanying the obituary, Robert appeared older, but otherwise hardly changed. Still tall and slim, he had cropped hair, now white, and a moustache in place of the beard I had known.

'Everything under control until the end,' said the title of the obituary.

He was a restless individualist, travelled all over the world with his bike, knew everything about military binoculars and thought many times about Elspeth.

I was so shocked to see my name. I'd often thought about Robert over the years, but to see that he had too was heartbreaking. Describing a man that I recognized immediately, the obituary revealed that Robert had led exactly the modest, honest, uncompromising life he'd wanted when he'd broken all ties with me.

Haunted by Herbert's email and the obituary, it took me a few days before I was ready to reply. 'I cannot bear to think of him in so much pain during his last months and cannot understand why he did not try to contact me,' I wrote. I explained that Robert and I kept in touch for a while after ending our trip together:

But after several months he told me he had met someone else and asked me not to contact him. He said it would be difficult for him and his new girlfriend would not understand. I respected his wishes and did not contact him, hoping that one day he would feel able to get in touch again. I had naturally assumed he must have married and any thoughts of me were long gone. It seems sometimes he was too much 'in control'. The tragedy of it all is that I have often thought of Robert over these past twenty years but kept my promise and stayed silent.

Four hours later, Herbert replied: 'I don't know anything about another girlfriend, I cannot remember the existing of such a person. The reason why he stopped the contact with you we shall never know.'

I was devastated. Mostly it was the sadness of Robert's life that struck me. He had led a solitary life, so to have been denied any kind of friendship with him after we had shared so much together felt very sad for both of us, but particularly tragic for Robert.

I wondered if Robert had ever left Holland again, whether he had ever ridden the many trips he'd spoken about when we were together. I discovered from biker friends of his that the UK was the only place he rode his bike outside Holland.

I felt sick. Maybe Robert had hoped he'd bump into me.

For five of the most wonderful, significant months of my life he had been my total soulmate, the love of my life. What we went through was extraordinary. To cut all ties after that had been very hard indeed, but now to discover that Robert had possibly put us both through an unnecessary exile from each other was beyond my comprehension.

In April, I travelled out to Holland to pay my respects at Robert's grave. Herbert put me in contact with Robert's neighbours, who invited me to stay. Although complete strangers to me, they were very welcoming and spoke very fondly of Robert, but when I looked out of their window at Robert's house, all I could think about was Robert crawling around in agony. Life sometimes seemed very cruel. While I was staying with them, Robert's neighbours showed me some of his belongings they had saved in a cardboard box.

'Do you mind if I have a look?' I said.

They lifted the flaps and I peered inside. There were a few items I didn't recognize as well as several that I did remember, but the surprise was that many of them were etched with my little logo of myself on a motorbike that Robert had noticed on my top box in Delhi.

Deeper in the box, I found some postcards that Robert had sent to his neighbours' daughter. On them, Robert had signed off with my logo.

'He used it all the time,' said the neighbours. 'He loved it. It was his own little sign.'

I swallowed to suppress the lump in my throat as much as to suppress the urge to tell them that Robert had copied my logo and that after all these years it showed that my trip had meant something – maybe everything – to at least one very special person in my life.

Six years later, in March 2015, I went to a meeting of overland bikers at the legendary Ace Café on the North Circular Road in London. At the meeting I finally met Bas, one of Robert's closest friends, with whom he had ridden dozens of bike trips. 'He often talked about you and your time together in India and Pakistan, Iran and Turkey,' said Bas.

'Do you know what happened to Robert's photographs of our time together?' I asked Bas. 'I'd love to see them.'

Bas knew nothing about the photos, but said he would send me some of his own photographs he'd taken of Robert. A few weeks later, they arrived in an email. Two of them showed Robert, standing beside two bikes with Dutch number plates loaded with tents and camping gear, parked on a cliff above the sea. The view looked like it could be of the south coast of England, which meant Robert might have passed close by the tower on his journey to the sea. When I thought of that, my chest felt tight, but when I looked at the third photo, I almost gasped. It showed Robert's beloved knife with its leather sheath. It was the Bowie knife that had been confiscated then returned to Robert by the chief of the police who turned over our room in Doğubayazit in Turkey, looking for drugs. The memories came flooding back and when I looked closely, there was my biker logo, carved lightly into the knife's handle. Of all Robert's belongings, his knife was among the most treasured, so the sight of my logo on it felt very significant.

Determined to find out if Robert's photos of our time together still existed, I continued my search, eventually locating them in the possession of one his oldest friends, a man called Wim.

'I will send you Robert's photographs and negatives,' Wim told me, 'and some other items that I think belong to you.'

A package arrived a short while later with a letter that said, 'I know these possessions are now in the right place.' I unpacked the contents – Robert's entire photo collection from his trip from Sydney to Holland and – a great surprise – his 1984 diary, mostly written in English. Flicking through it, I came across the page on which I had first drawn my little sketch of myself on my bike for him, in the tourist compound in Delhi, waiting for our permits to enter Punjab. A few pages further I found an entry in which Robert had written that HOLLAND stood for Hope Our Love Lasts And Never Dies.

It was a bittersweet moment. From what I'd heard from Robert's friends and now seen in his diary, it appeared Robert's love for me was just as resilient and everlasting as mine was for him. I had no regrets that I hadn't spent my life with him – I knew that we were incompatible in many ways. But although my feelings had changed towards him when we returned home, I had never stopped loving him. It was heartbreaking that Robert had prevented us from enjoying and sustaining a loving friendship. But now, thirty years after my trip had been forgotten by almost everyone, I knew that there was one very special person for whom it had always meant as much as it did for me. Now, at last, I knew that everything – accidents, illnesses, medical emergencies, hardships, heartbreaks, not to mention more than 35,000 miles and two years on the road – had, after all this time, been worth every wretched and every glorious minute.

My journal started as a diary but soon became one of my most valuable possessions. As well as using it to write down my thoughts, I noted useful addresses, phone numbers, travellers' cheque numbers, and recorded petrol purchases and fuel consumption. I also used the pages at the back of my journal to keep meticulous records of the all maintenance and servicing I carried out on my bike during my trip. When I left Singapore I decided to also keep a record of my petrol costs and the amount of fuel I purchased. This was mainly to help me budget for my journey home and to keep an eye on fuel consumption as petrol was an unavoidable fixed cost.

Equipment to take:

- Washing up liquid [for tyre changing]
- Gasket sealant/mastic
- Haynes manual
- Insulating tape
- Chain and lock
- Petrol tubing
- WD40
- Funnel
- Bulbs and fuses [headlight, indicators and brake light]
- Inner tubes x 2
- Cables: throttle, front brake, clutch, speedometer
- Contact breakers[points] x 4

- Spark plugs x 4
- Spare oil – engine and gearbox
- Spark plug caps x 2
- HT/plug leads x 2
- Condenser
- H_2O containers
- Rocker arm/spindle x 2
- Oil filters x 4
- 'C' clips / bolts / washers / wire
- Ignition coil
- Fork seals
- Push rod seals
- Graphite grease
- Gaskets: cylinder head and base
- Spare wheel spokes/spoke spanner
- Tyre valves
- Tools – spanners, socket set, screwdrivers, pliers, Allen keys, adjustable spanner, torque wrench, tyre levers, tyre gauge, plug spanner, mole grips, mallet, hammer, feeler gauge, solder wire, wire cutters, electrical tester, small file.
- Special BMW tools:
  - Exhaust flange tool
  - Steering head bearings adjustment/removal spanner,
  - Swing arm adjustment spanner
  - Peg spanner to remove fork filler caps

[After leaving Sydney I added to this list a pop rivet gun, spare rivets (3 sizes) and spare pieces of aluminium for repairs.]

Bike maintenance and service schedule [figures show mileage]

ENGINE OIL (Change)	GEARBOX OIL (change)	BEVEL & DRIVESHAFT OIL	NEW TYRES F – front R– rear	AIR FILTER (CLEAN)	NEW OIL FILTER	NEW CABLES	NEW PLUGS
33,100	33,100	33,100	33,100 (F)	33,100	37,045	37,000 (Clutch)	36,625
36,500	37,045	37,045 (DS)	41,500 (R)	59,900	45,000	37,035 (Front brake)	41,500
37,045	46,200	41,500 (B)	45,400 (F)	64,800	51,500	41,900 (Throttle right)	51,500
38,000	53,000	46,200 (DS)	53,000 (R)	68,220	59,000	49,980 (Throttle left)	53,000
41,500	65,819	53,000	60,003 (R)	73,200	63,800	52,000 (Throttle right))	59,000
45,000	73,200	65,819	60,104 (F)		69,190	59,800 (Speedo)	73,200
46,200	94,380	73,200	72,000 (R)		73,200	73,200 (Throttle right)	
51,500		69,190 (replace both seals)					
53,100							
55,300							
59,000							

ENGINE OIL (Change)		NEW POINTS	NEW BATTERY	VALVE BUSHES	FORK OIL (change)	ROCKER ARMS & SPINDLES	HT PLUG LEADS
61,300		37,045	44,898 (June 82)	51,500	37,300	52,500	45,000
63,800		41,500	73,100 (Oct 84)		45,500		67,600
66,900		45,020			53,100		
69,190		49,990					
73,200		58,000					
		63,800					
		73,200			Rewire 59,400		

Fuel (place purchased and cost)

MALAYSIA		
Place Purchased	**Cost (Malaysian $)**	**UK gallons**
Johor Bahru	$20.00 @ $4.80/gallon	4.2
Melacca	$10.00 @ $4.60/gallon	2.2
Kuala Lumpur	$8.00 @ $4.65/gallon	1.7
Cameron Highlands	$15.00 @ $4.80/gallon	3.1
Alor Setar	$12.00 @ $4.80/gallon	2.5
Total	**Mal $65.00 [US $28.60 in 1984]**	**13.7 gallons**

THAILAND	**Cost (Thai Baht)**	**litres**
Ranot	160 baht@ 11.94/litre	13.4
Phunphin	140 baht@ 11.94/litre	11.7
Prachuap	200 baht@ 11.94/litre	16.7
River Kwai	175 baht@ 11.94/litre	14.6
Pak Chong	220 baht@ 11.94/litre	18.4
Pak Chong	150 baht@ 10.94/litre	13.7
Kampheng Phet	100 baht@ 10.94/litre	9.1
Sukhothai	175 baht@ 10.94/litre	16.0
Chiang Mai	180 baht@ 11.94/litre	15.1
Golden Triangle	100 baht@ 11.94/litre	8.4
Phayao	210 baht@ 12.10/litre	17.4
Tak	170 baht@ 12.10/litre	14.0
Uthai Thani	170 baht@ 12.10/litre	14.0
Ratchaburi	200 baht@ 10.95/litre	18.3
Chumphon	200 baht@ 11.95/litre	16.7
Phatthalung	220 baht@ 12.95/litre	17.0
Total	**2770 baht (US $49 in 1984)**	**234.5 litres**

INDIA + NEPAL (summary)	**Cost (Indian rupees)**	**litres**
Calcutta to Kathmandu	339 rupees@6.50/litre	52.2
Kathmandu to Delhi	1195 rupees@6.75/litre	177.0
Delhi to Srinagar	387 rupees@6.65/litre	58.2
Srinagar to Pathankot, Punjab [close to border]	625 rupees@6.95/litre	89.1
Total	**2546 rupees (US $234 in 1984)**	**376.5 litres**

PAKISTAN	Cost (Pakistan rupees)	litres
Lahore	71 rupees@7.1/litre	10.0
Multan	105 rupees@6.17/litre	17.0
Loralai	154 rupees@6.52/litre	23.6
Quetta	105 rupees@7.0/litre	15.0
Nushki	55 rupees@6.87/litre	8.0
Dalbandin	80 rupees@6.66/litre	12.0
Total	570 rupees (US $40 in 1984)	85.6 litres

IRAN	Cost (Iranian rials)	litres
Zahedan	700 rials @29/litre	24.0
Zahedan	250 rials @35/litre	7.0
Bam	450 rials @27/litre	16.3
Kerman	330 rials @33/litre	10.0
Yazd	500 rials @31/litre	16.0
Isfahan	520 rials @32.5/litre	16.0
Saveh	600 rials @31.5/litre	19.0
Zanjan	540 rials @31/litre	18.0
Marand	510 rials @30/litre	17.0
Maku	200 rials @25/litre	8.0
Total	4600 rials (US $8.3 in 1984)	151.3 litres

TURKEY	Cost (Turkish lira)	litres
Erzurum	3500 lira @176/litre	19.8
Erzincan	1800 lira @200/litre	9.0
Sarkisla	3200 lira @188/litre	17.0
Niğde	3100 lira @155/litre	20.0
Silifke	3450 lira @191/litre	18.0
Alanya	2850 lira @196/litre	14.5
Denizli	4000 lira @190/litre	21.0
Efes	3300 lira @188/litre	17.5
Burhaniye	3500 lira @190/litre	18.4
Ipsala	3000 lira @187/litre	16.0
Total	31700 lira (US $79 in 1984)	171.2 litres

GREECE	Cost (Greek drachma)	litres
Kavala	890 drachma @57.4/litre	15.5
Border	300 drachma @ 58/litre	5.2
Total	1190 drachma (US $10 in 1984)	20.7 litres

YUGOSLAVIA	Cost (Yugoslavian dinars)	litres
Kumanovo	2000 dinars @100/litre	20.0
Slavonski Brod	2000 dinars @100/litre	20.0
Total	4000 dinars (US $10 in 1984)	40.0 litres

HOLLAND	Cost (Dutch guilders)	litres
Rotterdam	35 guilders (US $10 in 1984)	4.5 litres

ENGLAND	£1.00!	